# CHEF PAUL PRUDHOMME'S

# SEASONED AMERICA

# Chef Paul Prudhomme's
# SEASONED
# AMERICA

William Morrow and Company, Inc.  New York

Copyright © 1991 by Paul Prudhomme

Interior and jacket photographs copyright © 1991 by Will Crocker

It is the policy of William Morrow and Company, Inc., and its imprints and affiliates, recognizing the importance of preserving what has been written, to print the books we publish on acid-free paper, and we exert our best efforts to that end.

Library of Congress Cataloging-in-Publication Data has been ordered.
Prudhomme, Paul.
CHEF PAUL PRUDHOMME'S SEASONED AMERICA
ISBN 0-688-05282-7                                                           91-14014
                                                                                CIP

Printed in the United States of America

First Edition

1 2 3 4 5 6 7 8 9 10

BOOK DESIGN BY LINEY LI

# Acknowledgments

★

It took three years to complete this project, and during that time it became apparent to me who deserves much of the credit for its success.

Thanks first to my editor at William Morrow, Ann Bramson, whose idea resulted in this book.

Special thanks to my project manager, Jessie Tirsch, for her extensive research, dynamite writing skills, and for organizing all facets of the book.

My undying gratitude to my cooking assistant, Pat Scanlan, for her patience (she needed a lot of this!) and her sense of humor.

And more thanks . . .

To Sean O'Meara, our computer expert, for tirelessly retesting the recipes, and for his superb palate. Thanks, also, to Sean's Sunday Brunch Club.

To all the wonderful people who home-tested recipes for us: John and Ellyn Alexander, Sandy Crowder, Marti Dalton, Deborah Elliott, Suzette Fleury, Missy LaGarde, Paula and Joe LaCour and Elsie Messina, Shawn McBride, Pat Mullins, Dudley and Gretchen Passman, and Kate Ross.

To photographer Will Crocker and to Martha Crocker, and to our food stylist, Peggy Green, who brought her special skills to us all the way from Houston.

To Margie Blaum, for seeing to it that I had time for everything, and for her charming critiques.

To Shawn McBride for keeping me on track, and to her Mom, Audrey Granger, for her outstanding German potato salad.

To John McBride for all his efforts to get this book going.

To Chef Paul Miller, Don LeBlanc, Chef Robert Holmes, Michael Calagna, Janice Rozetcki, and the entire staff at K-Paul's Louisiana Kitchen for their cooperation and support.

And finally, to my wonderful wife, K Prudhomme, for her creative input and unwavering support—as always.

# Contents

★

# List of

# Color Photographs

★

BETWEEN PAGES 212 AND 213

# CHEF PAUL PRUDHOMME'S

# SEASONED AMERICA

# Introduction

★

When I set out at seventeen to see the world, I wound up eating and cooking my way through a good part of this country. Not only did I learn a lot about life in general, I learned there are many cultures that make up the great melting pot of American cuisine—and most of them aren't Cajun.

The people I met everywhere opened my eyes for me. They weren't eating gumbo in San Francisco, they were eating cioppino. In Florida, no one had heard of jambalaya, but they ate loads of *arroz con pollo*. The fish of choice in Colorado was trout, not catfish.

As I traveled, I learned that every region is different, and each one has a distinctive repertoire of dishes and cooking techniques. An old family recipe would be brought from someone's ancestral homeland and lovingly translated and modified according to the fresh ingredients and cooking facilities available here. I discovered that American food *is* Cajun food. But it's also German food, French food, Jewish, Chinese, Italian, Mexican, Cuban, Irish, Native American, and so much more. There are more flavors and subtle nuances than any one journalist or historian could ever chronicle.

There were surprises everywhere I went: some wonderful surprises, and some not so wonderful. There were foods that seemed so foreign to me I had a difficult time becoming accustomed to their taste and textures. Often, I'd try a dish I didn't care for several times out of curiosity, because everyone else in that part of America seemed to love it. Soon I'd begin to appreciate its simplicity, but wonder why the cook hadn't browned the onions, or added garlic or salt, basil, oregano, or thyme. If the right seasonings were added or better cooking techniques were employed, the simplest dish could grow into something really exciting. It was my first understanding of how to cross American cultures to create emotion in food. For instance, ground chile peppers are standard seasoning for Southwestern cooking, but if you add them—with restraint—to a more subtle dish from, say, the Midwest, you can have a sensational new taste experience.

Over the years, recipes have changed as they've been handed down through the generations. And chefs, cooks, and food experts have helped deliver many dishes from ridicule or banishment by adapting them to suit the tastes of a changing world. Take Cajun food, for instance, which in recent years enjoyed a period of extreme popularity throughout the United States. At the height of its chic, if you said you didn't care for Cajun food, people looked at you as if you were slightly deranged. But if the authentic, traditional Cajun dishes hadn't evolved somewhat from the original recipes, they never would have survived to gain acceptance in other cultures.

Even jambalaya, which is such a popular dish today, would have been regarded with contempt had it not changed. When I was a kid, it was made with short-grain rice that was grown in Louisiana rice fields, and it was incredibly starchy. I could never expect someone who grew up in New York City to enjoy a gooey clump of seasoned rice that comes out of the pot as one mass of starch. Because I was raised on jambalaya prepared just that way, I loved it, and I knew there was a great idea there—but I had to change my jambalaya to make it more acceptable to a wide variety of palates that weren't Cajun.

As far as I'm concerned, this all makes for happiness and a broader range of cooking tastes and techniques from which to choose. It makes me sad to know that many people who cook feel locked in to the ingredients and instructions of every recipe they attempt. No one should ever feel locked in to a recipe: There are always alternative ways to create a dish and get great results. And no one should feel locked out of a recipe either, simply because some of the ingredients are unavailable. Almost every recipe that exists has variations or potential variations and can be made with a variety of ingredients. If you can't get veal for a certain dish, try chicken. If lobster is unavailable, use crab. And almost any recipe can be adapted to suit the individual palate. If you're sensitive to spices, add chile peppers a little at a time until you have the heat you can tolerate. (See page 10 for tips on techniques.) All you need to know are a few basics, like how to work with seasonings and what enhances what. And all you need to do is use your imagination and be willing to take the risk.

My purpose in writing this book is to help us all understand how delicious traditional American food can be. Learning together how to get the best results with each dish, especially when using seasonings creatively, will help us get emotion and excitement into everything we cook. And once you get the reasoning behind the process and apply what you know, you'll find it gets easier and easier to develop your own ideas. You'll feel freer to experiment with seasonings and to substitute ingredients where necessary or where you see fit. I want you to feel as if each recipe in this book is your own. My goal is that you have fun in the kitchen, while turning out heavenly dishes that bear your own signature.

Ultimately, then, my family and yours can create happy American food for generations to come—food that has the mystery of the past, the knowledge of the present, and enough emotion and excitement to carry us into the future.

# My Way

★

Herbs and spices have long been considered by many Americans as foreign substances to be regarded with suspicion or avoided. In many conversations I've had around the country I've been made aware of a resistance toward adding any new herbs or spices to a regional or traditional family dish. (Wouldn't grandma turn over in her grave if she knew we spiced up her bland meatballs?)

But the key to seasoning is to add an herb or spice that will really complement and push up the flavors of a dish—and to add it at the right time and in the correct amount. Select the herbs and spices you want to taste in the dish and add some almost as soon as you begin to cook, right after you add the first onions, celery, or bell peppers, for instance. Ultimately, your seasonings will become a part of the dish, the way a perfume becomes a part of an individual. As you continue to add ingredients to the pot or skillet, add your seasonings in small amounts and taste frequently to be sure you're not covering up the taste of the most important ingredient in the dish—the chicken, beef, pork, or seafood. The true function of herbs and spices, is to heighten and enrich all the other flavors in a dish, not mask them. What's more, properly used seasonings give the food a fragrance that prepares your tastebuds to accept the full depth of those flavors.

5

## ☆ Building a Dish

If all the ingredients in each recipe could be thrown into a pot at one time, the heat turned on, and the food cooked a certain amount of time, with outstanding results, anyone could be a masterful cook. But much of the skill in cooking involves knowing how to "build" or "construct" a dish.

Imagine you were building a house, and all the components for the construction were dumped on the site at one time. What a mess! Now consider each dish you prepare as a house or a building. If all the ingredients are thrown together, they too will be dumped on your tastebuds in a confusing jumble, with no refinement or finesse.

The endeavor of a well-constructed dish is the same as that of a well-constructed building: to give the building, or dish, maximum strength and beauty by adding the right elements in the right order. A house has a foundation, floors, walls, windows, and doors and you can easily see the analogy in almost every recipe you prepare.

To begin with, a strong foundation for a dish of food can't possibly be created by using water alone—that would be like leaving out the dry cement mix for a building foundation. Plain water will dilute the taste of every other ingredient in the dish and will do nothing to hold up the walls of flavor. But if you first turn that water into a rich, wonderful stock, the strength of your foundation is assured.

The vegetables in a dish could be compared to the nails, rivets, and wire in a building, since they will hold the other ingredients together if they're prepared properly. They give the dish a center and strengthen the foundation. To get the best performance from vegetables like onions, celery, bell peppers, carrots, and mushrooms, among others, put them in a hot skillet or pot with the fat or liquid you're using at a sizzle (at least 350°). Approximately one-quarter of the total vegetables in the dish should be added at the start of the cooking. If you cook them until they just start to brown and then add some herbs and spices and allow them to caramelize, a tremendous taste change will take place. In the browning process, starches and acids turn into natural sugars, giving the vegetables a wonderful sweetness that adds depth to the final result.

As the cooking progresses and you add more vegetables and other ingredients at intervals, you'll be adding the walls, windows, doorways, and roof to the dish. The second and third additions of vegetables are the doorways. Adding them in stages should produce a different taste with every bite. With your first mouthful, a door may open and let in a taste of onion. With the next, the onion may leave and bell peppers enter, as the doorway lets the excitement of changing tastes go in and out.

The herbs and spices are the windows: They let in the sunshine, but it's up to each individual to determine just how much sunshine is to be added. In this book I've allowed the windows to be of maximum size to let in the most sparkle and sunshine possible for each dish, without causing the walls of the construction (the main ingredient in the dish) to crumble and disappear.

The focus of these elements—the foundation, windows, and doors— is, of course, the main part of the construction—the walls and roof. In a dish, the main part or ingredient is usually chicken, beef, pork, or seafood of some kind. The body of the building must be strengthened by the foundation and made emotional by the doors and windows.

The interior, if done well, should create maximum comfort and plea- sure. For the best results, be sure not to overstir, overcook, or overseason, so that every ingredient will have as much color and texture as possible.

A perfect example of building a dish with interesting tastes and textures can be found in Milwaukee Potato Soup (page 72). The potatoes are used in several ways: Some are grated and used as a thickening base. Not using any other kind of starch for thickening means that the rich potato flavor of the base will relate directly to the other potato flavors and textures in the soup. The grated potatoes will eventually disintegrate into the stock, forming a strong foundation. Later, some potatoes that have been cut in a small dice and others cut in a larger dice are added to give the soup "walls" with two different kinds of potato taste and textures. And all of this flavor is strength- ened further with the addition of doorways and windows—onions, celery, nutmeg, mustard.

Finally, the dressing on the outside of a building, or what is known as "architecturals," gives us an emotional impression before we enter the door. The same is true of any dish before we take the first bite. The "architecturals" of a dish might be a simple garnish of parsley or a slice of lemon dipped in paprika, some beautifully carved vegetables on the plate, the side dishes served with the main course, the dressing on the salad. Most important of the architecturals is, of course, the dish itself, which has been perfectly prepared and cooked for maximum eye appeal as well as taste. These visuals prepare us for what lies ahead: the sturdiness of the foundation, the doors that let wonderful tastes in and out, the windows full of sunshine. These are the flavors, textures, and strengths of a dish that is well constructed, and one you're not likely to forget.

# *Techniques*

★

In order to make cooking from this book easy, fun, and successful, there are several basic techniques you can quickly master and a few little rules that will save you a lot of trouble later.

1. Always prepare, or "prep," *every* ingredient as directed for *every* recipe. Many wonderful recipes have been ruined because the cook stopped to beat an egg or chop an onion at a critical moment. The recipes are set up to give you an idea of what to do and when to do it. Read each recipe through completely to get an overall idea of what you'll be doing. Then, one by one, prepare your ingredients. For example: Make the seasoning mix first, if there is one; chop the onions, bell peppers, celery; grate anything that needs grating, like cheese or potatoes; toast the nuts or cornmeal. Set each ingredient in its own cup, bowl, or container within reach, and read the recipe again. Take out all the pots, pans, and tools you'll need. Start the oven preheating, if necessary. Now, prop up the recipe in a convenient spot for easy reference, roll up your sleeves, and have fun!

2. When it comes to chopping or grating vegetables, we believe hand grating and chopping with a very sharp knife are best. Doing it the old-fashioned way leaves the vegetables with more of their texture and juices intact and, consequently, sweeter. Processing in a food processor or blender can turn vegetables into a bitter mush. If you *must* use a machine, be sure

the blades are changed and/or sharpened regularly for the best results. We have nothing against food processors and blenders, and in fact use them in a number of recipes in this book. But using them to do the right job is the key.

3. The easiest way to peel tomatoes is to immerse the tomatoes in a pot of boiling water until the skins split open, about a minute or two (depending on the ripeness of the tomatoes). Immerse the tomatoes in a bowl of ice water until they're cool enough to handle, then slip off their skins.

4. Caramelizing onions, peppers, and other vegetables means cooking them slowly in fat until they become a pretty, golden brown color. When cooked this way first, they add a natural sweetness and an indescribably wonderful flavor to your dish.

5. If you prefer to use olive oil or margarine in any of the recipes that call for butter, simply substitute an equal amount.

6. If you can't find ready-ground chile peppers, buy whole dried chile peppers and process them in the bowl of a food processor until finely ground. If the peppers aren't brittle enough for grinding, roast them first in a 200° oven for about 10 minutes, or until crisp. Cool a few minutes, split open, and remove the seeds, then process.

7. If allergies or personal taste conflict with a recipe, it's better to omit the offending ingredient, unless you're knowledgeable enough to make the correct substitution.

8. If you just *can't* find the fresh ingredient called for in a recipe you may substitute a canned, frozen, or dried version of the same ingredient —for instance, ground ginger for fresh or canned tomatoes for fresh— but don't expect the result to be the best it can be. There is often a huge difference in flavors and textures between fresh and the next best substitute.

9. Dark and light brown sugar can be substituted one for the other, as can dark and light molasses, but there will be a slight difference in the flavor.

10. If you don't own a proper thermometer and you're going to be frying foods in oil, you must take the time to keep the oil—and subsequently, the food—from burning. To test if the oil is hot without a thermometer, toss in a pinch of all-purpose flour. If the flour sizzles and turns

brown immediately, the oil should be just right. If the flour sinks to the bottom, the oil isn't hot enough for frying; if it turns black, the oil's too hot. If you do own a thermometer, the oil is "hot" at 350°, "very hot" at 375° to 390°.

**11.** If you don't have a food processor, you can still prepare most of the recipes in this book that call for a processor. Using a processor just makes preparation faster. In some cases you can substitute a blender: For instance, you could purée strawberries in either a blender or a food processor. On the other hand, you cannot make dough in a blender. To make an excellent dough by hand, just mix together the dry ingredients and cut in the butter one pat at a time with a fork. Then add any liquid ingredients, such as eggs or milk, and mix thoroughly with a large spoon.

**12.** To make stock: Put 2 quarts cold water in a large pot and add 1 medium onion, unpeeled and quartered; 1 large garlic clove, unpeeled and quartered; and 1 rib celery. Add bones and excess meat (no livers) for a beef or poultry stock, or shells, carcasses, and/or fish heads for seafood stock. Bring to a boil over high heat, reduce the heat to low, cover, and simmer as long as possible—30 minutes to 4 hours—replacing the water in the pot as needed to keep it covering the other ingredients. Makes about 1 quart; increase water depending on the amount of ingredients you're adding to the pot.

**13.** There really is no substitute for good homemade stock. But if the price of making stock is too high or your time is too short, at least collect the peelings and trimmings from the vegetables used in the recipe, place them in a pot of water, and simmer for as long as possible. *Any* kind of stock is better than using either plain water—or canned soups, which are too salty.

**14.** If you're cautious about your fat intake, you can reduce it somewhat by defatting your stocks. Even without the fat, a good stock will add a tremendous amount of flavor and richness to any dish. After you've cooked a rich stock, refrigerate it overnight. Next day, pack a strainer with ice— preferably crushed, but ice cubes work, too. Place the strainer over a pot large enough to hold all the stock. Remove the stock from the refrigerator and pour it in a steady, circling stream, the thickness of a pencil, over the ice. In order to remove all the fat, you may have to repeat the process once or twice. Once the fat is gone, place the pot of stock over high heat, bring to a boil, and cook until the stock has reduced by two thirds. In other words, if you start with 3 quarts of stock, you should have 1 quart when you're finished. If more than a week's storage is needed, pour the cooled defatted stock into ice cube trays and place in the freezer. When frozen solid, remove the cubes of stock, wrap each in plastic wrap, and store in the freezer in plastic bags for future use.

**15**. Because we're not perfect, some of these recipes will leave you with some leftover seasoning mix. Don't throw it away—use it to create savory scrambled eggs tomorrow morning, or add it to the next meal's mashed potatoes. Or you think of something even better. Keep thinking—you're going to be a terrific cook.

# BREAD
## *and*
# BREAKFAST

Whatever its guise—muffins, rolls, biscuits, tortillas, bagels—bread has long been a vital part of our national food fix. Early cookbooks devoted a great deal of space to the baking of bread, but since this was the most demanding and time-consuming of kitchen tasks, it was one of the first food chores to be turned over to professionals outside the home.

Today we bake bread at home again for the pleasure and taste of it. Fortunately, it's a lot easier to do today, since our recipes have been simplified and we now have wonderful time-saving equipment. Baking your own bread is especially gratifying because of the exciting variations you can try and because bread is such a good carrier of versatile flavors. When you bake one of our breads, think about how you can personalize the recipe by adding your own signature: caramelized onions, roasted nuts, or almost anything else you can think of—there are millions of ways. Do a little experimenting, and you'll have a bread with your name on it!

Breakfast in America has come a long way—from nearly unpalatable grains and starchy foods, including the Indians' cornmeal mush and the early settlers' quickly made porridge called "hasty pudding"—through periods of affluence and self-indulgence, when we stuffed ourselves every morning with rich foods like bacon, sausages, eggs, biscuits, jams, and butter. Nowadays people are much more health-conscious and concerned about making the meal a lighter one. But even those Americans who eat scanty breakfasts during the week are likely to sit down to a fussier morning meal on the weekends—especially Sunday, which has become a popular time to entertain by way of a fairly new vehicle called brunch.

# Deep South Spoon Bread

MAKES 6 TO 8 SERVINGS

★

As Southern as the hush puppy, spoon bread is actually more of a pudding or soufflé than a bread. It is, however, often the subject of controversy since Southerners argue endlessly about its preparation and consistency. Some bake it on a griddle, others in a casserole or baking dish. But in every case, spoon bread is a delicious mixture of cornmeal, butter, eggs, and milk. When it's finished baking, spoon it out and enjoy.

*1 cup yellow cornmeal*
*¾ teaspoon salt*
*½ cup corn flour*
*1 tablespoon baking powder*
*7 eggs*

*8 tablespoons (1 stick) unsalted butter*
*2 (12-ounce) cans evaporated milk*
*½ teaspoon cream of tartar*
*5 tablespoons sugar*

Preheat the oven to 350°.

Combine the cornmeal, salt, corn flour, and baking powder in a large mixing bowl and blend well.

Separate the eggs and place the whites in a food processor and the yolks in a small bowl.

Melt the butter in a 10-inch skillet over high heat. Add the evaporated milk and, using a wire whisk, whip constantly until the milk just starts to boil, about 4 minutes. Pour the milk slowly into the cornmeal mixture, whipping thoroughly with the whisk as you pour. Stir a small amount of this mixture into the egg yolks, then turn the egg yolk mixture into the larger bowl and mix thoroughly with the cornmeal.

Process the egg whites until frothy, about 20 seconds. With the food processor running, add the cream of tartar and sugar and process until the mixture is very frothy. Gently fold the egg white mixture into the cornmeal/milk mixture. Pour into a casserole dish approximately 10 by 10 by 2 inches deep. Bake 25 minutes, then turn the oven heat up to 450° and bake until golden brown, about 5 minutes.

Serve immediately, since the texture changes when cooled.

# Sally Lunn

MAKES 1 LOAF

★

There are lots of versions of the story of the origin of Sally Lunn. In one, a woman named Sally Lunn sold tea cakes in eighteenth-century England. In another, the French words *soleil* and *lune*, meaning "sun" and "moon," are the source. Recipes for Sally Lunn bread began appearing in American cookbooks early in the nineteenth century. Wherever it all began, the bread tastes wonderfully delicious.

8 tablespoons (1 stick) unsalted
   butter, in all
2 cups chopped onions
1 tablespoon black pepper
1 teaspoon salt
1 teaspoon dried thyme leaves
½ cup milk

3 eggs
¼ cup plus 1 tablespoon dark
   brown sugar
2 (¼-ounce) packages active dry
   yeast
2¾ cups all-purpose flour

Melt *4 tablespoons* of the butter in an 8-inch skillet over high heat. When the butter sizzles, stir in the onions, pepper, salt, and thyme. Cook, scraping the bottom of the skillet occasionally, until the onions are golden brown, about 7 to 8 minutes. Remove from the heat, stir in the milk, and set aside.

Place the eggs, brown sugar, and the *remaining 4 tablespoons* butter, cut into about 6 pats, in the bowl of a food processor and process until well blended, about 45 seconds. Add the yeast and process 90 seconds. Add the flour and process 75 seconds. Scrape the sides of the processor bowl (the dough will be thick and sticky). Add the onion mixture and process until thoroughly blended, about 15 seconds. (The dough will now be wet and sticky.) Turn the dough into a 9- by 5- by 2¾-inch loaf pan, set in a warm place and allow to rise, about 1½ hours, or until doubled in volume.

Meanwhile preheat the oven to 350°.

Bake until golden brown, about 45 minutes.

Serve warm, with butter if desired.

# Indiana Amish Onion Cake

MAKES 8 SERVINGS

*Color photograph 1*

★

The first Amish and Mennonite immigrants arrived in Indiana in the 1830s and 1840s bringing with them their plain, wholesome methods for preparing food. Many of their dishes are the result of irresistible flavor combinations, such as the onions, poppy seeds, and sour cream in this German onion cake. It's really a bread, meant to be served alongside a roast or other main course, but would make a great lunch served with a salad.

SEASONING MIX
1 tablespoon poppy seeds
1½ teaspoons paprika
1¼ teaspoons salt
1 teaspoon onion powder
¾ teaspoon dried marjoram
   leaves
¾ teaspoon black pepper
½ teaspoon white pepper
½ teaspoon dried dill weed

☆

15 tablespoons unsalted butter,
   softened, in all
3½ cups chopped onions
2 cups all-purpose flour
2 tablespoons white sugar
¼ cup cornstarch
1 tablespoon plus 1 teaspoon
   baking powder
5 eggs, in all
1 cup milk
1 cup sour cream
1 tablespoon dark brown sugar
Vegetable oil cooking spray

Preheat the oven to 450°.

Combine the seasoning mix ingredients thoroughly in a small bowl. Makes 3 tablespoons plus ¼ teaspoon.

Melt *4 tablespoons* of the butter in a 10-inch skillet over high heat. When the butter is sizzling, add the onions and cook, stirring occasionally, until the onions are light brown, about 8 to 10 minutes. Stir in *1 tablespoon plus 1 teaspoon* of the seasoning mix and cook until the onions are golden brown, about 5 to 7 minutes. Remove from the heat and set aside.

Place the flour, white sugar, cornstarch, baking powder, and the *re-*

*maining* seasoning mix in the bowl of a food processor and process until well blended. With the food processor running, add *8 tablespoons* (1 stick) of the butter, cut into pats and process until the texture of soft crumbs, about 1 minute. Add *3* of the eggs, one at a time, and blend 15 seconds, then add the milk in a thin stream and blend quickly to form a soft and sticky dough.

Using a wire whisk, beat the *remaining 2* eggs in a small bowl. Cut the *remaining 3 tablespoons* butter into small pieces. Add the butter to the beaten eggs and blend well with the whisk. Whip the sour cream into the egg mixture until well combined (there will still be bits of butter visible). Beat in the brown sugar.

Coat a 10-inch round cake pan or springform pan with cooking spray.

Spread the dough evenly over the bottom of the cake pan (tap the pan on the kitchen counter to even the dough). Spread the onion mixture evenly over the dough, then spread the sour cream mixture evenly over the onions.

Bake until golden brown on top, about 20 to 23 minutes. Let cool slightly, then cut into wedges and serve warm.

# Indian Pumpkin Griddle Cakes

MAKES ABOUT 22 (3-INCH) GRIDDLE CAKES

*Color photograph 2*

Since the early Plains Indians had to make do with primitive cooking conditions, a flat bread baked on stones was frequently on the menu. Since corn and pumpkin were staples in the Indian diet, it's easy to see how these wonderful griddle cakes came to be. You can serve them with maple syrup if you like, but they have so much flavor of their own they taste great with just melted butter drizzled over, accompanied by country sausage.

SEASONING MIX
½ teaspoon ground allspice
¼ teaspoon ground nutmeg
¼ teaspoon ground cinnamon

☆

2 eggs
2 cups yellow cornmeal
¼ cup packed light brown sugar
½ teaspoon salt
1 teaspoon baking soda
4 tablespoons unsalted butter
1½ cups milk
1 cup canned pumpkin
1 tablespoon vanilla extract
Vegetable oil cooking spray

Combine the seasoning mix ingredients thoroughly in a cup. Makes 1 teaspoon.

Whip the eggs with a wire whisk in a medium mixing bowl until frothy.

Thoroughly combine the cornmeal, sugar, salt, and baking soda in a large mixing bowl.

Melt the butter in a small saucepan over low heat and let it brown slowly, about 4 to 5 minutes. Stir in the milk and heat just to the boiling point. Pour the milk into the cornmeal mixture and blend thoroughly with a spoon. Add the pumpkin and blend with a whisk. Stir in the seasoning mix and vanilla. Whisk in the eggs.

Heat a large heavy skillet or griddle over high heat until very hot. Lift the skillet from the heat, coat it with cooking spray, and return to the heat. Drop the batter onto the skillet in large kitchen spoonsful, 2 to 3 at a time, and fry until lightly browned on the bottom, about 1 to 2 minutes. Turn the griddle cakes over and brown on the other side. (The skillet should be wiped clean, reheated, and resprayed between batches of griddle cakes.)

Serve immediately with sausage or bacon.

1.

# Indiana Amish Onion Cake

2.

## Indian Pumpkin Griddle Cakes

*page 19*

3.

## Kentucky Fried Tomatoes with Cream Gravy

4.

# Huevos Rancheros

*page 24*

5.

# Jalapeño Pie

*page 25*

6.

# West Coast Egg Foo Yung

*page 27*

7.

# Hangtown Fry

*page 29*

8.

# Red Flannel Hash

*page 35*

9.

# Deviled Crab

*page 46*

10.

## Oklahoma Honey Chicken

*page 56*

11.

# Waikiki Chicken

*page 59*

12.

# Delancey Street Chopped Liver

*page 61*

13.

# New England Butternut Bisque

*page 68*

14.

# New England Clam Chowder

*page 84*

15.

# Florida Fish House Grouper Chowder

*Clockwise from top left:*

# Kentucky Fried Tomatoes
# with Cream Gravy

MAKES 6 SERVINGS

*Color photograph 3*

★

Fried green tomatoes constitute an American classic. They're popular in the Midwest and on the Atlantic Coast, but our favorites are from the South, where the tart green tomatoes are dredged in cornmeal. Don't slice your tomatoes too thick or they won't cook all the way through. These are great for breakfast, with eggs, or delicious as lunch.

SEASONING MIX
2 teaspoons salt
1½ teaspoons dry mustard
1 teaspoon white pepper
1 teaspoon garlic powder
1 teaspoon dried sweet basil
   leaves
½ teaspoon black pepper
½ teaspoon onion powder
½ teaspoon ground coriander
¼ teaspoon ground nutmeg

☆

¾ cup all-purpose flour
¼ cup yellow cornmeal
½ teaspoon salt
14 slices (about ¼- to ⅓-inch-
   thick) very hard, very green
   tomatoes (about 3 or 4
   tomatoes)
8 slices bacon, diced
1 cup vegetable oil
1 cup chicken stock (see page 11)
1½ cups heavy cream, in all
6 English muffins, split

Combine the seasoning mix ingredients thoroughly in a small bowl. Makes 2 tablespoons plus 2¼ teaspoons.

Combine the flour and cornmeal in a small mixing bowl. Add the salt and *1 tablespoon plus 1 teaspoon* of the seasoning mix and blend well.

Sprinkle the tomato slices on one side only with a total of *1 tablespoon* of the seasoning mix, and pat it in with your hands.

Fry the bacon in a 12-inch skillet over high heat, stirring occasionally, about 3 minutes. Reduce the heat to medium and cook until the bacon is browned and crisp, about 4 to 5 minutes. Remove the bacon with a slotted spoon, drain, and set aside. Pour off the fat from the pan, reserving ¼ cup of the drippings.

Heat the reserved bacon drippings and the vegetable oil in the same skillet over high heat until very hot, about 5 minutes. While the fat is heating, dredge the tomato slices in the flour/cornmeal mixture one at a time; reserve the leftover flour mixture. When the fat is hot, add 6 of the tomato slices, or as many as fit in a single layer. Fry over high heat, turning twice, until browned, about 10 minutes. If the tomatoes seem to be browning too quickly, reduce the heat slightly. Remove with a slotted spatula and drain on paper towels. Fry the *remaining* tomato slices and drain. (Do not drain the fat from the skillet.) Chop 2 of the fried tomato slices and set aside.

Add *3 tablespoons* of the reserved seasoned flour mixture to the oil in the skillet, and cook, whisking with a wire whisk, about 3 minutes. Add the chopped fried tomatoes, the stock, and the cooked bacon and cook, whisking, about 2 minutes. Add *1 cup* of the cream and the *remaining* seasoning mix and cook, whisking, 3 minutes. Whisk in the *remaining ½ cup* cream and remove from the heat.

To serve, toast the muffin halves. Place a tomato slice on each half and cover with ¼ cup of the gravy.

# San Francisco Frittata

## MAKES 4 SERVINGS

★

The frittata is an Italian omelet that found its way to California more than a hundred years ago. This version can be made successfully with whatever filling you like or whatever ingredients you find fresh in your area, as well as some pork, in any form—be creative. Some people put potatoes or spaghetti in their frittatas; we used a combination of fresh vegetables and sweet Italian sausage. One of the things that distinguishes the frittata from a French omelet is that a French omelet is folded over, while the frittata is served open.

1 teaspoon salt

1 teaspoon poppy seeds

3/4 teaspoon dried sweet basil
   leaves

1/2 teaspoon garlic powder

1/2 teaspoon onion powder

1/2 teaspoon white pepper

1/2 teaspoon celery seeds

1/4 teaspoon black pepper

☆

6 large eggs

4 tablespoons unsalted butter,
   in all

1/2 pound sweet Italian sausage,
   casings removed

1/2 cup chopped onions

2 baby artichokes, trimmed and
   finely chopped

3 baby zucchini, sliced in half
   lengthwise

3 baby summer squash, sliced in
   half lengthwise

12 snow peas

1/2 cup sliced red bell peppers
   (sliced crosswise)

1/2 cup thinly sliced fresh
   mushrooms

12 fine green beans (haricots
   verts), cut in half

1/4 large avocado, peeled and cut
   into strips

1 cup shredded Monterey Jack
   cheese

Preheat the broiler.

Combine the seasoning mix ingredients thoroughly in a small bowl. Makes 1 tablespoon plus 2 teaspoons.

Whip the eggs with *2 teaspoons* of the seasoning mix in a medium-size mixing bowl, until frothy.

Melt *2 tablespoons* of the butter in a 10-inch ovenproof skillet over high heat. When the butter begins to sizzle, add the sausage and cook, breaking up any lumps with a spoon, until lightly browned about 3 minutes. Add the onions, stir, and cook 1 minute. Stir in all of the remaining vegetables, the avocado, and *2 teaspoons* of the seasoning mix and cook 1 minute. Stir in the *remaining* seasoning mix and the remaining *2 tablespoons* butter and cook 1 minute. Pour in the seasoned eggs and cook until almost set, about 3 minutes. Sprinkle the cheese evenly over the top, transfer the skillet to the broiler, and broil until the frittata is browned and puffy on top and the cheese has melted, about 2 minutes.

Serve with thick slices of warm Italian bread.

# Huevos Rancheros

MAKES 3 SERVINGS

*Color photograph 4*

★

Here's a good way to celebrate Sunday, Mexican-American style. Huevos rancheros, or "ranch eggs," came to America with the Mexican immigrants and quickly became a popular dish for brunch or lunch or even a light dinner. The cool flavors of the avocado and sour cream contrast beautifully with the spicy salsa. What a great way to eat eggs!

**SALSA**

1 medium fresh Anaheim pepper,
  seeded and diced (see Note)
1 large fresh jalapeño pepper,
  chopped (see Note)
1 medium green bell pepper,
  julienned
1 medium yellow onion,
  julienned
2 large fresh tomatoes, coarsely
  chopped
2 teaspoons minced fresh garlic
1/2 cup loosely packed chopped
  fresh cilantro
2 tablespoons distilled white
  vinegar

2 tablespoons fresh lemon juice
2 tablespoons fresh lime juice
2 tablespoons dark brown sugar
1 teaspoon salt
1 tablespoon ground ancho chile
  pepper (see Note)

1 large ripe avocado (preferably
  California, or Calavos)
2 tablespoons fresh lime juice
1/2 cup corn oil
6 small corn tortillas
6 eggs
3 tablespoons sour cream
1/2 cup grated Monterey Jack
  cheese

**FOR THE SALSA,** combine all the ingredients thoroughly in a bowl. Makes about 4 cups. (Any leftover salsa can be refrigerated for about 1 week in an airtight container.)

Preheat the broiler.

Peel the avocado, cut it in half, and slice it crosswise. Place the slices on a plate and sprinkle with the lime juice to prevent discoloration.

Heat the oil in a small skillet until hot. Briefly dip 2 of the tortillas, one at a time, into the oil, just to soften them. Place the tortillas, slightly overlapping, in an ovenproof skillet or on a heatproof plate. Arrange 2 of the avocado slices on top of each tortilla to form a ring.

Poach or lightly fry *2* of the eggs and place 1 in the center of each avocado ring. Place *1 tablespoon* of the sour cream between the eggs. Spoon ⅓ of the cheese in a circle around the eggs and, using a slotted spoon, spoon a circle of salsa around the cheese. Place under the broiler until the cheese is brown and bubbly, about 2 minutes. Repeat the process with the remaining ingredients.

Serve with sour cream and some of the remaining salsa. Enjoy!

NOTE: Try to find the fresh chile peppers we used, but if you can't, substitute peppers of similar heat intensities. Jalapeños are moderately hot and Anaheims are very mild.

If you can't find ground ancho peppers, use whatever chile pepper is available in your area. Just be sure to use only pure ground chile peppers, not commercial chili powder.

Be sure to wear rubber gloves when handling hot peppers.

# Jalapeño Pie

### MAKES 6 TO 8 SERVINGS
*Color photograph 5*

★

A Texas treat, jalapeño pie was nothing more than a cheese omelet with peppers . . . until we got hold of it. The cornmeal base gives it some real substance, and the ground chile peppers in the seasoning mix bring out the very best in the jalapeños.

SEASONING MIX

2 teaspoons ground guajillo
    chile pepper (see Note)
1 teaspoon ground arbol chile
    pepper (see Note)
1 teaspoon salt
1 teaspoon dried cilantro
    leaves
1 teaspoon ground cumin
1 teaspoon onion powder
½ teaspoon garlic powder
½ teaspoon white pepper
½ teaspoon black pepper

☆

¾ cup yellow cornmeal
1 teaspoon baking powder
1 tablespoon dark brown sugar
1 cup milk
4½ tablespoons unsalted butter,
    in all
½ cup hot water
1½ cups sliced onions, separated
    into rings
12 fresh jalapeño peppers,
    stemmed, seeded, and sliced
    crosswise into rings
3 tablespoons vegetable oil
8 eggs
2 cups grated sharp Cheddar
    cheese

Preheat the oven to 350°.

Combine the seasoning mix ingredients thoroughly in a small bowl.
Makes 2 tablespoons plus 2½ teaspoons.

Toast the cornmeal in an 8-inch skillet over high heat until just golden
brown. Turn the cornmeal into a medium-size mixing bowl, add the baking
powder, brown sugar, and *1 tablespoon plus 1 teaspoon* of the seasoning
mix, and mix well.

Heat the milk with *2½ tablespoons* of the butter in a small saucepan
over high heat until the milk comes just to a boil and the butter is melted.
Whisk the milk into the cornmeal mixture with a wire whisk. Add the hot
water and whisk until thick and smooth. Set aside.

Melt the *remaining 2 tablespoons* butter in an 8-inch skillet over high
heat. When the butter sizzles, add the onions, jalapeño peppers, and *1½
teaspoons* of the seasoning mix. Cook, stirring occasionally, until the onions
are lightly browned, about 3 to 4 minutes.

Heat the oil in an ovenproof 10-inch skillet until very hot but not
smoking. Stir in the cornmeal mixture. As soon as it sizzles, remove from
the heat and allow to sit 1 minute.

Spread the onions and peppers on top of the cornmeal mixture. Break the eggs into a mixing bowl, add the *remaining* seasoning mix, and whip with a wire whisk until frothy. Pour the eggs over the onions and peppers, sprinkle the grated cheese on top, and bake until golden and puffy, about 30 to 35 minutes.

Let cool a few minutes, cut into wedges, and serve with sour cream, if desired.

NOTE: These are the peppers we used. You can use whatever is available in your area, but be sure to get pure ground chile peppers, not commercial chili powder.

# West Coast Egg Foo Yung

MAKES 8 SERVINGS

*Color photograph 6*

A great way to start the day—or finish it—is with this Chinese-American specialty. Egg foo yung is said to have been created by a Chinese cook working on the Central Pacific Railroad in the mid-1850s. Although the dish has no exact counterpart in classic Chinese cuisine, it is definitely in the style of many traditional Chinese dishes. The flavors of fresh seafood and vegetables quick-cooked in an omelet are practically irresistible. When asked what he tasted first when he tried one, Sean O'Meara, our computer wizard, replied, "The foo."

SEASONING MIX

1 tablespoon sugar

2 teaspoons salt

1½ teaspoons dry mustard

1 teaspoon black pepper

1 teaspoon white pepper

1 teaspoon dried sweet basil
  leaves

1 teaspoon onion powder

½ teaspoon garlic powder

½ teaspoon ground ginger

☆

6 to 12 tablespoons peanut oil,
  in all

1 cup diced ham (about 4
  ounces)

1 tablespoon plus 1 teaspoon
  minced fresh ginger

1 cup chopped green onion tops

1½ teaspoons minced fresh
  garlic

4 cups fresh sunflower, mung, or
  soybean sprouts (see Note)

1 pound lump crabmeat, picked
  over for shells and cartilage

1 pound peeled small shrimp

8 eggs

Combine the seasoning mix ingredients thoroughly in a small bowl. Makes 3 tablespoons plus 2½ teaspoons.

Place *3 tablespoons* of the oil and the ham in a 10-inch skillet over high heat and cook, stirring occasionally, until the ham is lightly browned, about 4 minutes. Add the fresh ginger, green onion tops, and garlic and cook until the vegetables are lightly browned, about 4 to 5 minutes. Transfer the contents of the skillet to a large bowl and gently fold in the sprouts, crabmeat, shrimp, and seasoning mix.

Beat the eggs in another bowl until light and fluffy. Fold the eggs into the seafood mixture until well blended.

Heat *3 tablespoons* of the oil in an 8- or 10-inch skillet over high heat. When the oil is hot, ladle about ½ cup of the egg mixture per omelet into the skillet and cook the omelets 2 at a time until golden brown on both sides, adding oil as needed. Drain on paper towels.

Serve immediately, with soy sauce if desired.

NOTE: If you can't find these sprouts, you can use whatever is available in your area, such as radish or alfalfa sprouts. The ones mentioned, however, are larger and juicier, and give the omelets an exciting texture.

# Hangtown Fry

MAKES 4 TO 6 SERVINGS

*Color photograph 7*

★

There are so many stories about this dish, it's hard to know which version to believe. Food historians do agree, however, that it got its name during the Gold Rush. It was supposedly created in the Cary House restaurant in Hangtown, California (whose name was a tribute to its "hang-now, ask-questions-later" reputation). The story goes that a lucky miner wanted the most expensive dish in the restaurant, and the price of eggs and oysters being what they were during this period of outrageous inflation, eggs and oysters were what he got. The bacon is *lagniappe,* which means a little something extra down here in New Orleans. We think you'll find our version exotic enough to serve your guests for Sunday brunch.

SEASONING MIX
*1 teaspoon salt*
*1 teaspoon garlic powder*
*1 teaspoon onion powder*
*1 teaspoon dried tarragon leaves*
*½ teaspoon white pepper*
*½ teaspoon black pepper*
*½ teaspoon dried sweet basil leaves*
*¼ teaspoon ground nutmeg*

*½ pound bacon, diced*
*10 eggs*
*2 tablespoons heavy cream*
*½ cup unsalted saltine cracker crumbs (about 12 crackers)*
*12 large or 16 small oysters, shucked and drained*
*1 tablespoon unsalted butter*
*¼ cup chopped fresh parsley*
*¼ cup grated Parmesan cheese*

☆

Combine the seasoning mix ingredients thoroughly in a small bowl. Makes 1 tablespoon plus 2¾ teaspoons.

Fry the bacon in a 12-inch skillet over high heat, stirring occasionally, until crisp and browned, about 6 to 8 minutes. Remove the bacon from pan with a slotted spoon and drain on paper towels. Pour off the bacon fat from the pan, reserving 5 tablespoons; if there aren't 5 tablespoons of fat, add enough vegetable oil to make up the difference.

Preheat the broiler.

Whip the eggs with a wire whisk until very frothy. Add the cream and *1 tablespoon* of the seasoning mix and beat until well blended.

Combine *1 teaspoon* of the seasoning mix with the cracker crumbs. Sprinkle the *remaining* seasoning mix over the drained oysters and rub in well with your hands. Then roll the oysters in the cracker crumbs.

Heat the butter and the reserved bacon fat in a 10-inch ovenproof skillet. When the fat is sizzling hot, add the oysters and fry until golden brown on one side, about 3 to 4 minutes. Turn the oysters with a spatula or tongs and fry 3 minutes. Sprinkle the browned bacon and the parsley over the oysters. Whip the eggs again, pour them evenly over the oysters, and cook until loosely set, about 30 seconds. Lower the heat to medium low and gently pull the slightly set egg mixture in from the sides of the skillet with a flat-sided spoon, letting the liquid eggs run under. Let the eggs cook another 20 to 30 seconds, then pull the egg mixture in from the sides of the pan again. Continue to do this until the entire omelet is loosely set.

Sprinkle the Parmesan cheese over the top of the omelet and place under the broiler until light golden brown and puffy, about 1 minute. (Watch very closely to prevent burning.) Serve immediately.

# Basin Street Crab Dumplings

MAKES 6 SERVINGS

★

Although we think of these as a Louisiana version of crab cakes, Sean O'Meara, our computer expert, calls them "Cajun latkes." They're easy to make and versatile as can be. A treat for breakfast—with or without eggs—a super lunch, or a wonderful first course for dinner, crab dumplings may become a family standard.

SEASONING MIX

1½ teaspoons dried chopped
   chives
1 teaspoon dried parsley flakes
1 teaspoon salt
½ teaspoon onion powder
½ teaspoon garlic powder
½ teaspoon paprika
½ teaspoon dried cilantro leaves
½ teaspoon dried sweet basil
   leaves
½ teaspoon white pepper
¼ teaspoon black pepper
¼ teaspoon dry mustard
¼ teaspoon ground nutmeg

1 egg
2 tablespoons heavy cream
1½ cups grated potatoes
½ cup grated onions
3 tablespoons all-purpose flour
1 pound lump crabmeat, picked
   over for shells and cartilage
1 cup vegetable oil

☆

Combine the seasoning mix ingredients thoroughly in a small bowl. Makes 2 tablespoons plus 1¼ teaspoons.

Combine the egg, cream, and seasoning mix in the container of a blender and process on medium or "whip" speed until thoroughly blended, about 15 seconds.

Combine the potatoes, onions, flour, and the egg mixture in a large mixing bowl and mix thoroughly with a large spoon. Gently fold in the crabmeat, taking care not to break it up too much.

Heat the oil in a 12- or 14-inch nonstick skillet until very hot, about 5 to 6 minutes. Slip 6 quarter-cupfuls of the crab mixture into the oil, flattening each dumpling slightly, and adding only as many dumplings at a time as will fit without crowding. Fry, turning several times, until golden brown on both sides, about 5 to 6 minutes. Remove from the skillet and keep warm while you fry the remaining dumplings. (Make sure the oil is hot before adding the second batch of dumplings.) Serve immediately.

# Cape Codfish Cakes

### MAKES ABOUT 20 CAKES, OR 10 SERVINGS

★

Cod, considered almost sacred for hundreds of years, was an important food fish for the early settlers and a source of livelihood and even riches for Massachusetts traders in the seventeenth and eighteenth centuries. Every year enormous amounts of cod were preserved with salt and stored away for the winter. A favorite Sunday morning dish was made from the preserved fish—codfish balls or cakes. These were sometimes served with a tomato sauce, but we felt that the dish has so much flavor of its own, we didn't want to spoil it by adding anything.

SEASONING MIX
1 tablespoon plus 1 teaspoon
    garlic powder
1 tablespoon plus 1 teaspoon
    onion powder
1 tablespoon plus 1 teaspoon
    dried sweet basil leaves
1 tablespoon dried cilantro
    leaves
2 teaspoons dried thyme leaves
1½ teaspoons white pepper
1½ teaspoons black pepper
1 teaspoon ground cumin
1 teaspoon ground nutmeg

¾ pound salted codfish
    (salt cod)
3 cups diced potatoes
14 slices bacon, diced
5 tablespoons grated onion
1 teaspoon minced fresh garlic
6 egg yolks
1 cup heavy cream
3 tablespoons dried chopped
    chives
¼ cup olive oil

☆

Combine the seasoning mix ingredients thoroughly in a small bowl. Makes 7 tablespoons plus 1 teaspoon.

Soak the codfish in water to cover overnight, changing the water at least 3 or 4 times.

Drain the salted codfish and cut it into large dice.

Bring a large saucepan of water to a boil, add the potatoes, and cook until just tender, about 5 minutes. Remove from the heat and drain. Turn the potatoes into a large bowl and mash until fairly smooth. Set aside.

Fry the bacon in a 10-inch skillet over high heat, stirring occasionally, until browned about 10 to 12 minutes. Remove the bacon with a slotted spoon and drain on paper towels.

Heat the fat remaining in the skillet over high heat, and when the fat is hot, add the onion, garlic, and *3 tablespoons* of the seasoning mix. Mix thoroughly with a spoon and remove from the heat.

Combine the codfish, egg yolks, the cooked bacon, and the grated onion mixture in the bowl of a food processor. Process until blended, about 45 seconds. With the machine running, add the heavy cream in a thin stream. Pour the contents of the food processor over the mashed potatoes. Add the chives and *1 tablespoon* of the seasoning mix and fold together until thoroughly blended. Cover and refrigerate 1 hour.

Using a ¼-cup measure, scoop out the chilled codfish mixture from the bowl and shape into cakes.

Heat the olive oil in a 14-inch nonstick skillet over high heat. (If you use a smaller skillet, start with less oil.) When the oil is hot, add as many of the codfish cakes as will fit without crowding and fry, flipping the cakes several times, until golden brown on both sides, about 10 minutes. Drain on paper towels. Repeat with the remaining cakes, adding more oil as necessary and heating it until hot before adding more cakes.

These are wonderful for breakfast, served with eggs, or for lunch or a light dinner with salad or a hot vegetable. Serve them hot or cold, but don't reheat them, as they tend to dry out.

# Country Ham with Red-Eye Gravy

MAKES 6 SERVINGS

★

This dish is sure to keep any self-respecting Southerner hunkered over his plate, sopping up his gravy with a biscuit until the last drop's gone. It got its name from the "red eye" that seems to appear in the midst of the ham drippings. Traditionally, that's all this gravy is: ham drippings, often flavored with a little coffee. We took a little poetic license with it and came up with the following recipe. Serve with eggs, grits, or biscuits—or all of them. Or try my special favorite—red-eye gravy over doughnuts!

SEASONING MIX
1 tablespoon dark brown sugar
2 teaspoons paprika
1 teaspoon dry mustard
1 teaspoon garlic powder
1 teaspoon onion powder
1 teaspoon white pepper
1 teaspoon dried thyme leaves
¹/₂ teaspoon ground allspice

☆

¹/₄ cup all-purpose flour
6 (¹/₄-inch-thick) slices ham
5 slices bacon, diced
2 cups chicken stock
2 cups double-strength black
   coffee
1 tablespoon dark brown sugar
¹/₂ cup heavy cream

Combine the seasoning mix ingredients thoroughly in a small bowl. Makes 3 tablespoons plus 1½ teaspoons.

Combine the flour and all the seasoning mix in a shallow pan.

Trim the fat from the ham and cut each slice in half.

Cook the bacon in a 12-inch skillet over high heat until lightly browned, about 6 minutes. Turn the heat down to medium and cook 2 minutes. Remove the bacon with a slotted spoon and set aside.

Turn the heat back up to high under the skillet. Dredge each piece of ham in the flour/seasoning mix, shaking off the excess flour, and fry the ham in batches until browned, about 1 minute per side. Drain on paper towels.

Add the remaining flour mixture to the skillet. Using a wire whisk, whip in the chicken stock. Add the cooked bacon and whisk, occasionally scraping the bottom of the skillet, until the gravy is a rich, brown color, about 3 minutes. Whisk in the coffee and then the brown sugar and cook, whisking constantly, until the gravy comes just to the boiling point. Whisk in the cream and bring to a boil. Add the ham and cook until the sauce bubbles again, about 1 minute.

Serve the ham with some of the gravy—and serve the rest on fried bread, grits, or biscuits.

# Red Flannel Hash

MAKES 4 SERVINGS

*Color photograph 8*

★

New Englanders turn their leftover Sunday boiled dinner into this tasty, colorful dish, which is perfect for breakfast and also wonderful served with a salad for lunch or a light dinner. The beets, of course, make it red—and red makes me think of the color of the long johns I'd wear if I were spending the winter in New England.

**SEASONING MIX**

*1 teaspoon salt*

*1 teaspoon white pepper*

*1 teaspoon dried sweet basil leaves*

*¾ teaspoon dry mustard*

*½ teaspoon black pepper*

*½ teaspoon garlic powder*

*½ teaspoon onion powder*

*½ teaspoon dried oregano leaves*

*¼ teaspoon ground nutmeg*

*6 slices bacon, diced*

*1¾ cup chopped onions, in all*

*1 cup chopped celery*

*4 tablespoons unsalted butter*

*2 cups diced peeled potatoes*

*1½ cups diced peeled fresh beets*

*2½ cups diced cooked corned beef*

*½ cup loosely packed chopped fresh parsley*

☆

Combine the seasoning mix ingredients thoroughly in a small bowl. Makes 2 tablespoons.

Preheat the broiler.

Cook the bacon in a 12-inch ovenproof skillet over high heat, about 5 minutes. Add *¾ cup* of the onions, stir, and cook until the onions start to brown, about 4 minutes. Add the celery, butter, *1 tablespoon* of the seasoning mix, and the *remaining 1 cup* onions. Cook, stirring occasionally, about 6 minutes. Stir in the potatoes, beets, corned beef, parsley, and the *remaining* seasoning mix and cook until the mixture is sticking hard to the bottom of the skillet but not burning, about 7 to 10 minutes.

Place the skillet under the broiler and broil until brown and bubbly, about 3 to 4 minutes. Serve immediately with eggs.

# Philadelphia Scrapple

### MAKES ENOUGH TO SERVE AN ARMY

★

Scrapple gets it name from the scraps of pork that are combined with cornmeal to make this tasty pudding. It was a way for the thrifty early Philadelphians to use every bit of the butchered hog—and it remains a good way to do the same thing today. Scrapple is assembled in a loaf pan and refrigerated, then sliced and fried. Some like it with eggs in the morning, or even syrup or molasses. But it's so good, you can eat it without any accompaniment.

SEASONING MIX
1/4 cup salt
2 teaspoons paprika
2 teaspoons pure ground chile
 pepper (any type), optional
2 teaspoons ground sage
2 teaspoons dry mustard
2 teaspoons garlic powder
2 teaspoons onion powder
1 1/2 teaspoons white pepper
1 teaspoon black pepper
1 teaspoon ground savory
1 teaspoon dried marjoram
 leaves
1 teaspoon dried sweet basil
 leaves
1/2 teaspoon ground cardamom

1 (3- to 3 1/2-pound) Boston butt
 or pork shoulder
5 tablespoons vegetable oil, in all
4 cups chopped onions
2 1/2 cups chopped celery
2 cups chopped green bell
 peppers
1 tablespoon minced fresh garlic
10 to 12 cups chicken stock (see
 page 11), in all
2 1/4 cups yellow cornmeal
1/2 cup chopped fresh parsley
1 cup chopped green onion tops
2 tablespoons unsalted butter

☆

**DAY 1:** Combine the seasoning mix ingredients thoroughly in a small bowl. Makes 1/2 cup plus 2 tablespoons.

Cut 8 deep slits in the pork. Fill each slit with about *1 teaspoon* of the seasoning mix, pushing it in with your fingers. Sprinkle *1 tablespoon* of the seasoning mix all over the pork and rub in well with your hands.

Heat *3 tablespoons* of the oil in a large heavy pot over high heat. When the oil is very hot, add the pork, cover, and cook 3½ minutes. Turn the meat over, scatter the onions, celery, and bell peppers around the meat, and cover the pot. Cook, without lifting the lid, 10 minutes. Uncover and remove the pork. Stir in the garlic and the *remaining* seasoning mix and cook 3 minutes. Add *8 cups* of the chicken stock and return the pork to the pot. Cover, bring to a boil, reduce the heat to medium, and cook 1 hour. Add *2 cups* more stock, cover, and cook 1 hour more. Remove from the heat and remove the pork from the pot.

Preheat the oven to 350°.

When the pork is cool enough to handle, use your fingers to shred the meat into a bowl. There should be about 4½ cups shredded pork.

Strain the stock from the pot into a large measuring container and add enough of the *remaining* chicken stock to make 6½ cups liquid. Pour the stock back into the pot, add the shredded pork, cover, and cook over high heat, stirring occasionally, 17 minutes. Using a wire whip, whisk in the cornmeal. Remove from the heat and stir the mixture with a spoon until thick and thoroughly blended. Add the parsley and green onions, stir well, and pour into 2 ungreased loaf pans. Bake 30 minutes.

Let cool to room temperature, cover, and refrigerate overnight.

**DAY 2:** Remove the scrapple from the refrigerator, unmold, and cut into 2-inch-thick slices.

Heat the *remaining 2 tablespoons* oil in a small skillet over high heat. When the oil is hot, add the butter. When the butter is sizzling, brown the scrapple 2 or 3 slices at a time on both sides, about 1½ to 2 minutes in all.

Serve with eggs, grits, or potatoes and drizzle syrup or molasses on top, if you desire.

# APPETIZERS
## *and*
# NIBBLES

Appetizers, nibbles, and finger foods should be geared for the occasions at which they're served since they help set the atmosphere. For instance, at a party for business associates and clients you might want to serve only those finger foods that are relatively neat to eat and easy to handle. And it's probably simplest to offer foods that can be served at room temperature. Lower East Side Latkes, with a dipping bowl of sour cream or applesauce, or a simple cheese platter are just two appropriate choices.

For a big, casual buffet for family and friends you can take more risks, have a larger variety, and focus on foods that are fun and exciting, such as Pennsylvania Dutch Cheese Pie or Oklahoma Honey Chicken. Before your guests arrive, set out nibbles that are served cold or at room temperature, like Delancey Street Chopped Liver. When people start arriving, you can bring out the hot stuff, such as Waikiki Chicken Fingers and Tamale Pie.

At a sit-down dinner party, the appetizer or first course is extremely important because it sets the tone for the rest of the meal. Try not to select an appetizer that's very elaborate if your main course is complicated. On the other hand, if you're serving a simple roast for dinner, a more exciting first course like Scalloped Oysters would be just right.

# Pennsylvania Dutch Cheese Pie

MAKES 8 TO 10 APPETIZER SERVINGS
OR 6 SIDE-DISH SERVINGS

★

We all know that Monterey Jack cheese was created in Monterey, California, and Vermont and New York are famous for Cheddar cheese. But it was the Pennsylvania Dutch—long before the quiche rage—who became known for baking cheese into pies. And real men *do* eat Pennsylvania Dutch cheese pie.

SEASONING MIX
3 tablespoons sugar
1 teaspoon salt
1 teaspoon ground nutmeg
1 teaspoon dry mustard
1 teaspoon ground coriander
¾ teaspoon caraway seeds

☆

CRUST
1½ cups all-purpose flour
1 tablespoon plus 1 teaspoon
   Seasoning Mix (see above)
1½ teaspoons dry mustard
1 cup shredded Monterey Jack
   cheese
8 tablespoons (1 stick) unsalted
   butter, softened, cut into 8 pats
2 eggs, beaten

All-purpose flour
Vegetable oil cooking spray
Dried beans

FILLING
4 tablespoons unsalted butter
1½ cups chopped onions
3 tablespoons plus ¾ teaspoon
   Seasoning Mix (see above)
1½ cups heavy cream
4 eggs
4 cups grated Cheddar cheese

2 cups grated Monterey Jack
   cheese

Combine the seasoning mix ingredients thoroughly in a small bowl. Makes ¼ cup plus 1¾ teaspoons.

**FOR THE CRUST,** combine the flour, seasoning mix, mustard, and cheese in a mixing bowl and blend thoroughly with your hands. Cut in the butter with a fork, a pat at a time. Add the beaten eggs and blend with a large spoon or your hands until thoroughly incorporated. Refrigerate 2 hours.

Preheat the oven to 350°.

Sprinkle a clean surface with flour and roll out the dough to a thickness of ¼ inch. Fold the dough in half and then in half again. Reflour the work surface and roll the dough out again, reflouring from time to time.

Spray a 9-inch round cake pan with cooking spray. Fit the dough in the pan, leaving a ¼-inch overhang over the sides. Cover the dough with waxed paper, weight down with dried beans, and bake 20 minutes. Remove the pie shell from the oven and turn the heat down to 300°. Remove the waxed paper and beans from the dough.

**FOR THE FILLING,** melt the butter in an 8-inch skillet over high heat. When the butter starts to sizzle, add the onions and cook, stirring occasionally, until the onions are lightly browned, about 7 to 8 minutes. Stir in the seasoning mix and cook until brown bits appear in the skillet, about 1 minute. Stir in the cream, scrape the bottom of the skillet, and bring just to a boil. Remove from the heat.

Place the eggs and cheese in the bowl of a food processor and process 15 seconds. Add the onion mixture and process until well blended, about 1½ minutes. Makes 4 cups.

Pour the filling into the partially baked pie shell and bake until set, about 45 minutes.

Preheat the broiler.

Sprinkle the cheese over the pie and broil until browned and bubbly on top, about 5 minutes. Let cool a few minutes, then cut into wedges and serve.

# New York Oyster Pan Roast

MAKES 4 SERVINGS

Oyster pan roast is a well-known dish at the Oyster Bar at New York City's Grand Central Station, where it's been served to happy customers for many years. Here's an easy-to-make variation on the original theme.

SEASONING MIX

2 teaspoons salt
¾ teaspoon dried sweet basil
    leaves
½ teaspoon onion powder
½ teaspoon garlic powder
½ teaspoon dried thyme leaves
½ teaspoon white pepper
¼ teaspoon dried oregano leaves
¼ teaspoon dried marjoram
    leaves
⅛ teaspoon cayenne pepper

☆

1 pint shucked oysters, with their
    liquid, in all
4 tablespoons unsalted butter
2½ cups chopped peeled
    tomatoes (3 or 4 medium
    tomatoes)
1 cup chopped onions
2 medium bay leaves
1 teaspoon fresh lemon juice
½ cup heavy cream

Combine the seasoning mix ingredients thoroughly in a small bowl. Makes 1 tablespoon plus 2⅜ teaspoons.

Slice *4* of the oysters and set aside.

Heat a heavy 12-inch skillet over high heat. When the skillet is very hot, add the butter, tomatoes, onions, and bay leaves and cook, stirring occasionally, until the mixture thickens, about 4 to 5 minutes. Stir in *1 tablespoon* of the seasoning mix and cook, stirring occasionally, 6 to 7 minutes. Add the sliced oysters, stir, and cook 1 minute. Stir in the lemon juice and cook 1 minute. Add *1 teaspoon* of the seasoning mix and cook, scraping the bottom of the skillet whenever a crust forms, about 3 minutes. Stir in the *remaining* oysters and their liquid, the cream, and the *remaining* seasoning mix and cook 3 minutes. Remove from the heat.

Serve immediately with hot, crusty bread and a salad.

# Scalloped Oysters

MAKES 6 SERVINGS

★

Scalloped oysters were the forerunner of the oyster chowder. As a first course for a dinner party, however, the dish rates higher than chowder because of its elegance, festive appearance, and its ease of preparation. Coming to the table brown and bubbly from the oven, it promises greatness, and this perfectly seasoned version always pays off.

SEASONING MIX
2 teaspoons paprika
1 teaspoon dried sweet basil
   leaves
1 teaspoon dried cilantro leaves
¾ teaspoon dried thyme leaves
¾ teaspoon garlic powder
¾ teaspoon onion powder
½ teaspoon salt
½ teaspoon white pepper
½ teaspoon black pepper
¼ teaspoon ground nutmeg

1 cup soft fresh bread crumbs
   (see Note)
1 cup fine unsalted cracker
   crumbs
¼ cup olive oil
1 cup chopped onions
1 cup heavy cream
36 freshly shucked (preferred) or
   canned oysters
1½ cups grated Monterey Jack
   cheese

☆

Preheat the oven to 450°.

Combine the seasoning mix ingredients thoroughly in a small bowl. Makes 2 tablespoons plus 2 teaspoons.

Combine the bread crumbs, cracker crumbs, and *1 tablespoon plus 1 teaspoon* of the seasoning mix in another bowl. Spread this mixture evenly over the bottom of a 9-inch round cake pan.

Heat the olive oil in a small skillet over high heat. When the oil is hot, add the onions and the *remaining* seasoning mix. Cook, stirring and shaking the skillet from time to time, until the onions are browned, about 6 minutes. Add the cream and cook just until heated through, about 2 minutes. Remove from the heat.

Arrange the oysters over the bread crumb mixture in the cake pan

Pour the contents of the skillet over the oysters and sprinkle with the grated cheese. Bake until golden brown and bubbly, about 20 minutes. Let cool about 10 minutes before serving.

NOTE: The best soft bread crumbs are made from fresh French bread.

# Deviled Crab

MAKES 6 SERVINGS

*Color photograph 9*

Deviled dishes, mentioned in print as early as 1786, became popular in the nineteenth century. Although the word "deviled" originally indicated a dish that was fiery because it was prepared with hot seasonings, today deviled foods aren't necessarily hot—merely spicy. Deviled crabs are made almost everywhere in the South, but are also enjoyed in abundance from the Gulf Coast to the Chesapeake Bay. If you don't have scallop shells, these can be baked in ovenproof ramekins.

SEASONING MIX
*1½ teaspoons salt*
*1½ teaspoons garlic powder*
*1 teaspoon onion powder*
*1 teaspoon dry mustard*
*1 teaspoon paprika*
*1 teaspoon dried sweet basil*
*    leaves*
*½ teaspoon dried thyme leaves*
*½ teaspoon white pepper*
*¼ teaspoon black pepper*
*¼ teaspoon cayenne pepper*
*¼ teaspoon ground allspice*
☆

*9 tablespoons unsalted butter,*
*    in all*
*1½ cups chopped onions*
*1 cup chopped celery*
*2¾ cups seafood stock (see page*
*    11), in all*
*1 tablespoon all-purpose flour*
*1 cup chopped green onions*
*4 egg yolks*
*1 pound lump crabmeat, picked*
*    over for shells and cartilage*
*6 tablespoons bread crumbs*

Preheat the oven to 400°.

Combine the seasoning mix ingredients thoroughly in a small bowl. Makes 2 tablespoons plus 2¾ teaspoons.

Melt *4 tablespoons* of the butter in a 10-inch skillet over high heat. When the butter sizzles, add the onions and celery, and cook, stirring once, until the vegetables are just beginning to brown, about 4 to 5 minutes. Add the seasoning mix, stir well, and cook until the mixture is sticking to the bottom of the skillet, about 3 to 4 minutes. Add ½ *cup* of the seafood stock, scrape up the crust on the skillet bottom, and cook 2 minutes. Add another ½ *cup* of the stock, scrape the skillet, and cook 2 minutes. Stir in the flour and cook, scraping the bottom of the skillet whenever a crust forms, until the mixture sticks hard, about 2 minutes. Add another *1 cup* of the stock, scrape up the brown crust, and bring to a simmer. Cook until the mixture thickens, about 3 to 5 minutes. Stir in the *remaining ¾ cup* stock and cook 3 minutes. Add *2 tablespoons* of the butter and the green onions, stir well, and cook 3 minutes. Remove from the heat.

Beat the egg yolks lightly. Whisk 3 or 4 spoonfuls of the hot mixture into the yolks. Return the mixture to the skillet, whisking constantly. Add the crabmeat and mix thoroughly. Makes about 4 cups.

Fill each of 6 scallop shells with about ⅔ cup of the crab mixture. Top each with *1 tablespoon* of the bread crumbs, dot with ½ *tablespoon* of the butter, and place on a baking sheet. Bake until golden brown, about 20 minutes.

Serve hot, with salad and bread.

# Island Beach Oyster Pie

MAKES 6 SERVINGS

★

Inhabitants of the Atlantic coastline, and the little islands that dot the waters just offshore can't seem to eat enough mollusks, especially oysters and clams. They eat them raw, roasted, fried, steamed, and stewed, and they bake them in a crispy crust with potatoes and vegetables. We've seasoned our pie with a wonderful blend of herbs and spices, and it is a big hit with everyone who tastes it. It can easily be made with either clams or mussels as well as oysters.

**SEASONING MIX**

1½ teaspoons salt
1½ teaspoons dried sweet basil leaves
1 teaspoon garlic powder
1 teaspoon onion powder
1 teaspoon dried thyme leaves
1 teaspoon dried cilantro leaves
½ teaspoon black pepper
½ teaspoon white pepper

☆

**DOUGH**

2 cups all-purpose flour
2 tablespoons sugar
1½ teaspoons Seasoning Mix (see above)
½ teaspoon salt
¼ cup chopped green onion tops
¼ cup chopped celery
½ teaspoon minced fresh garlic
10 tablespoons (1¼ sticks) unsalted butter, cut into pats
5 tablespoons milk

**FILLING**

2 cups diced potatoes
1 pint shucked oysters (about 2 dozen medium) with their liquid (or 1 pint shucked clams or mussels)
4 tablespoons unsalted butter
1 cup chopped onions
1 cup chopped green bell peppers
2 tablespoons plus ½ teaspoon Seasoning Mix (see above)
½ teaspoon dried rosemary, crushed
5 tablespoons all-purpose flour
1 cup quartered small fresh mushrooms
½ teaspoon minced fresh garlic
2 hard-boiled eggs, chopped fine

**FINISH**

All-purpose flour
Vegetable oil cooking spray

Combine the seasoning mix ingredients thoroughly in a small bowl. Makes 2 tablespoons plus 2 teaspoons.

**FOR THE DOUGH,** place the flour, sugar, seasoning mix, salt, green onions, celery, and garlic in the bowl of a food processor and process until thoroughly blended, about 1½ to 2 minutes. With the food processor running, add the butter a pat at a time, and process until thoroughly blended, about

45 seconds. Turn the dough into a large mixing bowl, and break up any lumps with your hands. Stir in the milk with a wooden spoon and stir until smooth, then form into a ball of dough. Cover and refrigerate 30 minutes to 1 hour.

**FOR THE FILLING,** bring 2 quarts of water to a boil in a large pot over high heat. Add the potatoes, bring the water back to a boil, and cook until just tender but still firm, about 4 minutes. Drain and set aside.

Measure out 1 cup of the oyster liquid. If there is less than 1 cup, add water to the oysters, allow to sit about 10 minutes, and strain enough of this juice into the oyster liquid to make 1 cup. Set aside.

Melt the butter in a 10-inch skillet over high heat. When the butter begins to sizzle, add the onions, peppers, and seasoning mix. Cook, stirring once or twice, about 3 minutes. Stir in the rosemary and cook until a light brown crust starts to form on the bottom of the skillet, about 3 minutes. Add the flour and scrape up the crust until the flour is thoroughly blended into the vegetables. Stir in the reserved 1 cup oyster liquid and stir until the mixture is thick and pasty, about 1 minute. Add the potatoes, mushrooms, garlic, eggs, and drained oysters and cook, stirring until thoroughly blended, until just heated through, about 2 to 3 minutes. Remove from the heat and let cool.

Preheat the oven to 350°.

Sprinkle a clean surface with flour. Remove the dough from refrigerator and divide it in half. Roll out each half to a large circle about ¼ inch thick.

**TO FINISH,** coat a 9-inch round cake pan with cooking spray. Line the pan with 1 circle of dough, allowing the dough to hang over the edges. Pour the filling into the pan and cover with the second circle of dough. Fold the edges of the dough together, seal, and crimp. Punch a few holes in the top to allow steam to escape. Bake until golden brown, about 1 hour.

Turn the pie out onto a serving plate. Cut into wedges and serve warm.

# Maryland Crab Cakes

MAKES 8 CRAB CAKES: 8 APPETIZER SERVINGS
OR 4 MAIN-COURSE SERVINGS

★

Maryland is one of the top-ranking states for fresh seafood, and crab cakes have become almost a state signature. These juicy, spicy concoctions have been big favorites in that area since the eighteenth century. While Worcestershire and Tabasco sauces can usually be found in any traditional recipe for Maryland crab cakes, we found that the seasonings and herbs we've added, along with the fresh soft bread crumbs, give these cakes a flavor and texture that make them melt in your mouth.

**SEASONING MIX**
2 teaspoons salt
2 teaspoons paprika
1 teaspoon garlic powder
1 teaspoon onion powder
1 teaspoon dry mustard
1 teaspoon dried sweet basil
　leaves
¾ teaspoon white pepper
½ teaspoon black pepper
½ teaspoon dried thyme leaves

☆

**CRAB CAKES**
5 cups soft bread crumbs, in all
　(use fresh bread—French
　preferably—and grate or
　process)
7 tablespoons unsalted butter
2 cups chopped onions
1 cup chopped green bell peppers

1 cup chopped celery
1 cup chopped fresh parsley,
　in all
1 tablespoon Worcestershire
　sauce
1 teaspoon Tabasco sauce,
　optional
1 teaspoon minced fresh garlic
½ cup seafood stock (see page
　11) or bottled clam juice
1 pound lump crabmeat, picked
　over for shells and cartilage
3 eggs, lightly beaten
1 cup heavy cream

**SAUCE**
2 cups heavy cream, in all
½ cup chopped green onion tops
1 cup vegetable oil

Combine the seasoning mix ingredients thoroughly in a small bowl. Makes 3 tablespoons plus ¾ teaspoon.

**FOR THE CRAB CAKES,** toast *3 cups* of the bread crumbs in a 12-inch skillet over high heat, shaking the skillet occasionally, until the crumbs are light brown, about 5 to 6 minutes. Remove the crumbs and set aside. (The volume of crumbs will have reduced to approximately 2¼ cups.)

Return the skillet to high heat and add the butter, onions, bell peppers, and celery and cook, stirring once or twice, until the vegetables start to brown, about 6 minutes. Stir in *2 tablespoons* of the seasoning mix, ½ *cup* of the parsley, the Worcestershire sauce, Tabasco, and garlic and cook over high heat until the mixture is sticking to the bottom of the pan, about 5 minutes. Add the seafood stock or clam juice, scrape up the crust on the bottom of the skillet, and remove from the heat.

Place the toasted bread crumbs in a medium-size mixing bowl. Add the crabmeat and the *remaining* seasoning mix and ½ *cup* chopped parsley. Then add the vegetable mixture from the skillet, the eggs, and cream, and stir gently, without breaking up the lumps of crabmeat. Remove ½ cup of the mixture and set aside to use in the sauce. Refrigerate the remaining mixture 1½ hours.

**FOR THE SAUCE,** combine *1 cup* of the cream and the reserved ½ cup crab mixture in an 8-inch skillet over high heat. Cook, whipping constantly with a wire whisk, about 3 minutes. Whisk in the *remaining 1 cup* cream and cook 2 minutes. Add the green onions and bring the sauce to a boil, whisking occasionally, about 2 minutes. Remove from the heat and keep warm.

**TO FINISH,** remove the crab mixture from the refrigerator.

Heat the oil in a 10-inch skillet over high heat. While the oil is heating, place the *remaining 2 cups* bread crumbs in a bowl. Measure out ½ cup of the crabmeat mixture, form it into a flat cake, and dredge in the crumbs. Repeat with remaining mixture to form 8 crab cakes.

When the oil is hot, add 4 of the crab cakes to the skillet, lower the heat to medium, and fry until browned, about 3 minutes each side. Drain on paper towels. Remove from the skillet, turn up the heat to high, and repeat with the remaining crab cakes.

To serve as an appetizer, pour a generous ¼ cup of the sauce onto each of 8 plates and place a crab cake in the middle. To serve as a main course, allow ½ cup sauce and 2 crab cakes per person.

# Decatur Street Shrimp
# and Rice Cakes

MAKES 5 FIRST-COURSE SERVINGS OR
10 HORS D'OEUVRE SERVINGS

★

Shrimp and rice are two of the most familiar ingredients in Louisiana cooking. They're found in gumbos, jambalaya, and any number of other regional dishes. Sweet fried rice cakes are known as *calas*. We've left out the sweetness and added shrimp, seasonings, and all kinds of other good things to turn these wonderful fried cakes into a first course or party finger food.

SEASONING MIX
2 teaspoons salt
2 teaspoons paprika
2 teaspoons onion powder
2 teaspoons garlic powder
2 teaspoons dried sweet basil
 leaves
1 teaspoon black pepper
1 teaspoon white pepper
1 teaspoon dry mustard
1 teaspoon dried oregano leaves
1 teaspoon dried thyme leaves

☆

2 cups seafood stock (see
 page 11)
1 cup uncooked converted rice

1 pound peeled shrimp (about
 1½ pounds unpeeled shrimp)
9 tablespoons unsalted butter,
 in all
2 cups chopped onions
1 cup chopped green bell peppers
1 cup chopped celery
1 small bay leaf
1½ cups sliced fresh mushrooms
5 eggs, in all
½ cup chopped green onion tops
¼ cup chopped fresh parsley
Vegetable oil cooking spray
2 tablespoons water
1½ cups all-purpose flour
¾ cup vegetable oil

Combine the seasoning mix ingredients thoroughly in a small bowl. Makes 5 tablespoons.

Bring the seafood stock to a boil in a medium saucepan. Add the rice, cover, and bring back to a boil. Reduce the heat to low and simmer until the rice is tender and all the stock has been absorbed, about 15 minutes. Remove from the heat and set aside.

Chop enough shrimp to make ½ cup—about 4 or 5, if they're medium-large. Cut the remaining shrimp into "nibble-size" pieces.

Melt *5 tablespoons* of the butter in a 10-inch skillet over high heat. When the butter sizzles, add the onions, bell peppers, and celery and cook until soft, about 3 minutes. Stir in *2 tablespoons* of the seasoning mix and cook, stirring occasionally, 4 minutes. Add the ½ cup chopped shrimp, the bay leaf, and mushrooms and stir. Cook, scraping the pan occasionally when the mixture sticks, until the vegetables are browned and caramelized, about 9 to 10 minutes. Remove the bay leaf and add the shrimp/vegetable mixture to the cooked rice, mixing with a spoon until thoroughly blended. (Be sure to scrape all of the mixture from the skillet.)

Place half the rice mixture in the bowl of a food processor. Add *3* of the eggs and the *remaining 4 tablespoons* butter, cut into pats, and process until thoroughly puréed, about 25 seconds. Turn the puréed mixture back into the rest of the rice. Add the green onions, parsley, the cut-up shrimp, and the *remaining* seasoning mix and blend well with a spoon.

Coat a baking sheet with cooking spray.

Form cakes from the shrimp/rice mixture by scooping out ½-cup portions and flattening them slightly with your hands. You should get 10. Place the cakes on the baking sheet and refrigerate 2 hours.

Make an egg wash by beating together the *remaining 2* eggs and the water in a shallow bowl.

Place the flour in another shallow bowl or pie plate.

Heat the oil in a 10-inch skillet. While the oil is heating, remove the shrimp/rice cakes from the refrigerator and dip each cake in the flour, then the egg wash, then the flour again. When the oil is very hot, fry the cakes until golden brown, about 2 to 3 minutes each side. Drain on paper towels.

Serve 2 cakes per person as a first course, or pass a plate of the cakes at a cocktail party.

# Smoked Soft-Shell Crawfish Bienville

MAKES 6 SERVINGS

★

Almost everyone who's ever been to New Orleans has had crawfish in one form or another. Down here, this little creature is revered, and you'll see signs, books, and tee shirts testifying to its glory. There are crawfish boils and crawfish festivals and crawfish-eating contests. Crawfish are lovingly stirred into bisques, stews, and etouffées. And recently, when hard-shell crawfish are out of season, die-hard "mudbug" lovers have been found devising recipes for soft-shell crawfish. If your fish market can't order soft-shell crawfish for you, find one that can. You'll thank yourself.

SEASONING MIX

1 tablespoon plus 1 teaspoon
   paprika
2½ teaspoons salt
2½ teaspoons dry mustard
2 teaspoons white pepper
2 teaspoons garlic powder
2 teaspoons dried sweet basil
   leaves
1½ teaspoons black pepper
1½ teaspoons onion powder
1¼ teaspoons dried thyme leaves

☆

BIENVILLE SAUCE

8 tablespoons (1 stick) unsalted
   butter, cut into pats
¼ cup all-purpose flour
8 slices bacon, diced
1½ cups chopped onions
1 cup chopped celery
½ cup chopped green bell
   peppers
1 cup sliced fresh mushrooms

¼ cup chopped smoked ham
2 tablespoons plus 1 teaspoon
   Seasoning Mix, in all (see
   above)
2 cups seafood stock (see page
   11), in all
1 teaspoon minced fresh garlic
¾ cup chopped green onion tops
½ cup chopped fresh parsley
1 cup heavy cream
8 shucked oysters, with their
   liquid
½ pound peeled shrimp (about
   ¾ pound unpeeled shrimp)

CRAWFISH

24 soft-shell crawfish
2 eggs
2 tablespoons milk
1 cup all-purpose flour
1 cup bread crumbs
2 cups vegetable oil

Combine the seasoning mix ingredients thoroughly in a small bowl. Makes 6 tablespoons plus 1¼ teaspoons.

**FOR THE SAUCE,** melt the butter in an 8-inch skillet over high heat. When the butter starts to foam and bubble, remove from the heat and whisk in the flour. Continue to whisk until the mixture is thoroughly blended into a roux. Set aside.

Fry the bacon in a 10-inch skillet over high heat until browned, about 6 to 8 minutes. Remove the bacon with a slotted spoon and set aside.

Add the onions, celery, green peppers, and mushrooms to the hot bacon fat in the skillet. Cook, stirring occasionally, until the onions are golden brown, about 6 minutes. Add the ham and *2 tablespoons* of the seasoning mix and cook, stirring occasionally, until a crust forms on the bottom of the skillet, about 7 minutes. Stir in *1 cup* of the seafood stock, scrape the bottom of the skillet clean, and bring to a rolling boil. Stir in the garlic, green onions, parsley, and the *remaining 1 teaspoon* seasoning mix. Cook, stirring occasionally, 5 minutes. Add the *remaining 1 cup* stock and scrape up the crust on the bottom of the skillet. Stir in the cream, bring to a rolling boil, and cook, stirring occasionally, 3 minutes. Add the oysters and shrimp and cook, stirring occasionally, 3 minutes.

Meanwhile, reheat the roux in the small skillet, whisking frequently, about 1 minute. Whisk this mixture into the sauce and bring to a boil, whisking constantly. Remove from the heat and keep warm.

**TO CLEAN THE CRAWFISH,** slice the heads open from underneath, behind the mouth to the top. Remove the insides of each head, including the 2 hard calcium pellets the crawfish uses to form a new hard shell after shedding the old one.

**TO PREPARE THE CRAWFISH,** place them in a bowl, sprinkle with *2 teaspoons* of the seasoning mix, and toss to coat.

Beat the eggs, milk, and *1 tablespoon* of the seasoning mix in a small bowl.

Thoroughly combine the flour and *2 teaspoons* of the seasoning mix in a shallow bowl.

Thoroughly combine the bread crumbs and *2 teaspoons* of the seasoning mix in another shallow bowl.

Heat the oil in a 10-inch skillet over high heat until very hot, about 7 to 10 minutes. While the oil is heating, dip the seasoned crawfish, one at a time, into the flour mixture, then the beaten eggs, then the bread crumbs. Fry the crawfish, 4 at a time, until golden brown, about 1 minute on each side; stand away from the skillet while the crawfish are frying because they tend to spatter and pop. Drain the crawfish on paper towels and keep warm.

To serve, spoon ¾ cup of the sauce onto each plate and top with 4 crawfish.

# Oklahoma Honey Chicken

MAKES 8 SERVINGS

*Color photograph 10*

The taste of this popular finger food is reminiscent of a wonderful Midwestern barbecue, but the soy sauce gives it a somewhat Oriental flair. When we make these for our office, we have to keep Carol Leonard, who is one of our accountants, from eating them all.

SEASONING MIX
*1½ teaspoons ground ginger*
*1¼ teaspoons salt*
*¾ teaspoon paprika*
*¾ teaspoon onion powder*
*¾ teaspoon pure ground*
  *California Beauty chile pepper*
  *(see Note)*
*½ teaspoon ground sage*
*¼ teaspoon garlic powder*
*¼ teaspoon ground cumin*
☆

*16 chicken drumettes, (wings*
  *with the tip and first joint cut*
  *off)*
*4 tablespoons unsalted butter*
*½ cup finely chopped onions*
*2 teaspoons finely minced fresh*
  *garlic*
*½ cup dry sherry*
*2 tablespoons soy sauce*
*½ cup chicken stock*
  *(see page 11)*
*½ cup honey*

Preheat the broiler.

Combine the seasoning mix ingredients thoroughly in a small bowl. Makes 2 tablespoons.

Sprinkle *1 tablespoon* of the seasoning mix over the wings and work it in well with your hands.

Melt the butter in a heavy 12-inch skillet over high heat. When the butter sizzles, add the seasoned wings. Brown the chicken on one side, turn it, add the onions and garlic, and cook until the wings are brown on both sides, about 10 to 12 minutes in all. Add the sherry, soy sauce, chicken stock, and the *remaining* seasoning mix and bring to a hard boil. Remove from the heat, stir in the honey, and let sit 3 minutes.

Remove the chicken wings from the sauce with tongs, place on the broiler pan in a single layer, and broil, turning once, until brown and crispy, about 2 minutes on each side. Pour the sauce into a bowl.

Serve the wings immediately and pass the sauce for dipping.

NOTE: This is the chile pepper we used. You can use whatever is available in your area, but be sure to buy pure ground chile peppers, not commercial chili powder.

# Buffalo Chicken Wings

## MAKES 8 SERVINGS

★

The best finger food to come along in years, Buffalo chicken wings were concocted at the Anchor Bar in Buffalo, New York. They were an instant success and are now an attraction at bars all over America. Our version has a somewhat different seasoning, which we think gives the wings a deeper flavor. And the blue cheese dressing is so good, you'll probably catch your guests licking it off their fingers.

*2 teaspoons salt*
*2 teaspoons paprika*
*1 teaspoon cayenne pepper*
*1 teaspoon onion powder*
*1 teaspoon garlic powder*
*¾ teaspoon white pepper*

☆

*10 tablespoons (1¼ sticks)*
  *unsalted butter, in all*
*1 tablespoon plus 1 teaspoon*
  *Tabasco sauce, in all*
*24 chicken wings, tips removed,*
  *room temperature*
*2 cups vegetable oil*
*Blue Cheese Dressing (recipe*
  *follows)*
*Celery sticks, optional*

Combine the seasoning mix ingredients thoroughly in a small bowl. Makes 2 tablespoons plus 1¾ teaspoons.

Melt *5 tablespoons* of the butter with *2 teaspoons* of the Tabasco sauce in a small saucepan over low heat. Pour into a small shallow bowl or pie plate, and let cool slightly.

Place the chicken wings in a large bowl, sprinkle with *2 tablespoons* of the seasoning mix, and add the butter/Tabasco mixture. Work the seasonings and butter mixture into the wings with your hands, distributing the seasoning evenly. (Be sure to have the chicken wings at room temperature; if they're cold, the marinade mixture will congeal and won't coat the chicken evenly.) Set aside to marinate while you heat the oil.

Heat the oil in a large heavy skillet over high heat. When the oil is very hot, add as many wings as will fit easily in a single layer. Fry until crisp and golden brown, about 8 to 12 minutes, turning several times. Drain on paper towels. Repeat with the remaining wings.

Meanwhile, make a finishing sauce by melting the *remaining 5 tablespoons* butter with the *remaining 2 teaspoons* Tabasco and the *remaining* seasoning mix in a small saucepan. Dip the cooked wings into the finishing sauce and place on a serving platter. Serve with the Blue Cheese Dressing and celery sticks, if desired.

## BLUE CHEESE DRESSING

★

*2 eggs*
*1 tablespoon fresh lemon juice*
*1 tablespoon apple cider vinegar*
*¼ cup chopped onions*
*¼ cup chopped celery*
*½ teaspoon salt*

*½ teaspoon white pepper*
*⅛ teaspoon cayenne pepper*
*½ teaspoon minced fresh garlic*
*1 teaspoon Worcestershire sauce*
*2 cups vegetable oil*
*½ cup crumbled blue cheese*

Place all the ingredients except the oil and cheese in a blender and process 15 to 20 seconds. Continue processing while you drizzle in the oil in a slow, steady stream. Process another 45 seconds and pour into a bowl. Add the blue cheese, mix well, and refrigerate until ready to use.

# Waikiki Chicken

MAKES 8 TO 10 HORS D'OEUVRE SERVINGS
OR 4 MAIN-COURSE SERVINGS
*Color photograph 11*

This luscious dish has its roots dug firmly into Hawaiian soil. The macadamia nuts identify it positively with soft island breezes, hula dancing and luaus. Be sure to let the chicken cool somewhat before eating it, or the nuts will burn your tongue. You can also serve Waikiki Chicken as a main course: Leave the chicken breasts whole (as pictured in the color insert) and increase the frying and baking times by about 3 minutes each. Serve the chicken with the sauce spooned over it.

SEASONING MIX

2 tablespoons salt

4 teaspoons paprika

2 teaspoons garlic powder

2 teaspoons onion powder

2 teaspoons dried thyme leaves

2 teaspoons dried sweet basil
  leaves

1½ teaspoons white pepper

1 teaspoon black pepper

1 teaspoon ground allspice

☆

¼ cup fresh lemon juice

2 tablespoons Worcestershire
  sauce

¼ cup dry sherry

1¼ cups chopped green onions,
  in all

¾ cup chopped fresh parsley,
  in all

1½ teaspoons minced fresh
  garlic, in all

4 whole boneless, skinless
  chicken breasts (8 halves),
  cut into 2½-inch-long strips

1½ cups finely chopped
  macadamia nuts (see Note)

3 cups unseasoned bread
  crumbs

5 tablespoons sugar, in all

3 eggs

1 cup all-purpose flour

1 cup vegetable oil

1 cup chopped onions

3 cups chicken stock, in all

½ cup chutney (specialty
  section of grocery store)

1 tablespoon prepared Dijon
  mustard

Combine the seasoning mix ingredients thoroughly in a small bowl. Makes 7 tablespoons plus ½ teaspoon.

Combine the lemon juice, Worcestershire sauce, sherry, ¼ *cup* of the green onions, ¼ *cup* of the parsley, *1 teaspoon* of the garlic, and *2 table-spoons* of the seasoning mix in a medium-size bowl. Add the strips of chicken and marinate them at room temperature, turning them several times, about 1 hour.

Preheat the oven to 350°.

Combine the nuts, bread crumbs, *3 tablespoons* of the sugar, and *3 tablespoons* of the seasoning mix in a mixing bowl.

Drain the chicken and reserve ¼ cup of the marinade.

Make an egg wash by beating together the eggs, the *remaining 2 tablespoons* sugar, and the reserved marinade. Spread the flour in a shallow pan or bowl.

Heat the oil in a 12-inch skillet over high heat until very hot. Dip the chicken strips in the flour, then the egg wash, and then the bread crumb/ nut mixture (reserve the excess egg wash and bread crumb mixture), and fry until golden brown on both sides, but not cooked all the way through, about 5 to 6 minutes. Remove the chicken to a baking sheet and bake 3 to 5 minutes, or until cooked through. Keep warm.

To make the sauce, add the onions to the hot oil in the skillet and cook 1 minute over high heat. Using a wire whisk, whip in ½ cup of the reserved bread crumb mixture and cook 2 minutes. Add *2 cups* of the chicken stock and cook, whisking often, about 2 minutes. Whisk in the *remaining* seasoning mix and *1 cup* stock and cook 2 minutes. Add ½ cup of the reserved egg wash and cook, whisking constantly, until the sauce begins to boil, about 2 minutes. Whisk in the chutney, mustard, and the *remaining 1 cup* green onions and *½ cup* chopped parsley. Cook 1 minute and remove from the heat.

Pass the chicken with toothpicks and use the sauce for dipping.

NOTE: You can substitute almonds or cashews for the macadamia nuts.

# Delancey Street Chopped Liver

MAKES ENOUGH TO SERVE A CROWD

*Color photograph 12*

★

As every Jewish grandma knows—especially those who reside in New York City, for some reason—the secret to great chopped liver is chicken fat. It gives the liver a flavor that could never be achieved with any substitute and a texture that's incredibly silky. In fact, this one's so smooth it's like a fine pâté. The herbs and spices we've added may take this chopped liver out of grandma's kitchen, but you won't be sorry.

3 tablespoons sugar

1 tablespoon salt

2 teaspoons paprika

1½ teaspoons white pepper

1½ teaspoons dried thyme leaves

1 teaspoon black pepper

1 teaspoon garlic powder

1 teaspoon onion powder

1 teaspoon dry mustard

1 teaspoon ground cumin

½ teaspoon ground nutmeg

☆

1 pound unrendered chicken fat, diced

3 cups chopped onions, in all

1 cup chopped celery

2 teaspoons minced fresh garlic

2 pounds beef liver, cut into slices

1 cup chicken stock (see page 11)

¾ pound chicken livers

½ cup finely chopped fresh parsley

5 eggs

Vegetable oil cooking spray

Combine the seasoning mix ingredients thoroughly in a small bowl. Makes 7 tablespoons plus 1½ teaspoons.

Cook the chicken fat in a heavy 4-quart pot over high heat until rendered, about 9 minutes. Add *2 cups* of the onions, the celery, garlic, and *2 tablespoons* of the seasoning mix. Stir well and cook 6 minutes. Add the *remaining 1 cup* onions and cook 2 minutes. Add the beef liver slices and cook 2 minutes. Stir in the chicken stock and cook 4 minutes. Stir in the chicken livers and parsley. Crack the eggs into a dish without breaking the yolks and slide them into the pot on top of the other ingredients; don't stir. Cover the pot and cook over high heat until the eggs are set, about 7 minutes. Remove from the heat.

Transfer the beef and chicken livers to the bowl of a food processor and pulse 20 to 25 times, or until coarsely puréed. Add the remaining mixture from the pot and the *remaining* seasoning mix and process until thoroughly blended and creamy.

Spray a bowl or decorative mold with cooking spray. Turn the liver mixture into the bowl or mold and smooth the top. Cover and refrigerate overnight.

Unmold and serve with crackers or on a bed of lettuce.

# La Jolla Tamale Pie

## MAKES 6 TO 8 SERVINGS

★

Tamales, long a traditional food in Mexico, are corn husks stuffed with meat. In the early part of this century, Californians living near the Mexican border turned this old favorite into a pie, putting lots of good things to eat between layers of cornmeal mush. The blend of seasonings in our version elevates the tamale pie to a dish you'll be proud to serve to company.

SEASONING MIX
1 tablespoon plus 2 teaspoons
   salt
1 tablespoon ground cumin
1 tablespoon dried cilantro
   leaves
2¼ teaspoons white pepper
2¼ teaspoons ground New
   Mexico chile pepper (see Note)
1½ teaspoons ground arbol chile
   pepper (see Note)
1½ teaspoons ground pasilla
   chile pepper (see Note)
1½ teaspoons black pepper
1½ teaspoons garlic powder
1½ teaspoons onion powder
1½ teaspoons dried thyme leaves
¾ teaspoon dried oregano leaves

1½ pounds lean ground pork
¼ cup olive oil, in all
3 cups chopped onions, in all
2 cups chopped green bell
   peppers, in all
2¼ cups yellow cornmeal, in all
4 tablespoons unsalted butter
2 teaspoons minced fresh garlic
5½ cups beef stock (see page 11),
   in all
2 tablespoons dark brown sugar
1 cup sliced pitted large black
   olives
Vegetable oil cooking spray

☆

Preheat the oven to 350°.

Combine the seasoning mix ingredients thoroughly in a small bowl. Makes ½ cup plus 1¼ teaspoons.

Combine the pork and *2 tablespoons* of the seasoning mix in another bowl and blend well with your hands.

Heat *3 tablespoons* of the olive oil in a 12-inch skillet over high heat. When the oil is hot and sizzling, add *2 cups* of the onions, *1 cup* of the bell peppers, and *3 tablespoons* of the seasoning mix. Cook, stirring occasionally, until the onions are golden, about 4 to 6 minutes. Stir in *1 cup* of the cornmeal and the butter and cook, stirring occasionally, until the cornmeal is dark and sticking to the bottom of the skillet, about 4 to 5 minutes. Add the garlic and *1 tablespoon* of the seasoning mix, scrape the skillet bottom, and cook 2 minutes. Stir in *3½ cups* of the beef stock and scrape the bottom of the skillet clean. Using a wire whisk, whip the mixture as you bring it to a rolling boil. As soon as the mixture starts to bubble, whisk in *¾ cup* of the cornmeal. Reduce the heat to medium and simmer about 11 minutes, whisking occasionally. Stir in the brown sugar and cook 3 minutes. Remove from the heat.

Meanwhile, heat the remaining *1 tablespoon* olive oil in a 10-inch skillet over high heat. When the oil is hot, about 3 minutes, add *1 tablespoon* of the seasoning mix and the *remaining 1 cup* each onions and bell peppers. Cook, stirring occasionally, until the vegetables are browned, about 6 minutes. Move the vegetables to one side of the skillet and add the seasoned pork to the cleared space. Break up any lumps of meat with a spoon and cook until lightly browned, about 2 minutes. Stir the pork into the vegetables and cook, stirring occasionally, until the pork and vegetables are well browned, about 5 minutes. Stir in the *remaining* seasoning mix and cook 3 minutes. Stir in the *remaining ½ cup* cornmeal. Cook until a crust forms on the bottom of the skillet, scrape it up, and cook until another crust forms, about 4 minutes in all. Stir in *1 cup* of the beef stock and the olives and scrape the bottom of the skillet clean. Cook 4 minutes. Add the *remaining 1 cup* stock, scrape the skillet bottom, and remove from the heat.

Coat a 10-inch cake pan or springform pan with cooking spray and spread 2 cups of the cornmeal mixture over the bottom of the pan. Spread 2 cups of the pork filling over the cornmeal. Spread the remaining cornmeal mixture, evenly over the pork, then spread the remaining pork mixture over the cornmeal. Bake until brown, about 30 minutes.

Cut the pie into wedges and serve warm.

NOTE: These are the ground chile peppers we used; you can use whatever is available in your area, but don't use commercial chili powder.

# SOUPS
## *and*
# STEWS

Although soups are often thought of merely as meal starters, and stews have a reputation for being inelegant, both recently have come into their own at even the fanciest of dinner parties. The realization has finally dawned that we love eating "pot" food.

When I was growing up, we had to eat the animals that no longer produced. And since these animals were usually old, the meat was tough and had to be cooked many hours before it became tender. For much the same reason, soups and stews were the iron foundation of the early settlers' diets. Today we don't eat them out of necessity, but because soups and stews are emotional foods. We eat them to feel good, because they evoke a sense of being cared for, hugged, and loved. The memory evoked is often "Grandma's making a wonderful soup" or "Ma's cooking my favorite stew"; and not only the tastes, but the smells, too, are truly memorable.

# New England Butternut Bisque

MAKES 8 FIRST-COURSE SERVINGS

*Color photograph 13*

★

Butternut squash is a staple in New England, where it turns up in stuffings, pies, and soups, as well as side dishes. This soup is a natural in the autumn and, in fact, makes a special first course for Thanksgiving dinner. In addition to the seasonings we've used to give it some zip, we've dressed it up with a little cinnamon and vanilla to bring out the natural sweetness of the delicious squash.

SEASONING MIX
*3 tablespoons dark brown sugar*
*1½ teaspoons salt*
*1 teaspoon dry mustard*
*1 teaspoon white pepper*
*¾ teaspoon onion powder*
*¾ teaspoon ground cinnamon*
*½ teaspoon garlic powder*
*¼ teaspoon ground mace*
*¼ teaspoon ground nutmeg*

*1 large or 2 medium butternut*
*    squash, peeled, seeded, and all*
*    membrane removed*
*3 tablespoons unsalted butter*
*1 cup chopped onions*
*1 cup chopped celery*
*5 cups chicken stock (see page 11)*
*3 cups heavy cream*
*3 tablespoons chopped fresh*
*    parsley*

☆

Combine the seasoning mix ingredients thoroughly in a small bowl. Makes 5 tablespoons.

Grate enough of the squash on the large holes of a hand grater to yield 3 cups. Cut half the remaining squash into small dice, half into medium dice—there should be about 2 cups small dice and 2 cups medium dice. Set the diced squash aside.

Melt the butter in a large heavy pot over high heat. When the butter sizzles, add the onions, celery, and the grated squash, and cook, occasionally scraping the bottom of the pot, about 13 to 15 minutes. Stir in *4 tablespoons* of the seasoning mix and cook, scraping the pot bottom once or twice, 3 to 4 minutes. Add the chicken stock, the diced squash, and the *remaining* seasoning mix. Bring to a boil, reduce the heat to low, and simmer, scraping the bottom of the pot from time to time, until the squash has disintegrated somewhat, about 40 minutes. Turn up the heat to high and stir in the cream. Bring to a boil, reduce the heat to low, and simmer 15 minutes. Remove from the heat and stir in the parsley. Makes about 9 cups.

Let the soup cool a few minutes and serve.

# Massachusetts Corn Chowder

## MAKES 10 TO 12 MAIN-COURSE SERVINGS

★

Since the earliest colonial days, New England cooking has relied heavily on corn, and corn chowder is as native to that area as a clam bake. Our chowder is thickened with grated potatoes and always turns out sweet, even if the corn we use isn't. Sitting down to a hearty bowl of corn chowder would be a great way to appreciate the contributions of our ancestors on a winter's night.

**SEASONING MIX**
2 teaspoons salt
1¼ teaspoons onion powder
1 teaspoon garlic powder
1 teaspoon dried thyme leaves
1 teaspoon dry mustard
1 teaspoon paprika
¾ teaspoon dried marjoram
   leaves

☆

½ *pound bacon, diced*
1 *cup chopped celery*
3 *cups chopped onions,* in all
2 *cups grated potatoes*
6 *cups chicken stock (see page*
   *11),* in all
7 *cups fresh corn kernels (about*
   *14 ears),* in all ~ 4 - 17oz cans
2 *cups finely diced peeled*
   *potatoes*
~~1 tablespoon dark brown sugar,~~
   ~~optional (see Note)~~
2 *cups heavy cream*

Combine the seasoning mix ingredients thoroughly in a small bowl. Makes 2 tablespoons plus 2½ teaspoons.

Place the bacon in a large heavy pot over high heat, cover, and cook, uncovering the pot occasionally to stir, until the bacon is crisp, about 5 to 6 minutes. Remove the bacon with a slotted spoon and drain on paper towels.

Pour off all but 3 tablespoons of the bacon fat from the pot and heat the fat over high heat. Add the celery and *2 cups* of the chopped onions. Scrape the pot bottom, cover, and cook until the onions are golden, un-covering the pot to scrape the bottom once or twice, about 3 to 4 minutes. Stir in the grated potatoes, cover, and cook just until the potatoes start to brown and stick to the pot bottom, about 2 minutes. Add *2 cups* of the chicken stock and scrape the bottom of the pot well. Stir in *2 tablespoons* of the seasoning mix, cover, and cook 1 minute. Add *2 cups* more chicken stock and scrape the pot bottom clean. Cover and bring to a rolling boil. Reduce the heat to medium and cook, uncovering occasionally to stir, about 2 minutes. Then use a wire whisk to break up the potatoes and blend them into the stock. Turn the heat up to high and add the corn, the *remaining 1 cup* onions and *2 cups* stock, and the *remaining* seasoning mix. Scrape the bottom of the pot and bring to a boil. Cover and cook, uncovering now and then to stir, about 8 minutes. Remove the lid and beat the mixture with a whisk. Cook, stirring occasionally, 6 minutes. Add the diced potatoes, stir, and cook 3 minutes. ~~If you're using the brown sugar, stir it into the soup.~~ Stir in the cream and bring to a boil. Reduce the heat and simmer 1 minute. Remove from the heat, finely crumble the cooked bacon, and stir it into the soup.

Serve piping hot with crusty bread and a green salad.

NOTE: If the corn you're using doesn't have a sweet taste, add the sugar; if the corn is sweet, omit the sugar.

# Yukon Mushroom and Wild Rice Soup

MAKES 8 TO 10 FIRST-COURSE SERVINGS

★

This is a delicious soup from Alaska, but it might as easily have been created in Minnesota, where much of our wild rice, actually a grass, is cultivated in rice paddies. If you can't find the dried and fresh mushrooms used here, substitute what is available to you. The seasoning mix we've devised will work just as well with other wild mushrooms.

SEASONING MIX

2 teaspoons salt
1 teaspoon paprika
3/4 teaspoon onion powder
3/4 teaspoon garlic powder
1/2 teaspoon white pepper
1/2 teaspoon ground savory
1/2 teaspoon dried sweet basil
    leaves
1/4 teaspoon black pepper

☆

4 tablespoons unsalted butter
2 cups chopped onions
1 cup chopped celery
2 bay leaves
5 ounces uncooked wild rice
1 ounce dried chanterelle
    mushrooms
1 teaspoon minced fresh garlic
8 cups chicken stock (see page
    11), in all
6 large fresh shiitake mushrooms,
    stems removed and the tops
    cut into 1/4-inch slices

Combine the seasoning mix ingredients thoroughly in a small bowl. Makes 2 tablespoons plus 1/4 teaspoon.

Melt the butter in a heavy, 3-quart pot over high heat. When the butter sizzles, add the onions and celery, bay leaves, and *1 tablespoon* of the seasoning mix and cook, stirring occasionally, 10 minutes. Stir in the wild rice and the chanterelles and cook 2 minutes. Add the *remaining* seasoning mix, the garlic, and *6 cups* of the stock. Stir well and bring to a boil. Reduce the heat to low, cover, and simmer 18 minutes.

Add the shiitake mushrooms, cover, and cook 3 minutes. Turn the heat up and stir in the *remaining 2 cups* stock. Bring to a boil, cover, reduce the heat to low, and simmer, 45 minutes.

Ladle into soup bowls and serve immediately.

# Milwaukee Potato Soup

MAKES 16 FIRST-COURSE SERVINGS

★

In 1898, a woman named Lizzie Black Kander began giving cooking classes at The Settlement in Milwaukee, Wisconsin, and a hearty potato soup was part of the first lesson. It stuck to the ribs and it was good, but it needed some added dimension, and our seasoning mix with a hint of cinnamon and nutmeg seems to do the trick deliciously. We also treated the potatoes three different ways to give the soup the maximum amount of texture to support the flavor. This recipe is a perfect example of how to "build" a dish (see pages 6 to 8).

SEASONING MIX
*1 tablespoon plus 1 teaspoon salt*
*2 teaspoons dry mustard*
*1 teaspoon onion powder*
*1 teaspoon garlic powder*
*1 teaspoon white pepper*
*½ teaspoon ground nutmeg*
*½ teaspoon ground cinnamon*

☆

*7 large potatoes, in all*
*12 tablespoons (1½ sticks) unsalted butter, in all*
*1 cup grated onions, (grated on the large holes of a hand grater)*
*1 cup chopped celery*
*5 cups chicken stock (see page 11), in all*
*6 cups milk*
*2 cups sliced onions (the slices halved)*
*1 cup heavy cream*

Combine the seasoning mix ingredients thoroughly in a small bowl. Makes 3 tablespoons plus 1 teaspoon.

Peel the potatoes and shred enough of them on the large holes of a hand grater to get 3 cups. Cut 3 of the remaining potatoes into small dice and the remaining 2 potatoes into medium dice. There should be about 8 cups diced potatoes in all.

Place a large heavy pot over high heat. Add *8 tablespoons (1 stick)* of the butter, the shredded potatoes, grated onions and celery, and cook, scraping the bottom of the pot when the mixture begins to stick, about 8 to 10 minutes. Stir in *2 tablespoons* of the seasoning mix and cook, scraping up the potato/onion mixture when it sticks to the bottom of the pot, about 2 minutes. The mixture will begin to stick hard, but don't let it get dark brown or the soup will be too dark. Add *1 cup* of the chicken stock and scrape up the crust on the bottom of the pot. (The mixture will look somewhat pasty.) Add *3 cups* more stock, scrape the bottom of the pot, and bring to a rolling boil. Stir in the milk, the *remaining 1 cup* stock, and the *remaining* seasoning mix and cook 2 minutes. Add the diced potatoes, cover the pot, and cook 2 minutes. Add the sliced onions, cover, and cook, uncovering to scrape the bottom of the pot from time to time as the mixture sticks, about 12 minutes. Reduce the heat and simmer, covered, uncovering occasionally to scrape the pot bottom, about 19 minutes. Uncover and simmer 12 minutes, scraping from time to time and whisking with a wire whisk. Cut the *remaining 4 tablespoons* butter into pats, add the cream and butter to the soup, and whisk until the butter is thoroughly blended, about 6 minutes. Remove from the heat and serve immediately.

# Cream of Tomato Soup

MAKES 10 TO 12 FIRST-COURSE SERVINGS

Largely as a result of its membership in the deadly nightshade family, as well as its ties to Spain and that country's "hot" customs, the tomato was somewhat distrusted by Americans until the start of the twentieth century, when it finally gained full acceptance. It's hard to pinpoint exactly where in this country tomato soup originated, especially since tomatoes are grown just about everywhere and just about everybody's mother has served tomato soup on a cold winter's night. The only real work involved in this recipe is the peeling and chopping of the tomatoes, but it's worth using fresh tomatoes for their flavor.

SEASONING MIX

1 tablespoon sugar
2 teaspoons salt
2 teaspoons paprika
1 teaspoon dried sweet basil
 leaves
3/4 teaspoon white pepper
3/4 teaspoon garlic powder
1/2 teaspoon onion powder
1/2 teaspoon black pepper
1/2 teaspoon ground nutmeg

1 cup heavy cream
4 tablespoons unsalted butter
1 1/2 chopped onions
1/2 cup chopped celery
11 cups peeled and chopped very
 ripe tomatoes (about 16)
 (see Note)
1 1/2 cups chicken stock
1/4 cup chopped fresh parsley

☆

Combine the seasoning mix ingredients thoroughly in a small bowl. Makes 3 tablespoons plus 2 teaspoons.

Bring the cream just to the boiling point in a small saucepan. Remove from the heat and set aside.

Melt the butter in a heavy 3-quart pot (do *not* use cast iron) over high heat. Add the onions and celery and cook, stirring occasionally, 12 minutes. Stir in *2 tablespoons* of the seasoning mix and cook 2 minutes. Stir in the tomatoes and the *remaining* seasoning mix, cover, and bring to a rolling boil. Uncover the pot, stir well, and cook hard about 3 minutes. Stir in the stock and bring to a boil. Cover, reduce the heat to low, and simmer 10 minutes. Uncover, turn up the heat to high, and cook 10 minutes more. Stir in the parsley and remove from the heat.

Put the soup into a food processor in 2 batches and process until coarsely puréed but not quite smooth. Pour into a large bowl and stir in the reserved cream. Makes about 10 cups.

Serve immediately with warm bread and butter—or grilled cheese sandwiches.

NOTE: You can use any variety, including Italian plum tomatoes, adjusting the number as necessary to get 11 cups chopped tomatoes. See page 10 for information on how to peel tomatoes easily.

# Black Bean Soup

MAKES 10 FIRST-COURSE SERVINGS

★

Beans, a food staple in Mexico, long ago traveled north into New Mexico, where they still retain their popularity, even in smart restaurants where the trendiest gourmet food is served. Of course, beans of many varieties are grown and cooked all over the United States. But the black bean seems to be most closely related to Spanish-influenced food, and black bean dishes are served mostly in Miami, where Cuban-Americans are cooking fantastic food, and in the Southwest. This particular recipe is Southwestern, and we've enhanced it with an exciting blend of ground chile peppers.

*1 pound dried black beans*

*SEASONING MIX*
*1 tablespoon salt*
*1 tablespoon ground ancho chile pepper (see Note)*
*2 teaspoons ground guajillo chile pepper (see Note)*
*2 teaspoons ground pasilla chile pepper (see Note)*
*2 teaspoons ground New Mexico chile pepper (see Note)*
*2 teaspoons onion powder*
*2 teaspoons garlic powder*
*2 teaspoons dried cilantro leaves*
*2 teaspoons dried thyme leaves*
*2 teaspoons dried oregano leaves*
*1 teaspoon white pepper*
*1 teaspoon ground nutmeg*
*1 teaspoon crushed chile quebrado (see Note)*

☆

*¼ cup yellow cornmeal*
*½ pound bacon, diced*
*4 cups chopped onions,* in all
*1 cup chopped celery*
*6 cups chicken stock,* in all
*2 cups chopped green bell peppers*
*1 tablespoon minced fresh garlic*
*¼ cup chopped fresh cilantro*

**DAY 1:** Put the beans in a large bowl, add 4 cups water, cover, and let soak overnight.

**DAY 2:** Combine the seasoning mix ingredients thoroughly in a small bowl. Makes ½ cup plus 1 teaspoon.

Toast the cornmeal in a small skillet over medium heat, stirring and shaking the pan frequently, until lightly toasted, about 3 to 5 minutes. Remove from the heat and set aside.

Drain the beans.

Fry the bacon in a large heavy pot (cast iron is best) over high heat, stirring occasionally, until golden brown, about 7 to 9 minutes. Stir in *2 cups* of the onions, the celery, and *¼ cup* of the seasoning mix, cover, and cook 3 minutes. Stir in *1 cup* of the stock and scrape up the crust on the bottom of the pot. Add the beans, cover, and cook, uncovering occasionally to scrape the pot bottom, about 18 minutes. Add *2 cups* more stock, scrape the pot bottom clean, and cook, stirring occasionally, 3 minutes. Add *2 cups* more stock, *2 tablespoons* of the seasoning mix, the bell peppers, garlic, and the *remaining 2 cups* onions. Cover and bring to a boil. Reduce the heat to low and simmer, stirring occasionally, about 27 minutes. Stir in the *remaining 1 cup* stock and the *remaining* seasoning mix, cover, and simmer 45 minutes. Stir in the toasted cornmeal and the cilantro, cover, and cook until the beans are tender, about 15 minutes.

Serve garnished with thin lemon slices or a dollop of sour cream, if desired.

NOTE: These are the chile peppers we used. You can use whatever is available in your area, but using 3 or 4 peppers of varying heats make this dish really special. Just be sure to buy pure ground chile peppers, not commercial chili powder.

# Iowa Blue Satin Soup

MAKES 4 TO 6 FIRST-COURSE SERVINGS

★

If you're looking for the finest blue cheese anywhere, go to Iowa, where the Maytag Dairy Farm turns out the critically acclaimed Maytag blue cheese. Not surprisingly, a lot of wonderful dishes centered around blue cheese have come out of Iowa, such as Blue Satin Soup. Ours is seasoned differently from the original, of course, and we found that sour cream mixed in at the end finishes the soup perfectly.

SEASONING MIX
3/4 teaspoon white pepper
3/4 teaspoon garlic powder
1/2 teaspoon onion powder
1/2 teaspoon dried marjoram
    leaves
1/2 teaspoon dried sweet basil
    leaves
1/4 teaspoon ground cardamom
1/4 teaspoon dried tarragon
    leaves
1/8 teaspoon ground cloves

☆

6 tablespoons unsalted butter,
    in all
1 1/2 cups chopped onions
1 cup chopped green bell peppers
3/4 cup chopped celery
2 cups chicken stock (see page 11)
3 cups milk
1 cup heavy cream
4 to 6 ounces blue cheese
    (preferably Maytag Blue)
2 tablespoons finely chopped
    fresh parsley
Croutons (see Note)
Sour cream
Chopped chives or green onion
    tops

Combine the seasoning mix ingredients thoroughly in a small bowl. Makes 1 tablespoon plus 5/8 teaspoon.

Melt *4 tablespoons* of the butter in a heavy 5-quart pot over high heat. When the butter sizzles, add the onions, bell peppers, celery, and *2 teaspoons* of the seasoning mix, and stir. Cover and cook, uncovering the pot occasionally to stir, until the onions are browned and all the vegetables are sticking to the bottom of the pot, about 8 to 10 minutes. Stir in the chicken stock, scrape up the crust on the pot bottom, cover, and bring to a boil. Reduce the heat to low and simmer, uncovering the pot occasionally to stir, until the mixture is dark brown, thick, and greatly reduced, about 15 to 17 minutes. Remove from the heat and let cool a few minutes.

Pour the mixture into the bowl of a food processor and process until thoroughly puréed, about 1 minute. Pour the mixture back into the pot and place over high heat. Stir in the milk, cream, and the *remaining* seasoning mix. Scrape the bottom of the pot, bring just to a boil, reduce the heat to low, and simmer, uncovered, 6 minutes.

Turn up the heat to medium and crumble the cheese into the soup, stirring with a whisk to break it up. Stir in the parsley. Keep the soup at a low bubble; if it begins to boil, turn the heat down. Whip in the *remaining 2 tablespoons* butter with a wire whisk. As soon as the butter has melted, remove from the heat. Makes about 6 cups.

To serve, ladle out individual bowls of soup. Place 1 or 2 croutons on top of each serving, add a dollop of sour cream, and sprinkle on a pinch of chopped chives or green onions.

NOTE: To make croutons, preheat the oven to 250°. Slice day-old French bread about 1 inch thick and cut off the crusts. Place the croutons on a baking sheet, brush with a little oil, and bake 20 to 25 minutes; turn, brush with oil, and bake another 25 minutes or until golden brown on both sides.

# Charleston She-crab Soup

MAKES 4 MAIN-COURSE SERVINGS OR
6 FIRST-COURSE SERVINGS

She-crab soup has been a delicacy of both Charleston, South Carolina, and Savannah, Georgia, since the early 1800s. The roe from the female crab gives the soup a richness and a special flavor that distinguishes it from other crab soups. If possible, buy fresh female crabs, boil them, and pick out the roe yourself. If not, buy lump crabmeat with roe. To bring out all the flavor of the crabmeat it's important to brown some of it well, so use a skillet at least 12 inches in diameter.

SEASONING MIX
1¾ teaspoons salt
½ teaspoon dry mustard
½ teaspoon dried sweet basil
  leaves
¼ teaspoon garlic powder
¼ teaspoon onion powder
⅛ teaspoon cayenne pepper
⅛ teaspoon ground nutmeg
⅛ teaspoon ground allspice

☆

4 tablespoons unsalted butter
1 pound lump crabmeat with
  roe, picked over for shells and
  cartilage, in all
2 tablespoons fresh lemon juice
½ teaspoon grated lemon zest
¼ cup finely chopped shallots or
  onions
4 cups heavy cream, in all
1 tablespoon chopped fresh
  parsley
Dry sherry, optional

Combine the seasoning mix ingredients thoroughly in a small bowl. Makes 1 tablespoon plus ⅝ teaspoon.

Place a 12-inch skillet over high heat and add the butter, *1 tablespoon* of the seasoning mix, and *½ cup* of the crabmeat. Cook 2 minutes, shake the skillet, and stir once, and cook another 30 seconds. Add the lemon juice and lemon zest. Stir well and cook until a brown crust has formed on the bottom of the skillet and the crabmeat is sticking, about 2 minutes. Add the shallots or onions and cook, stirring and scraping the skillet bottom frequently, until the mixture sticks hard, about 2 to 3 minutes. Stir in *1 cup* of the heavy cream and cook 30 seconds. Stir in the *remaining 3 cups* cream and cook 3 minutes. Stir in the *remaining* seasoning mix and cook 2 minutes more. Stir in the *remaining* crabmeat and the parsley and cook 4 minutes. Remove from the heat. Makes about 5½ cups.

Serve immediately, and pass the sherry if desired. One tablespoon per serving will taste wonderful.

# Opelousas Crawfish Stew

MAKES 6 TO 8 MAIN-COURSE SERVINGS

★

This is a dish that can be prepared even when crawfish are out of season, since it's made with crawfish tails, available frozen year-round. Although long a specialty of Louisiana, and a favorite in my hometown of Opelousas, crawfish are now being farmed in other parts of the country, and crawfish tails are probably available in your fish market. If you don't find them on your first try, ask the market to order some for you.

SEASONING MIX
2½ teaspoons salt
2 teaspoons paprika
1½ teaspoons onion powder
1½ teaspoons dried sweet basil
  leaves
1¼ teaspoons black pepper
1 teaspoon garlic powder
1 teaspoon dry mustard
½ teaspoon white pepper

☆

11 tablespoons unsalted butter,
  in all
2 cups chopped onions, in all
2 cups chopped green bell
  peppers, in all
1 cup chopped celery
4¾ cups chopped peeled, fresh
  tomatoes, in all
1½ teaspoons minced fresh garlic
2 pounds fresh or frozen
  crawfish tails, defrosted if
  frozen
2 cups seafood stock (see
  page 11)

Combine the seasoning mix ingredients thoroughly in a small bowl. Makes 3 tablespoons plus 2¼ teaspoons.

Melt *4 tablespoons* of the butter in a 12-inch skillet (preferably cast iron) over high heat. When the butter sizzles, add *1 cup* each of the onions and bell peppers and the celery, stir, and cook 1 minute. Stir in *1 tablespoon* of the seasoning mix and cook, stirring occasionally, until the onions are browned, about 8 to 9 minutes. Stir in *2 cups* of the tomatoes and the garlic. Cover and cook, uncovering several times to stir, until the mixture is pasty, about 10 minutes. Stir in *3 tablespoons* of the butter, the *remaining 2¾ cups* tomatoes, and the *remaining 1 cup* onions and bell peppers and scrape up any crust on the bottom of the skillet. Stir in *1 tablespoon* of the seasoning mix, cover, and cook, uncovering once to stir, about 7 minutes. Stir in the crawfish tails, the *remaining 4 tablespoons* butter, and the *remaining* seasoning mix. Add the seafood stock, stir well, cover, and bring to a boil. Remove from the heat.

Serve hot over rice.

# West Coast Oyster Stew

MAKES 6 FIRST-COURSE SERVINGS

Oysters were an important part of the American diet long before the United States came into being. They were a staple food of the coastal Indians and later were enjoyed by the colonists. Different oysters are found on the various coasts, such as the bluepoints and box oysters from Long Island and the Olympias from the West Coast. When you make this simple, luscious treat from the Northwest, be sure not to overcook the oysters. Oyster stew purists may be horrified at the thought of thyme in this old standard, but if you're one of those, try it anyway; we think you'll like it. Keep in mind that some oysters are brinier, or saltier, than others. If the oysters you buy are particularly briny or if they come with enough of their own liquid so you do not have to add water for the recipe, you might want to omit some of the salt called for.

*36 shucked oysters (about 1 pint), with their liquid*
*1 quart heavy cream*
*8 tablespoons (1 stick) unsalted butter,* in all
*½ cup chopped onions,* in all
*½ cup chopped celery,* in all

*1½ teaspoons salt (see Note)*
*½ teaspoon white pepper*
*⅛ teaspoon cayenne pepper, optional*
*¾ teaspoon dried thyme leaves*
*¼ cup chopped fresh parsley*

Strain off the liquid from the oysters and reserve 1 cup. If there's less than 1 cup of liquid with your oysters, add enough water to make 1 cup, pour over the oysters, and let sit 10 minutes; strain into a cup and set aside.

Heat the cream in a saucepan over high heat until small bubbles form around the edges. Remove from the heat and set aside.

Melt *4 tablespoons* of the butter in a large pot over high heat. When the butter sizzles, add *¼ cup* each of the onions and celery. Cook until the vegetables begin to brown, about 4 to 5 minutes. Add the *remaining ¼ cup* each onions and celery and cook until the vegetables are browned, about 2 minutes. Add the reserved oyster liquid, scrape the bottom of the pot, and bring to a boil. Reduce the heat to low and simmer 4 minutes. Stir in the salt, white pepper, and cayenne, if desired, and simmer 2 minutes. Stir in the thyme and simmer 4 minutes. Turn up the heat, add the oysters and the *remaining 4 tablespoons* butter, and bring to a simmer, stirring gently. Remove any skin that has formed on the cream, stir the cream into the oysters, and bring first to a simmer. When bubbles begin forming around the edges of the soup, stir in the parsley, heat until bubbles form again, and remove from the heat.

Serve immediately. Allow 1 cup stew per serving, including approximately 6 oysters.

NOTE: If the oysters are especially briny (salty) or if there's enough liquid with the oysters so that adding water is unnecessary, you may want to omit ½ teaspoon of the salt.

# Manhattan Seafood Chowder

MAKES 8 MAIN-COURSE SERVINGS

★

It was actually in Rhode Island that tomatoes were first added to chowders that had been made with milk or cream, but this new version somehow became known as "Manhattan." By the start of the twentieth century it was being served and eaten all over New York. Some people sneer at a tomato version of clam or fish chowder, but I love the combination of flavors, which, when seasoned properly, is irresistible. Most fish markets will probably order clams for you if they don't regularly carry them. If you can't find fresh clams in your area, use the whole shucked clams in cans from the supermarket.

SEASONING MIX

2 teaspoons salt

1 teaspoon onion powder

1 teaspoon garlic powder

1 teaspoon paprika

1 teaspoon dry mustard

1 teaspoon dried sweet basil leaves

1/2 teaspoon dried thyme leaves

1/2 teaspoon dried tarragon leaves

1/2 teaspoon dried rosemary

1/2 teaspoon white pepper

☆

30 shucked small hard-shell clams (littlenecks), with their liquid (see Note)

1/4 pound bacon, diced

1 1/2 cups chopped onions, in all

1 cup chopped celery

1 cup diced carrots

2 cups quartered tiny new potatoes

3 cups chopped peeled, fresh tomatoes (4 or 5 tomatoes)

2 cups seafood stock (see page 11), in all

1 cup chopped green onions

1 pound firm white fish fillets, such as tilapia, sole, grouper, or red snapper, cut into bite-size pieces

Combine the seasoning mix ingredients thoroughly in a small bowl. Makes 3 tablespoons.

Chop the clams into large rough pieces, or place in a food processor and pulse 5 or 6 times. Set aside.

Place a heavy 8-quart pot over high heat. Add the bacon and sauté until lightly browned, about 4 minutes. Add *1 cup* of the onions and the celery and cook until the vegetables begin to brown, about 5 to 6 minutes. Add the carrots and cook 4 minutes. Stir in *1 tablespoon* of the seasoning mix and the potatoes. Cover the pot and cook, stirring once, about 3 minutes. Add *2 teaspoons* of the seasoning mix, stir well, cover, and cook

2 minutes. Add the *remaining ½ cup* onions, stir, cover, and cook 1 minute. Stir in the tomatoes and *1 teaspoon* of the seasoning mix, cover, and cook 4 minutes. Add ½ cup of the reserved clam liquid and *1 cup* of the seafood stock, cover, and cook 4 minutes. Add the green onions, the *remaining 1 cup* stock and the *remaining* seasoning mix. Bring to a boil, add the fish and the chopped clams, cover, and cook 3 minutes. Remove from the heat and let sit 5 minutes. Makes about 9 cups.

Serve with oyster or common crackers and a salad.

NOTE: If you can't purchase the clams shucked and if you can't do it yourself, place the clams in a 12-inch skillet with 4 tablespoons water, cover, and steam just until the shells separate enough to get a knife between them, about 1 to 2 minutes. Don't let them steam fully open. Push the point of a knife with a short, sturdy blade between the shells and pry them apart. Pour the clam liquid into a small container and free the clams with the tip of the knife.

# New England Clam Chowder

MAKES 12 MAIN-COURSE SERVINGS
OR 16 FIRST-COURSE SERVINGS
*Color photograph 14*

There is probably no other dish native to New England about which New Englanders disagree more. No one is certain who first came up with the idea of cooking seafood in milk, but it seems likely that the combination arrived in Massachusetts in the seventeenth century with settlers from Old England. There always has been debate about how to properly thicken a clam chowder, and we agree with those who refuse to use flour, since it tends to neutralize the pungency of the clams. Our recipe depends on both diced and grated potatoes, which not only thicken the soup naturally but add a flavor of potato to every mouthful, complementing the clams perfectly.

SEASONING MIX
1¼ teaspoons white pepper
1¼ teaspoons black pepper
1¼ teaspoons onion powder
1¼ teaspoons garlic powder
1¼ teaspoons dry mustard
1¼ teaspoons dried sweet
    basil leaves
1 teaspoon dried thyme
    leaves
½ teaspoon dried oregano
    leaves
¼ teaspoon ground nutmeg
☆

½ pound salt pork, diced (see Note)
2 medium potatoes, peeled and
    grated
1 cup chopped onions
1 cup chopped green bell peppers
1 cup chopped celery
4 cups clam liquid (can be
    bottled clam juice), in all
6 tablespoons unsalted butter,
    in all
4 cups milk
4 cups diced peeled potatoes
2 cups heavy cream
4 dozen shucked hard-shell
    clams, with their liquid
¼ cup chopped fresh parsley
Salt, optional (see Note)

Combine the seasoning mix ingredients thoroughly in a small bowl. Makes 3 tablespoons plus ¼ teaspoon.

Place the salt pork in a large heavy pot (not cast iron) over high heat, cover, and cook until the pork is sticking hard to the bottom of the pot, about 8 minutes. Add the grated potatoes, the onions, bell peppers, celery, and *1 tablespoon plus 2 teaspoons* of the seasoning mix. Scrape the bottom of the pot well, cover, and cook 3 minutes. Add *3 cups* of the clam juice, scrape the pot bottom clean, and cook, scraping the bottom of the pot often, about 13 minutes. Stir in the *remaining 1 cup* clam juice, scrape the crust from the bottom of the pot, and cook 2 minutes. Add *3 tablespoons* of the butter and cook, scraping the pot bottom occasionally, about 2 minutes. Add the *remaining* seasoning mix and cook, whisking constantly to break up the potatoes and release their starch to thicken the chowder,

4 minutes. Stir in the milk and bring just to the boiling point, then add the diced potatoes and bring to a simmer. Reduce the heat to medium and cook, uncovered, scraping often, until the potatoes are tender, about 20 minutes. Watch the pot closely: If the soup begins to bubble too much, reduce the heat, so the milk won't curdle. Add the *remaining 3 tablespoons* butter and the heavy cream and whip with the whisk. Scrape the bottom of the pot, stir, turn up the heat a bit, and cook just until the soup begins to bubble gently. Add the clams, cook 1 to 2 minutes, and remove from the heat. Stir in the parsley and salt, if necessary. Makes about 16 cups.

Serve the chowder in deep soup bowls with crusty bread.

NOTE: Salt pushes the flavors of the other seasonings in this dish. Because salt pork differs depending on where it's processed, yours may be saltier or less salty than ours. If it comes thickly encrusted with salt, rinse some of it off and pat dry before dicing. Taste the chowder at the end, and, if necessary, add salt cautiously until the flavor is just right.

# Asopao de Camerones (Shrimp and Rice Soup)

MAKES 6 TO 8 MAIN-COURSE SERVINGS

★

About two thirds of the people who come to the mainland from Puerto Rico settle in New York City. Many of these Spanish-speaking people live in a section of the city known as Spanish Harlem, or *El Barrio*, which means "the neighborhood." The food cooked here is spicy, colorful, and enticing—real "feel-good" food. *Asopao* is a hearty, main-dish soup, loaded with shrimp, ham, and olives. We added green beans to ours, but you can use any kind of fresh beans or peas.

SEASONING MIX

*1½ teaspoons paprika*

*1 teaspoon salt*

*1 teaspoon onion powder*

*1 teaspoon garlic powder*

*1 teaspoon ground guajillo chile pepper (see Note)*

*1 teaspoon ground ancho chile pepper (see Note)*

*1 teaspoon dried oregano leaves*

*1 teaspoon dried sweet basil leaves*

*1 teaspoon dried thyme leaves*

*¾ teaspoon black pepper*

*½ teaspoon white pepper*

☆

*2 pounds unpeeled large shrimp, preferably with heads (1½ pounds if headless)*

*3 tablespoons olive oil*

*1½ cups chopped onions,* in all

*1 cup chopped green bell peppers,* in all

*1 cup chopped celery,* in all

*2 cups diced ham (about ½ pound),* in all

*2 tablespoons plus 2 teaspoons capers,* in all

*¼ cup plus 1 tablespoon chopped pimiento-stuffed green olives,* in all

*3 bay leaves*

*6 cups Shrimp Stock,* in all *(recipe follows)*

*1 teaspoon minced fresh garlic*

*½ cup raw converted rice*

*1 cup chopped peeled, fresh tomatoes*

*1 cup sliced green beans (cut into 2-inch pieces)*

*¼ cup chopped fresh parsley*

*½ cup chopped green onion tops*

Combine the seasoning mix ingredients thoroughly in a small bowl. Makes 3 tablespoons plus 1¾ teaspoons.

Peel the shrimp, reserving the heads and shells, and prepare the Shrimp Stock (see recipe below).

Sprinkle *2 teaspoons* of the seasoning mix over the shrimp and work it in well with your hands. Cover and set aside. You can refrigerate the shrimp while the stock is cooking, but take them out about ½ hour before you cook them, to bring them to room temperature.

Heat the oil in a heavy 5-quart pot over high heat, about 3 minutes. When the oil is hot, add *½ cup* each of the onions, bell peppers, and celery, *¼ cup* of the ham, *2 teaspoons* of the capers, *1 tablespoon* of the olives, *1 tablespoon* of the seasoning mix, and the bay leaves. Cook, stirring occasionally, until the onions and ham are browned, about 5 to 6 minutes. Stir in *1 cup* of the Shrimp Stock and the garlic and scrape the bottom of the pot. Cook, stirring occasionally, until the mixture is a rich brown color, most of the liquid has cooked away, and the vegetables are sticking to the bottom of the pot, about 7 minutes. Stir in the *remaining* seasoning mix, and the *remaining 1 cup* onions, *½ cup* each bell peppers and celery, and *1¾ cups* ham, and cook 2 minutes. Stir in the rice and cook until the rice starts to brown and a crust has formed on the pot bottom, about 2 minutes. Stir in the tomatoes, green beans, parsley, green onions, and the *remaining 2 tablespoons* capers and *¼ cup* olives. Scrape up the crust on the bottom of the pot and cook, scraping the pot bottom from time to time, about 5 to 6 minutes. Add the *remaining 5 cups* stock and scrape the bottom of the pot. Bring to a boil, reduce the heat to low, and simmer 4 minutes. Stir in the seasoned shrimp. Cover the pot, remove from the heat, and let sit 10 minutes. Makes about 10 cups.

Serve in big bowls with a hearty bread.

NOTE: These are the ground chile peppers we used. You can use whatever is available in your area, but be sure to buy pure ground chile peppers, not commercial chili powder.

### SHRIMP STOCK

Place 8 cups water in a large pot over high heat. Add the shrimp shells and heads (above) to the water. Bring to a boil, reduce the heat to low, and simmer, partially covered, 2 hours. Add water as needed to keep the liquid at a minimum of 6 cups. Strain.

# Florida Fish House Grouper Chowder

MAKES 8 MAIN-COURSE SERVINGS OR
12 FIRST-COURSE SERVINGS

*Color photograph 15*

★

A very popular fish in the South, especially in Florida, grouper can be cooked any number of ways. And if you travel through the state of Florida, you'll probably get to sample grouper chowder made a variety of ways as well. For this recipe, we like to start with a whole grouper so we can use the bones in our fish stock, the ideal way to make any fish soup. During the first stage of cooking, the grated potatoes will stick to the bottom of the pot, forming a wonderful crust on which to build the soup.

SEASONING MIX
2 teaspoons salt
2 teaspoons paprika
1½ teaspoons dried sweet basil
  leaves
1½ teaspoons garlic powder
1 teaspoon onion powder
1 teaspoon white pepper
1 teaspoon dry mustard
1 teaspoon dried thyme leaves
½ teaspoon dried tarragon leaves
½ teaspoon ground nutmeg
½ teaspoon black pepper
☆

1¼ pounds grouper fillets (see
  Note)
1 pound bacon, diced
2 cups chopped onions, in all
1½ cups chopped celery, in all
2 cups shredded potatoes (about
  1½ medium potatoes)
6 cups fish or seafood stock (see
  page 11), in all
½ teaspoon minced fresh garlic
2 (16-ounce) cans whole peeled
  tomatoes, cut in halves
4 cups diced potatoes, in all

Combine the seasoning mix ingredients thoroughly in a small bowl. Makes ¼ cup plus ½ teaspoon.

Check the fish carefully for any bones that might have been missed, then cut it into 1-inch cubes and set aside.

Cook the bacon in a covered 5-quart pot or roasting pan over high heat, uncovering occasionally to stir, until well browned, about 12 minutes. Add *1½ cups* of the onions and *½ cup* of the celery and cook 5 minutes. Stir in the shredded potatoes and *2 tablespoons* of the seasoning mix. Cook, uncovered, scraping up the crust that forms on the bottom of the pot, about 5 minutes. Add *¾ cup* of the stock and scrape up all the crust with a large metal spoon. Add *¼ cup* more stock, scrape up the crust again, and cook 2 minutes. Add *1 cup* more stock and cook another 2 minutes, scraping the bottom of the pot clean. Add the *remaining ½ cup* onions and *1 cup* celery and *3 cups* more stock. Stir well, bring to a boil, and cook 2 minutes. Stir in the garlic, tomatoes, and the *remaining* seasoning mix and cook 2 minutes. Add the *remaining 1 cup* stock and bring to a boil, then reduce the heat to low, cover, and simmer 25 minutes.

Turn the heat back up to high and add *2 cups* of the diced potatoes. Bring to a boil, reduce the heat to medium, cover, and cook 10 minutes. Turn the heat up, add the *remaining 2 cups* diced potatoes, and cook 5 minutes. Bring the mixture to a rolling boil, and add the fish. Remove from the heat, cover, and let sit 10 minutes.

Serve as a first course or, with salad and bread, as the main course.

NOTE: We started with a whole 3-pound grouper and cleaned, skinned, and filleted it so we could have the bones for our stock. You could have your fish market do this for you and give you the carcass separately.

# San Francisco Cioppino

MAKES 8 MAIN-COURSE SERVINGS

*Color photograph 16*

★

Cioppino, an aromatic fish stew from San Francisco, was probably created in the 1930s by the Italian immigrants in the area. Most likely, it gets its name from the English word "chop." Its main ingredients are seafood, tomatoes, and wine, but the possible variations are infinite. Be sure to have a big bowl on the table for everyone to toss their shells into, and lots of napkins and towels to wipe off fingers after they've been licked clean.

SEASONING MIX
*1 tablespoon salt*
*1 teaspoon white pepper*
*1 teaspoon dried basil leaves*
*¾ teaspoon dried thyme leaves*
*½ teaspoon black pepper*

*½ teaspoon dry mustard*
*½ teaspoon dried oregano leaves*
*¼ teaspoon dried winter savory*
*40 strands (approximately) saffron*

2 tablespoons olive oil

¾ finely chopped onions

½ cup finely chopped green bell peppers

½ cup finely chopped celery

½ cup finely chopped leeks (white and green parts)

5 small or 4 large bay leaves

6 cups seafood stock (see page 11), in all

Juice of 1 lemon

1¾ cups dry white wine, in all

1½ teaspoons minced fresh garlic

3 cups chopped peeled fresh tomatoes (about 5 tomatoes)

1 cup roughly chopped leeks

1½ cups diced onions (large rough dice)

2 cups diced green bell peppers (large rough dice)

1¾ cups diced celery (large rough dice)

12 small red new potatoes

1 live lobster, cut into sections

8 small hard-shell clams, scrubbed

12 ounces firm-fleshed fish fillets, such as red snapper or grouper, cut into 1-inch pieces

16 mussels, scrubbed and debearded

1 cup chopped fresh parsley

½ pound peeled shrimp

Combine the seasoning mix ingredients thoroughly in a small bowl. Makes approximately 2 tablespoons plus 2 teaspoons.

Heat the olive oil in a large heavy pot or kettle over high heat. When the oil is hot, add the finely chopped onions, bell peppers, celery, and leeks and cook 2 minutes. Add the bay leaves and *1 tablespoon* of the seasoning mix. Stir to coat the vegetables with the seasoning and then cook until the vegetables begin to brown, about 4 to 5 minutes. Stir in *1 cup* of the seafood stock, scrape up any brown crust on the bottom of the pot, and cook 8 minutes. Add *1 cup* more stock, scrape the pot bottom, and simmer until the liquid has reduced somewhat, about 10 minutes. Add the lemon juice, stir, and cook 1 minute. Stir in ½ *cup* of the wine and cook 2 minutes. Add the garlic and tomatoes and cook, stirring occasionally, about 12 minutes. Stir in *1 cup* more wine and *2 cups* more stock and bring to a boil. Add the rough-cut vegetables, the potatoes, and the *remaining* seasoning mix. Bring to a boil, cover the pot, reduce the heat to medium, and simmer until the potatoes are just fork-tender, about 12 to 14 minutes. Turn the heat up to high, stir in the *remaining 2 cups* stock and ¼ *cup* wine, and bring to a boil. Add the lobster and clams, pushing them down into the soup, cover, and cook 2 minutes. Add the fish and the mussels, cover, and cook 3 minutes. Stir in the parsley and shrimp and cook about 3 minutes, or just until the shrimp lose their translucence and the clams and mussels open.

Serve immediately with lots of French or Italian bread.

# Brunswick Stew

### MAKES 8 MAIN-COURSE SERVINGS

This stew probably originated in Brunswick County, Virginia, in the 1820s, when it would have been made with squirrel, but no vegetables. The modern palate can appreciate the changes that gradually evolved in the recipe. Ours produces a rich, lip-smacking feast that tastes even better the second day, so you might want to make it a day in advance.

SEASONING MIX
1 tablespoon salt
2 teaspoons paprika
¾ teaspoon onion powder
¾ teaspoon dry mustard
½ teaspoon black pepper
½ teaspoon garlic powder
½ teaspoon dried thyme leaves
½ teaspoon dried savory leaves
¼ teaspoon white pepper

☆

1 (4-pound) chicken, cut into
    serving pieces, all visible fat
    removed

2 tablespoons olive oil
1 pound potatoes, peeled,
    quartered, and cut into ¼-
    inch slices
4 cups chopped onions, in all
2 cups chopped green bell
    peppers, in all
4 cups chicken stock (see
    page 11), in all
2 cups chopped peeled fresh
    tomatoes (3 to 4 medium)
1 cup lima beans, preferably
    fresh, thawed if frozen
1½ cups corn kernels, preferably
    fresh (about 2 ears)

Combine the seasoning mix ingredients thoroughly in a small bowl. Makes 2 tablespoons plus 2¾ teaspoons.

Sprinkle *1 tablespoon plus 1 teaspoon* of the seasoning mix over the chicken pieces and rub it in thoroughly with your hands.

Heat the oil in a heavy 5-quart pot. When the oil is hot, add the chicken pieces, skin side down, and brown on both sides, about 10 to 12 minutes. Remove the chicken pieces to a bowl and set aside.

Add the potatoes to the hot oil, cover, and cook, uncovering to stir once or twice, about 10 to 11 minutes. Add *2 cups* of the onions, *1 cup* of the bell peppers, and the *remaining* seasoning mix, stir well, and cover the pot. Cook, uncovering occasionally to scrape up the crust on the bottom of the pot, about 4 minutes. (Don't let the potatoes get too dark.) Add *1 cup* of the chicken stock, scrape up any crust on the pot bottom, cover, and cook 5 to 6 minutes. Add *1 cup* more stock, scrape and stir well, cover, and cook 5 minutes. Return the chicken to the pot, stir in *1 cup* more stock, cover, and bring to a boil. Add the *remaining 2 cups* onions and *1 cup* bell peppers and the tomatoes. Stir in the *remaining 1 cup* stock, scrape up any crust on the bottom of the pot, and cook, uncovered, until the sauce begins to bubble. Reduce the heat to medium and simmer, uncovered, scraping occasionally whenever the potatoes and vegetables stick to the bottom of the pot, about 30 minutes. (If the sauce doesn't thicken to a stew consistency, turn up the heat for the last part of the cooking time.) Add the lima beans and corn and cook 8 minutes. Remove from the heat and let sit a few minutes before serving. (Or let cool, refrigerate overnight, and reheat before serving.)

Delicious with hunks of bread for gravy dipping.

# Pennsylvania Dutch Chicken Dumpling Soup

MAKES 6 TO 8 MAIN-COURSE SERVINGS

★

Rivvel soup is a traditional, old-fashioned recipe known to everyone who lives in Pennsylvania Dutch country. Rivvels are usually very small, but we've made ours into dumplings—something you can sink your teeth into. For maximum flavor, this soup should be served as soon as it's made; if it does have to sit any length of time before being served, remove the dumplings from the pot, or they'll absorb the soup and start disintegrating into the liquid.

**SEASONING MIX**
1 tablespoon salt
1 teaspoon dry mustard
1 teaspoon dried thyme leaves
¾ teaspoon onion powder
½ teaspoon garlic powder
½ teaspoon black pepper
¼ teaspoon white pepper
¼ teaspoon ground allspice
¼ teaspoon ground mace
⅛ teaspoon cayenne pepper

☆

1 large (5- to 6-pound) stewing hen, cut into pieces, all visible fat removed
3 tablespoons vegetable oil
3 cups chopped onions
2 cups chopped celery

10 sprigs fresh parsley
¼ cup snipped fresh dill
2 teaspoons minced fresh garlic
8 cups chicken stock (see page 11)

**DUMPLINGS**
2 cups all-purpose flour
1 tablespoon baking powder
1 tablespoon dark brown sugar
1 teaspoon salt
½ teaspoon black pepper
½ teaspoon ground sage
¼ teaspoon garlic powder
¼ teaspoon onion powder
2 eggs
⅔ cup milk
¼ teaspoon snipped fresh dill

**DAY 1:** Combine the seasoning mix ingredients thoroughly in a small bowl. Makes 2 tablespoons plus 1⅝ teaspoons.

Sprinkle *1 tablespoon plus 1 teaspoon* of the seasoning mix over the hen parts and rub it in well with your hands.

Heat the oil in a 12-inch skillet over high heat. When the oil is very hot, add the hen pieces and brown on all sides, about 12 minutes. Remove from the heat, remove the chicken from the skillet, and drain on paper towels.

Pour 2 tablespoons of the fat from the skillet into a large heavy pot over high heat. Add the onions, celery, parsley sprigs, and the *remaining* seasoning mix. Cook, scraping the pot bottom occasionally, until the onions are lightly browned, about 3 minutes. Add the dill and garlic, scrape the pot bottom, and cook 5 minutes. Add the hen pieces and *6 cups* of the chicken stock and bring to a boil. Reduce the heat to low and simmer, covered, until the meat is tender, about 1 hour. Transfer the chicken and the soup to separate containers and refrigerate overnight.

**FOR THE DUMPLINGS,** mix all the dry ingredients thoroughly in a medium bowl.

Whisk the eggs in a small bowl until very frothy. Add the milk and whisk until frothy and pale yellow. Add the dill.

Stir the wet ingredients carefully into the dry ingredients until thoroughly blended and a stiff dough is formed. Cover the bowl with a towel and refrigerate overnight.

**DAY 2:** Skim all the congealed fat from the top of the soup. Measure out the soup and add more stock to make 8 cups if necessary. Pour the soup into a large pot and bring to a simmer over medium heat.

Meanwhile, remove the skin from the chicken and pull the meat from the bones. Shred the meat into bite-size pieces.

When the soup is bubbling, turn the heat up to high and stir in the chicken meat. Gently (don't pack!) shape dumplings the size of golf balls and drop into the bubbling soup. Reduce the heat to medium, cover, and cook 3 to 4 minutes, or just until the dumplings rise to the surface of the soup. Don't overcook!

Serve immediately.

# Chicken, Shrimp, and Sausage Gumbo Hazel

MAKES 10 TO 12 MAIN-COURSE SERVINGS

★

My mother, Hazel Prudhomme, used to make gumbo when there was an occasion, such as a holiday or when special company was coming to our house. She made her gumbos with chicken and andouille, crawfish, rabbit, squirrel, or game meats. She never used shrimp, since we couldn't get any, and she rarely made a gumbo with both meat and seafood, as we've done here. Serve this over rice or potato salad, as Mom did, and you've got a sensational one-dish meal.

SEASONING MIX
1 tablespoon plus 1 teaspoon
   dried parsley flakes
2½ teaspoons salt
2 teaspoons paprika
1½ teaspoons dried thyme leaves
1½ teaspoons garlic powder
1¼ teaspoons black pepper
1 teaspoon dry mustard
¾ teaspoon white pepper
¾ teaspoon ground cumin
½ teaspoon onion powder

☆

1 (3- to 3½-pound) chicken, cut
   into 8 pieces, all visible fat
   removed

½ cup vegetable oil
1 pound andouille sausage, cut
   diagonally into pieces about 2
   inches long
¾ cup all-purpose flour
3 cups chopped onions, in all
2 cups chopped green bell
   peppers, in all
1 cup chopped celery
½ cup chopped fresh parsley
4 bay leaves
1 quart seafood stock (see
   page 11)
1 quart chicken stock (see
   page 11)
1 pound peeled shrimp (about
   1½ pounds unpeeled shrimp)

Combine the seasoning mix ingredients thoroughly in a small bowl. Makes 5 tablespoons plus ¾ teaspoon.

Sprinkle the chicken pieces all over with *1 tablespoon* of the seasoning mix and rub it in well with your hands.

Heat the oil in a 12-inch skillet (preferably cast iron) over high heat. When the oil begins to smoke, add the chicken skin side down, starting with the larger pieces, and cook, turning once, just until golden brown on both sides, about 4 to 5 minutes. Leave the thighs in longest, as they have the most fat to be rendered. Remove the chicken from the skillet and drain on paper towels.

Add the sausage to the oil in the skillet and cook, turning once, until browned, about 4 minutes. Remove the sausage and drain on paper towels. Pour ¾ cup of fat from the skillet into a measuring cup and discard the rest.

Place the skillet over high heat until hot, about 30 seconds. Add the reserved fat and heat until hot, about 1 minute. Add the flour *¼ cup* at a time, whipping constantly with a wire whisk until all of the flour is absorbed and the mixture has become a light chocolate-colored roux. Quickly stir in *2 cups* of the onions, *1 cup* of the bell peppers, and the celery. Add *2 tablespoons* of the seasoning mix, the parsley, and bay leaves and cook, stirring, until the roux is thick and dark chocolate-colored, about 3 to 4 minutes.

Bring the seafood and chicken stocks to a boil in a heavy 8-quart pot over high heat. When the stock is boiling, add the roux in 2 installments, whisking until the roux has thoroughly dissolved into the stock. Bring the mixture back to a hard boil, whisking often to ensure that the flour doesn't separate and burn, about 9 to 11 minutes. Scrape the bottom of the pot frequently with the whisk to be sure that the flour isn't sticking. Add the browned chicken and sausage, the *remaining* seasoning mix, and the *remaining 1 cup* each onions and bell peppers. Stir well, cover, and bring to a boil. Reduce the heat to low and simmer until the chicken is tender, about 45 minutes. Remove from the heat, stir in the shrimp, cover, and let sit 10 minutes. Makes about 12 cups.

Serve in shallow bowls over rice or potato salad.

# Brooklyn Borscht

MAKES 8 FIRST-COURSE SERVINGS OR
4 TO 6 MAIN-COURSE SERVINGS

*Color photograph 17*

★

Immigrants from Russia and Poland brought us borscht, a beet soup made with or without meat, served hot or cold, with or without a garnish of sour cream. Our borscht is rich with beef, beets, cabbage, and carrots and is definitely to be served hot. Its tangy flavor combined with its hearty texture are guaranteed to keep out the cold on a winter's night. Delicious!

**SEASONING MIX**
*2 teaspoons salt*
*2 teaspoons paprika*
*1 teaspoon white pepper*
*1 teaspoon dried thyme leaves*
*½ teaspoon onion powder*
*½ teaspoon garlic powder*
*½ teaspoon black pepper*
*½ teaspoon ground coriander*

☆

*¼ cup vegetable oil*
*1½ cups chopped onions*
*1½ pounds lean beef, cut into*
  *½-inch dice*
*1 cup shredded potatoes*
*¼ cup apple cider vinegar*
*5 cups beef stock (see page 11),*
  *in all*
*3 small bay leaves*
*1 cup shredded onions*
*3 cups shredded green cabbage*
*2 cups shredded carrots*
*2 cups shredded fresh turnips*
*2 cups shredded fresh beets*
*4 tablespoons unsalted butter*
*Sour cream, optional*

Combine the seasoning mix ingredients thoroughly in a small bowl. Makes 2 tablespoons plus 2 teaspoons.

Heat the oil in a heavy 8-quart pot over high heat. When the oil is very hot, add the chopped onions and cook, stirring once, until the onions are lightly browned, about 3 minutes. Push the onions to one side of the pot. Spread the meat evenly around the cleared space in the pot, sprinkle with *2 tablespoons* of the seasoning mix, and cook, without stirring, 3 minutes. Then stir the meat to turn and brown evenly and cook about 2 minutes. Stir the meat into the onions and cook 3 minutes. Stir in the potatoes and cook 3 minutes. Add the vinegar, scrape up the crust on the bottom of the pot, and cook until the vinegar evaporates, about 2 minutes. Add *1/2 cup* of the beef stock and scrape the bottom of the pot. Add the bay leaves and cook, allowing the potatoes to form another crust on the bottom of the pot, about 1 minute. Add *1 cup* more stock and cook, scraping occasionally, about 2 minutes. Stir in the *remaining 3 1/2 cups* stock, cover, and bring to a boil. Reduce the heat to low and simmer 18 minutes. Turn the heat up to high, add the shredded onions and cabbage, cover, and bring back to a boil. Reduce the heat to low and simmer 8 minutes. Add the carrots, turnips, beets, and the *remaining* seasoning mix. Stir, cover, and cook 10 minutes. Add the butter and cook, stirring constantly, until it melts.

Serve immediately, garnished with sour cream, if desired.

# Sopa de Albóndigas
# (Mexican Meatball Soup)

### MAKES 8 TO 10 MAIN-COURSE SERVINGS

★

Originally from Mexico, this soup has become a favorite in the American Southwest and on the old Spanish ranches in Southern California. Albóndigas, Mexican meatballs flavored with chopped vegetables, are traditionally served in a red sauce or a fresh tomato soup, like the one below. To make meatballs that are light and delicious, don't overmix the chopped meat when you combine it with the vegetables and eggs, and handle the meatballs lightly when you form them.

SEASONING MIX

2 teaspoons salt

2 teaspoons ground guajillo
  chile pepper (see Note)

1 teaspoon ground arbol chile
  pepper (see Note)

1 teaspoon onion powder

1 teaspoon garlic powder

1 teaspoon white pepper

1 teaspoon black pepper

1 teaspoon ground cumin

1 teaspoon paprika

3/4 teaspoon dried oregano
  leaves

1/4 teaspoon ground coriander

☆

1/2 pound ground pork

1/2 pound ground beef

1/2 cup very finely diced
  zucchini

2 tablespoons chipotle sauce
  (see Note)

3/4 cup beef stock (see page 11),
  in all

5 tablespoons vegetable oil,
  in all

2 cups chopped onions, in all

1 tablespoon plus 1 teaspoon
  minced fresh garlic, in all

1/4 cup chopped fresh cilantro or
  2 teaspoons dried cilantro
  leaves

2 eggs

1 cup chopped green or
  red bell peppers

2 cups chopped peeled fresh
  tomatoes

2 tablespoons unsalted butter,
  cut into 4 pats

1 (12-ounce) can tomato juice

2 tablespoons plus 1 teaspoon
  dark brown sugar

7 cups chicken stock (see
  page 11), in all

Combine the seasoning mix ingredients thoroughly in a small bowl. Makes
1/4 cup.

Combine the ground pork, ground beef, and zucchini in a large bowl,
sprinkle with *1 tablespoon* of the seasoning mix, and work it in thoroughly
with your hands.

Combine the chipotle sauce and *1/4 cup* of the beef stock in the container of a blender and process until thoroughly blended. Set aside.

Heat *2 tablespoons* of the oil in an 8-inch skillet over high heat. When
the oil is very hot, add *1 cup* of the onions, *2 teaspoons* of the garlic, and
*1 tablespoon* of the seasoning mix. Cook, stirring occasionally, until the
mixture is golden brown, about 3 to 4 minutes. Remove from the heat
and stir in the cilantro. Let cool a minute or two, then add to the ground
meat/zucchini mixture. Add the eggs and mix thoroughly. Place in the
refrigerator.

Heat the *remaining 3 tablespoons* oil in a large heavy pot over high heat. When the oil is very hot, add the bell peppers, the *remaining 1 cup* onions, and *1 tablespoon* of the seasoning mix. Cook, stirring occasionally, until the vegetables are lightly browned, about 6 minutes. Stir in the tomatoes and the *remaining 2 teaspoons* garlic and cook 2 minutes. Add the *remaining ½ cup* beef stock and cook 3 minutes. Add the butter and cook 3 minutes. Stir in the chipotle sauce mixture and cook 2 minutes. Stir in the *remaining* seasoning mix, reduce the heat to medium high, and cook, occasionally scraping the bottom of the pot, until the mixture has cooked down to a thick paste and is sticking to the bottom of the pot, about 11 minutes. Add the tomato juice and brown sugar, scrape the crust from the bottom of the pot, and cook until another crust forms, about 4 minutes. Turn the heat up to high, stir in *2 cups* of the chicken stock, scrape the bottom of the pot, and bring to a bubbling boil. Cook, scraping occasionally, about 9 minutes. Add the *remaining 5 cups* chicken stock and bring to a boil.

Remove the meat mixture from the refrigerator. Using your hands or a melon baller, gently form the mixture into 1-inch meatballs. Add them to the soup and bring to a boil, then reduce the heat to low, cover, and simmer until meatballs are tender, about 20 minutes.

Serve immediately with thick bread and a cool salad.

NOTE: These are the ground chile peppers we used. You can use whatever is available in your area, as long as you use pure ground chile peppers, not commercial chili powder.

Canned chipotle peppers, available in specialty food stores, are usually packed in tomato sauce or adobo sauce; either will work fine here. Do not attempt to taste them from the jar unless you're immune to fire!

# Vegetable Beef Soup

## MAKES 14 TO 16 FIRST-COURSE SERVINGS OR
## 8 TO 10 MAIN-COURSE SERVINGS

★

In America's early years, soups were considered functional as well as nourishing. For one thing, they easily accommodated scraps of leftover meats that might otherwise have been wasted. And an abundance of fresh vegetables at harvest times usually meant the surplus would find its way to the soup pot. When home canning became popular, vegetable soups made the charts as hearty winter fare, especially when there was meat in the pot, as there is in ours.

*1 pound dried baby lima beans*

**SEASONING MIX**
*1 tablespoon plus 1 teaspoon salt*

*1 tablespoon paprika*
*2 teaspoons dry mustard*
*2 teaspoons black pepper*
*2 teaspoons ground guajillo chile pepper (see Note)*
*2 teaspoons onion powder*
*2 teaspoons garlic powder*
*2 teaspoons dried sweet basil leaves*
*1½ teaspoons ground cumin*
*1 teaspoon dried thyme leaves*
*1 teaspoon white pepper*
☆

*2 pounds boneless top round or chuck, cut into ¾-inch cubes*
*3 tablespoons vegetable oil*
*4 cups chopped onions, in all*
*1 cup chopped green bell peppers*
*2 cups chopped celery, in all*
*6 tablespoons all-purpose flour*
*4 bay leaves*
*10 cups beef stock (see page 11), in all*
*1½ cups sliced carrots*
*1 cup chopped turnips (about 1 large turnip)*
*2 cups diced peeled, potatoes*
*3 cups chopped peeled fresh tomatoes, with their juices*
*1 teaspoon minced fresh garlic*
*2 cups corn kernels, preferably fresh (about 4 ears)*

**DAY 1:** Put the lima beans in a large bowl, add hot water to cover, cover the bowl with a plate, and let soak overnight.

**DAY 2:** Combine the seasoning mix ingredients thoroughly in a small bowl. Makes 7 tablespoons plus 1½ teaspoons.

Sprinkle *3 tablespoons* of the seasoning mix all over the meat and rub it in well with your hands.

Drain the beans.

Heat the oil in a large heavy pot over high heat. When the oil is hot, add the meat and brown on all sides, about 3 minutes. Add *2 cups* of the onions, the bell peppers, and *1 cup* of the celery. Stir well, cover the pot, and cook, uncovering occasionally to stir, until the meat and vegetables are well browned, about 9 to 11 minutes. Stir in the flour and bay leaves, cover, and cook, uncovering once or twice to scrape the flour from the pot bottom as it sticks, about 3 to 4 minutes. Add *1 cup* of the beef stock and scrape up the crust on the bottom of the pot. Stir in *7 cups* more stock, the drained lima beans and *2 tablespoons* of the seasoning mix. Bring to a boil, stirring frequently to keep the flour from sticking. Cover the pot, reduce the heat to low, and simmer, occasionally uncovering the pot to stir, about 45 minutes. Turn the heat back up to high and stir in the *remaining 2 cups* stock, the carrots, turnips, potatoes, tomatoes, garlic, corn, the *remaining 2 cups* onions and *1 cup* celery, and the *remaining* seasoning mix. Bring to a boil, reduce the heat to low, cover, and cook, uncovering occasionally to stir, about 30 minutes. Remove from the heat.

Serve immediately with hot bread. This soup is especially good ladled over hot rice.

**NOTE:** This is the ground chile pepper we used. You can use whatever is available in your area, but be sure you buy pure ground chile peppers, not commercial chili powder.

# South Miami Cuban Stew

MAKES 6 TO 8 MAIN-COURSE SERVINGS

★

When Cubans began emigrating in large numbers to Florida they brought along with them their own special culinary expertise and flavors that are now becoming an integral part of American cookery. Cuban food—and now Cuban-American food—is an unforgettable treat. This dish, which in Spanish is called *fileto saltedo*, tastes even better the second day, so you might want to plan to make it a day ahead.

SEASONING MIX
2 teaspoons salt
1 teaspoon garlic powder
1 teaspoon onion powder
1 teaspoon paprika
1 teaspoon celery seed
1 teaspoon mustard seed
1 teaspoon dried thyme leaves
3/4 teaspoon dried sweet basil
   leaves
3/4 teaspoon turmeric
1/2 teaspoon black pepper
1/2 teaspoon white pepper
1/2 teaspoon ground sage

☆

2 1/2 pounds top sirloin of beef,
   top round, or chuck, cut into
   3/4-inch cubes
1 tablespoon olive oil

1/2 pound chorizo (Spanish
   sausage), thinly sliced
6 1/2 ounces baked ham, diced
3 cups diced peeled, potatoes
2 1/2 cups chopped onions, in all
2 cups chopped green bell
   peppers, in all
1/2 cup chopped celery
1 1/2 cups chopped peeled fresh
   tomatoes
1 cup canned tomato sauce
1 tablespoon minced fresh
   garlic
1 large red bell pepper, cut into
   2 1/2-inch-long strips
1/2 cup fresh or frozen baby
   green peas, optional
4 cups beef stock (see page 11)
1/4 cup dry sherry

Combine the seasoning mix ingredients thoroughly in a small bowl. Makes 3 tablespoons plus 2 teaspoons.

Sprinkle *2 tablespoons* of the seasoning mix all over beef and work it in well with your hands.

Heat the oil in a large heavy pot over high heat. When the oil is hot, add the chorizo and ham and cook, stirring once or twice until browned on all sides, about 6 minutes. Remove the chorizo and ham with a slotted spoon and set aside. Add the beef to the pot and brown on all sides, about 6 minutes. Remove the beef with a slotted spoon and set aside. Add the potatoes, *1½ cups* of the onions, *1½ cups* of the green bell peppers, the celery, and *1 tablespoon* of the seasoning mix. Stir well, cover the pot, and cook 7 minutes. Remove the lid, stir, and cook, uncovered, until most of the juices have evaporated and a hard brown crust covers the bottom of the pot, about 4 to 6 minutes. Add the tomatoes and tomato sauce and scrape the bottom of the pot clean. Return the beef, chorizo, and ham to the pot, and add the *remaining 1 cup* onions and *½ cup* green bell peppers, the garlic, and red bell pepper. Stir in the beef stock and the *remaining* seasoning mix, cover, and bring to a boil. Uncover, reduce the heat to medium, and simmer until the meat is tender, about 22 minutes. Stir in the sherry and cook, uncovered, scraping the bottom of the pot occasionally to prevent sticking, about 30 minutes. Add the peas and simmer 5 minutes. Remove from the heat.

This is wonderful served over rice.

# Kentucky Burgoo

MAKES 20 TO 25 GENEROUS MAIN-COURSE SERVINGS

A very popular stew as far back as 1750, burgoo is a favorite at political rallies in the South. The person most often associated with burgoo is Gus Jaubert, a famous chef from Lexington, Kentucky, who prepared six thousand gallons of it for the Grand Army of the Republic in 1895. Our recipe will feed only a slightly smaller army. Before you start, be sure you have enough of the seasonings called for. It's best to make burgoo a day ahead to let all the flavors marry. It makes skimming the fat off easier, too. Be aware that this dish takes time. On the other hand, it's really worth it.

SEASONING MIX

2 tablespoons plus 2 teaspoons
    salt
1 tablespoon plus 2 teaspoons
    dried thyme leaves
1 tablespoon plus 2 teaspoons
    dried sweet basil leaves
1 tablespoon plus 1½ teaspoons
    garlic powder
1 tablespoon plus 1 teaspoon dry
    mustard
1 tablespoon plus ½ teaspoon
    onion powder
1 tablespoon plus ½ teaspoon
    paprika
1 tablespoon black pepper
1 tablespoon white pepper
2 teaspoons ground cumin

☆

1 (6- to 7-pound) stewing hen,
    cut up, all visible fat removed
1 pound beef stew meat, cut
    into ½-inch cubes
1 pound veal stew meat, cut
    into ½-inch cubes

4 quarts plus 3 cups (19 cups)
    chicken stock (see page 11),
    in all
8 tablespoons (1 stick) unsalted
    butter
2 pounds beef bones (ask your
    butcher)
¾ cup apple cider vinegar
7 cups chopped onions, in all
4 cups chopped celery, in all
1 fresh jalapeño pepper, seeded
    and chopped
6 small bay leaves
3 cups sliced fresh or frozen okra
3 cups chopped cabbage, in all
2 cups corn kernels, preferably
    fresh (about 4 ears)
4 cups chopped peeled fresh
    tomatoes
2 cups sliced carrots
½ cup chopped fresh parsley
2 cups fresh or frozen lima beans
2 cups chopped green bell
    peppers
1 tablespoon minced fresh garlic
¼ cup packed light brown sugar

**DAY 1:** Combine the seasoning mix ingredients thoroughly in a small bowl. Makes 13 tablespoons plus 2½ teaspoons.

Sprinkle the hen parts with *3 tablespoons plus 1 teaspoon* of the seasoning mix, and rub it into the skin with your hands.

Place the cubed veal and beef in a mixing bowl, sprinkle with *3 tablespoons* of the seasoning mix, and rub in well with your hands.

Put *2 quarts* of the chicken stock into a very large stockpot set over high heat and cover the pot. While the stock is heating, melt the butter in a slightly smaller pot over high heat. When the butter is sizzling, add as many of the larger hen pieces as will fit in a single layer, skin side down, and cook until golden brown, turning once or twice, about 10 minutes. If the temperature of the butter seems to cool down as the hen pieces cook, cover the pot for a few minutes to hold the heat in. Add the browned hen pieces to the stock in the larger pot, brown the remaining hen pieces and then the beef bones, and add these to the stock. Cover the stock and bring it to a rolling boil. Add *2 quarts* more stock, cover, and bring back to a boil. Reduce the heat to medium low and simmer 15 to 20 minutes. Add the vinegar and simmer 30 to 35 minutes.

Meanwhile, add the beef and veal stew meat to the fat remaining in the smaller pot and brown over high heat, stirring occasionally, about 5 to 7 minutes. Remove the meat with a slotted spoon and set aside. Pour off all but 1 tablespoon fat from the pot. Add *3 cups* of the onions, *2 cups* of the celery, the jalapeño pepper, and bay leaves. Stir well and cook until the onions are golden, about 7 to 9 minutes. Stir in the okra, *1 tablespoon* of the seasoning mix, *1 cup* of the cabbage, and the corn. Cover and cook 10 minutes. Stir in the tomatoes and scrape the bottom of the pot clean. Add *1 tablespoon* of the seasoning mix, cover, and cook, uncovering the pot to scrape up the crusts as they form on the pot bottom, about 15 minutes.

Transfer 2 cups of the stock from the larger pot to the smaller one. Scrape the bottom of the smaller pot, cover, and cook, uncovering several times to scrape the bottom of the pot, about 10 minutes. Stir in the *remaining 4 cups* onions, *2 cups* celery, and *2 cups* cabbage, the *remaining* seasoning mix, the carrots, parsley, lima beans, bell peppers, garlic, brown sugar, and the browned beef and veal. Cover and bring to a full boil.

Transfer the contents of the smaller pot to the larger one, add the *remaining 3 cups* chicken stock, and bring the stock to a boil. Ladle about 4 cups of the boiling stock into the smaller pot, scrape the bottom clean, and pour the stock and scrapings back into the larger pot. Cover, reduce the heat to medium low, and simmer, stirring occasionally, until the meat is tender, about 45 minutes to 1 hour. (Total cooking time for the hen should be a minimum of 2 hours.)

Let the burgoo cool to room temperature, then refrigerate overnight, in several containers if necessary.

**DAY 2:** Remove the burgoo from the refrigerator and skim off all the congealed fat from the top. Allow the stew to come to room temperature, reheat, and serve in big bowls with thick buttered bread.

# Cowboy Stew with Cornmeal Dumplings

MAKES 8 MAIN-COURSE SERVINGS

*Color photograph 18*

★

Out on the plains, the cowboys developed their own culinary wisdom, and some of their food was excellent. This stew is a perfect example of the hearty fare that was cooked up in many a chuck wagon. It has probably evolved somewhat since its earliest form, and we've changed it too—we think for the better. It's one of those meals where you just don't want to put your fork down. Or your spoon. Or your fingers!

SEASONING MIX

2 teaspoons salt

2 teaspoons ground arbol chile
   pepper (see Note)

1½ teaspoons dry mustard

1 teaspoon ground guajillo chile
   pepper (see Note)

1 teaspoon dried thyme leaves

1 teaspoon garlic powder

1 teaspoon onion powder

¾ teaspoon white pepper

½ teaspoon black pepper

½ teaspoon ground cumin

☆

STEW

2 pounds beef top round, cut
   into ½-inch cubes

12 slices bacon, diced

1 cup chopped onions

3 small bay leaves

Cornmeal Dumplings (recipe
   follows)

12 to 14 small white onions
   (about 1½ inches in
   diameter), peeled, or 36 tiny
   pearl onions, peeled

3 cups beef stock (see page 11),
   in all

8 tablespoons (1 stick) unsalted
   butter, cut into pats

¼ cup all-purpose flour

¼ cup dark molasses

2 cups brewed coffee

2 cups thickly sliced carrots

Combine the seasoning mix ingredients thoroughly in a small bowl. Makes 3 tablespoons plus 2¼ teaspoons.

**FOR THE STEW,** sprinkle *2 tablespoons* of the seasoning mix over the beef and rub it in thoroughly with your hands.

Cook the bacon in a large heavy pot over medium-high heat until brown and crisp, about 10 to 11 minutes. Remove with a slotted spoon.

Add the seasoned beef to the bacon fat left in the pot and cook over high heat until the meat is browned on all sides, about 3 to 4 minutes. Add the chopped onions and bay leaves, pushing them under the meat. Cover and cook, scraping the pot bottom occasionally, until the meat is a rich brown color and sticking to the bottom of the pot, about 18 to 20 minutes. Remove from the heat. Remove ¼ cup of the juices from the pot.

Prepare the dumplings; recipe follows below.

Set the pot of stew over high heat, add the whole onions and *1 cup* of the stock, and scrape the bottom of the pot. Stir in the butter, cover, and cook, uncovering once or twice to stir, about 8 minutes. (The gravy should become a deep brown color.) Stir in the flour and cook 1 minute. Stir in the molasses and coffee and scrape the bottom of the pot. Add the *remaining 2 cups* stock, scrape the pot bottom clean, and bring to a boil. Add the carrots and the *remaining* seasoning mix and bring to a boil.

Remove the dumpling batter from the refrigerator and use a large spoon to drop 10 dumplings onto the bubbling stew. Cover, reduce the heat to medium low, and cook 20 minutes *without opening the pot.*

Allow the stew to cool about 10 minutes before serving. Place 1 dumpling in each of 8 flat soup plates and ladle about 1 cup of the stew over it.

CORNMEAL DUMPLINGS
¾ *cup yellow cornmeal*
½ *cup all-purpose flour*
1½ *teaspoons baking powder*
1 *tablespoon Seasoning Mix*

*2 eggs*
¼ *cup reserved beef juices*
  *(at room temperature)*
¼ *cup dark molasses*
*Reserved fried bacon (see above)*

Thoroughly blend the dry ingredients in a mixing bowl. Using a large spoon, make a hole, or well, in the center. Add the eggs and mix with the spoon until the dry ingredients are thoroughly wet. Add the reserved beef juices and stir to blend. Stir in the molasses, add the fried bacon, and mix thoroughly. Refrigerate until ready to use.

NOTE: These are the chile peppers we used. You can use whatever is available in your area, but don't use commercial chili powder.

# Posole Stew

MAKES 8 TO 10 MAIN-COURSE SERVINGS

*Color photograph 19*

★

Posole is whole white hominy; it is also the name given to the festive Mexican stew popular in western Texas and New Mexico, which resembles a green chili stew. The basic ingredients are pork, hominy, and chile peppers, and they can be put together in a simple fashion or with a little more pizzazz, as we have done. Some cooks insist that the posole or hominy must be dried, while others assert that frozen or canned posole works best. We used canned posole, which was easiest to find. This dish tastes better the second day, so make it a day ahead and refrigerate overnight. When you're ready to serve, skim off any fat that has accumulated on top of the stew, heat, and serve.

SEASONING MIX

*2 teaspoons salt*

*1½ teaspoons dried oregano leaves*

*1 teaspoon ground guajillo chile pepper (see Note)*

*1 teaspoon ground arbol chile pepper (see Note)*

*1 teaspoon garlic powder*

*1 teaspoon onion powder*

*1 teaspoon ground cumin*

*1 teaspoon dried thyme leaves*

*¾ teaspoon dried cilantro leaves*

*½ teaspoon black pepper*

*½ teaspoon white pepper*

☆

*1 pound pork shoulder, cut into 1-inch cubes, all visible fat removed*

*1 pound lamb shoulder or leg of lamb, cut into 1-inch cubes, all visible fat removed*

*2 very thick slices slab bacon (about 6 ounces), diced*

*3 cups chopped onions,* in all

*2 cups chopped green bell peppers,* in all

*50 strands (approximately) saffron*

*1 pound linguiça (Portuguese sausage), kielbasa (Polish), or sweet Italian sausage, cut into 1-inch pieces*

*10 ounces mild chorizo (Spanish sausage), cut into 1-inch pieces*

*20 fresh Anaheim peppers (or other mild fresh, chile peppers), coarsely chopped (about 4 cups)*

*5 cups chicken stock (see page 11)*

*1 teaspoon minced fresh garlic*
*2 (1-pound, 13-ounce) cans white*
*hominy posole or pozole (whole*
*white hominy), drained (see*
*Note)*

*3 tablespoons chopped fresh*
*cilantro plus ½ cup fresh whole*
*cilantro leaves*

**DAY 1:** Combine the seasoning mix ingredients thoroughly in a small bowl. Makes 3 tablespoons plus 2¼ teaspoons.

Combine the cubed pork and lamb in a bowl. Sprinkle *1 tablespoon plus 1 teaspoon* of the seasoning mix over the meat and work it in well with your hands.

Fry the slab bacon in a large covered pot over high heat until lightly browned, uncovering once to stir, about 6 minutes. Strain off all but 3 tablespoons of the fat. Add *2 cups* of the onions, *1 cup* of the bell peppers, and the saffron to the pot, cover, and cook, uncovering the pot occasionally to stir, until the vegetables are beginning to brown and stick to the bottom of the pot, about 4 to 6 minutes (don't let them burn!). Stir in *1 tablespoon* of the seasoning mix and scrape the bottom of the pot with a metal spatula. Push the vegetables and bacon to one side of the pot and add all of the sausage to the cleared space. Cook, uncovered, stirring both the vegetables and the sausage occasionally, until the sausage is browned on all sides, about 6 to 7 minutes. Remove the sausage with a slotted spoon and drain on paper towels.

Add the cubed pork and lamb to the cleared space, cover the pot, and cook, uncovering occasionally to stir, until the meat is browned on all sides, about 4 to 5 minutes. Stir the Anaheim peppers into the vegetables, cover, and cook 3 to 4 minutes, stirring the meat occasionally. Stir the meat into the vegetables and add the *remaining* seasoning mix and the chicken stock. Mix thoroughly and scrape the bottom of the pot clean. Cover, bring to a boil, reduce the heat to low, and simmer 10 minutes. Stir in the garlic and the *remaining 1 cup* each onions and bell peppers. Scrape the pot bottom, cover, and simmer, uncovering occasionally to scrape the bottom of the pot, about 17 minutes. Add the posole and the reserved sausage. Cover, turn up the heat, and bring to a boil. Reduce the heat to low and simmer, uncovering occasionally to stir, about 45 minutes to 1 hour. Add the chopped cilantro, cover, and cook until the meat is very tender, about 30 to 45 minutes. Stir in the whole cilantro leaves, cover, and cook 2 more minutes. Remove from the heat, let cool to room temperature, and refrigerate overnight.

**DAY 2:** Skim the fat from the top of the stew, reheat slowly over low heat, and serve warm in bowls with thick peasant bread.

NOTE: These are the chile peppers we used, but you can use whatever is available in your area. Just be sure to buy pure ground chile peppers, not commercial chili powder.

Posole and pozole are available in specialty food shops and some supermarkets.

# MAIN DISHES
## *and*
# CROWD PLEASERS

U ntil fairly recently, Americans didn't think in terms of serving separate appetizers and main courses at home. Instead, all the food was put on the table at once and called dinner. But with the increasing popularity of restaurant dining and the quest to be stylish, meals began to be divided into courses, which were served at intervals.

Usually, the main course consists of or is centered around meat, poultry, or seafood of some kind, accompanied by starches and vegetables. Our ancestors usually overcooked their meats and poultry, in the hope of making them easier to chew. Today, the meat we eat is much younger and doesn't require as much cooking time.

Chicken and fish are becoming more and more popular because of their healthful image. Fish dishes are better than ever because Americans have finally learned that the secret to the best-tasting seafood is a minimum of cooking time. But chickens haven't exactly improved over the years. In the "good old days," they were raised in the farmer's barnyard and fed on scraps from the kitchen, just as my family raised chickens in our own back yard. The birds were fat and happy and tasted delicious. Nowadays it's hard to find a chicken that hasn't been formula-cultivated, but if you have a good butcher, you can probably get natural hens or free-range chickens, which are allowed to roam and scratch like chickens did in the old days. They're more expensive, but you may feel they're worth the difference in flavor.

I think the main course should always be the best, most exciting part of the meal, whether it's a simple dish, such as Midtown Meat Loaf, or a more complicated one, like Navajo Tacos. The main attraction is awaited at each meal with great anticipation, and it's your job to make the most of it.

# Pasta Primavera

MAKES 6 TO 8 SERVINGS

*Color photograph 20*

★

This is relatively new in the American culinary repertoire, as it has been popular only since the 1970s. Credit for its creation is given to, among others, Sirio Maccioni, owner of Le Cirque restaurant in New York City. In Italian, *primavera* means "springtime," and with lots of fresh vegetables quickly cooked, springtime is definitely what this dish brings to mind.

SEASONING MIX
2½ teaspoons dried sweet basil
   leaves
1½ teaspoons salt
1 teaspoon dried thyme leaves
¾ teaspoon white pepper
½ teaspoon garlic powder
½ teaspoon onion powder

☆

2 tablespoons olive oil
1 cup thin strips prosciutto
2 cups cauliflower florets

2 cups sliced fresh mushrooms
½ cup sliced carrots (cut on
   the diagonal)
2 cups sliced zucchini
6 tablespoons unsalted butter
1 teaspoon minced fresh garlic
1 cup asparagus tips or ¾ cup
   snow peas
1 cup chopped green onions
2 cups heavy cream
9 ounces of your favorite
   pasta

Combine the seasoning mix ingredients thoroughly in a small bowl. Makes 2 tablespoons plus ¾ teaspoon.

Heat the olive oil in a 12-inch skillet over high heat. When the oil is very hot, add the prosciutto, cauliflower, mushrooms, carrots, and zucchini. Add the butter and as it melts stir in the garlic and all the seasoning mix. Stir in the asparagus tips or snow peas and green onions. Stir well and cook just until the vegetables are crisp-tender, about 4 to 5 minutes. Stir in the cream and bring to a boil. Lower the heat to medium and cook until the sauce has thickened a bit, about 3 minutes.

Meanwhile, cook the pasta according to the package directions; drain. Add the cooked pasta to the skillet, toss well, and remove from the heat. Makes about 8 cups. Serve immediately with hot Italian bread.

20.

# Pasta Primavera

*page 116*

21.

# Baked Stuffed Tomatoes

*page 119*

22.

# Stuffed Eggplant

*page 121*

*(shown with Kansas Stuffed Squash    page 245)*

23.

# Indiana Dutch Cabbage Rolls

*page 123*

24.

# Louisiana Fried Catfish with Crabmeat Topping

*page 128*

25.

## Stuffed Rocky Mountain Trout

*page 132*

26.

## Seaside Stuffed Shrimp

*page 137*

27.

# Texas Shrimp and Rice

*page 139*

# Stuffed Peppers

MAKES 8 SERVINGS

★

When Americans discovered that they enjoyed eating large sweet bell peppers stuffed with other delicious foods, they devised all sorts of fillings that would be complemented by the flavor of these edible cups. Ours are stuffed with pork and an aromatic blend of dried herbs and spices. They're a special favorite of Pat Scanlan, who works with me in the test kitchen. Pat loves them for company because they look so pretty.

SEASONING MIX

1 tablespoon plus 1 teaspoon
   paprika
1 tablespoon plus 1 teaspoon salt
1 tablespoon plus 1 teaspoon
   dried tarragon leaves
2 teaspoons dried thyme leaves
2 teaspoons dried cilantro leaves
2 teaspoons dried sweet basil
   leaves
2 teaspoons garlic powder
2 teaspoons onion powder
2 teaspoons dry mustard
2 teaspoons white pepper
1¼ teaspoons black pepper
3 bay leaves, crumbled

☆

1 cup pine nuts
4 large green bell peppers
3 tablespoons unsalted butter

3 tablespoons olive oil
2 cups chopped onions, in all
1¾ cups chopped green bell
   peppers, in all
1¼ cups chopped celery, in all
1¼ cups small fresh mushrooms
1 pound ground pork
5 cups grated unpeeled potatoes
   (about 3 medium potatoes)
3½ cups chicken stock (see
   page 11), in all
1 (8-ounce) can tomato sauce
1¼ cups sliced fresh mushrooms
4 peeled fresh tomatoes, roughly
   chopped, with their juices
1 tablespoon dark brown sugar
1 teaspoon minced fresh garlic
1 teaspoon dried tarragon leaves
1 teaspoon dried sweet basil leaves
1 teaspoon salt

Combine the seasoning mix ingredients thoroughly in a small bowl. Makes about 9 tablespoons plus 2 teaspoons.

Toast the pine nuts in an 8-inch skillet over medium heat, flipping the nuts and shaking the pan almost constantly, until light brown, about 2 to 3 minutes. Remove from the heat and set aside.

Cut the peppers in half crosswise, forming 8 cups, and remove the seeds and ribs. Set aside.

Preheat the oven to 325°.

To make the stuffing, heat the butter and oil in a 12-inch skillet over high heat. When the fat is hot, add *1 cup* of the onions, *1 cup* of the chopped bell peppers, and *¾ cup* of the celery. Stir in *2 tablespoons* of the seasoning mix. Place the small whole mushrooms on top of the chopped vegetables and cook, without stirring, 3 minutes. Stir the mushrooms into the vegetables and cook, stirring once, until the vegetables are browned, about 5 to 6 minutes. Move the vegetables to one side of the skillet and add the pork to the cleared space. Break up any lumps of meat with a spoon, sprinkle with *1 tablespoon* of the seasoning mix, and cook, stirring the vegetables once, 3 minutes. Stir the pork and cook, stirring occasionally, until browned, about 3 minutes. Stir the pork into the vegetables and cook 3 to 4 minutes. Stir in the potatoes and cook, allowing a crust to form on the skillet bottom, about 4 minutes. Add *1½ cups* of the chicken stock and scrape the bottom of the skillet clean. Cook, gently scraping up each new crust as it forms, about 7 to 9 minutes; do not scrape up the final crust. Remove from the heat and stir in the toasted pine nuts.

Set aside 1 cup of the stuffing mixture. Stuff the bell pepper halves with the remaining mixture, using about ½ cup per pepper half. Set the stuffed peppers aside.

Return the skillet to high heat and add *1 cup* of the stock, the *remaining 1 cup* onions, *¾ cup* chopped bell peppers, and *½ cup* celery, and the reserved 1 cup stuffing. Scrape off the hard crust from the bottom and sides of the skillet and cook 2 minutes. Stir in the tomato sauce, sliced mushrooms, and the *remaining* seasoning mix and cook, scraping once to keep the mixture from sticking, about 3 to 4 minutes. Add the garlic, tarragon, basil, and salt and cook 1 minute. Remove from the heat.

Place half the chopped tomatoes in the bowl of a food processor and blend until puréed. Add half the contents of the skillet and process just until thoroughly blended, about 15 to 20 seconds. Pour this mixture into a large bowl, and repeat the process with the remaining chopped tomatoes and sauce from the skillet. Add this sauce to the bowl and mix together until thoroughly blended.

Pour the sauce into a large baking pan, about 11 by 16 inches. Stir in the *remaining 1 cup* stock. Stand the pepper cups in the sauce and bake 30 minutes. Baste the peppers with the sauce and bake 35 minutes more, basting the peppers 2 or 3 times. Let stand a few minutes before serving.

Serve with rice or pasta.

# Baked Stuffed Tomatoes

MAKES 8 SERVINGS

*Color photograph 21*

Tomatoes, once thought to be poisonous, became respectable in the nineteenth century, and in the twentieth were recognized as perfect for filling with all kinds of goodies. Here they're stuffed with rice, mushrooms, pork, and chicken livers, for a delicious and unexpected taste.

SEASONING MIX

2 teaspoons salt

1½ teaspoons ground guajillo chile pepper (see Note)

1½ teaspoons ground ancho chile pepper (see Note)

1½ teaspoons ground New Mexico chile pepper (see Note)

1½ teaspoons ground pasilla chile pepper (see Note)

1½ teaspoons onion powder

1¼ teaspoons garlic powder

1¼ teaspoons white pepper

1 teaspoon dry mustard

1 teaspoon paprika

¾ teaspoon black pepper

8 large pretty tomatoes

½ pound chicken livers

2 tablespoons olive oil

2 cups chopped onions

1 cup chopped green bell peppers

1 pound ground pork

2 cups chopped fresh mushrooms

3 tablespoons light brown sugar

1 teaspoon minced fresh garlic

9 tablespoons plus 1 teaspoon grated Parmesan cheese, in all

2 cups shredded Monterey Jack cheese

☆

Combine the seasoning mix ingredients thoroughly in a small bowl. Makes ¼ cup plus 2¾ teaspoons.

Cut the tops off the tomatoes, scoop out and reserve the pulp.

Place the chicken livers and *2 tablespoons* of the seasoning mix in the container of a blender and process until the livers are thoroughly puréed, about 15 to 20 seconds.

Preheat the oven to 400°.

Heat the oil in a 12-inch skillet over high heat. When the oil is hot, add the onions and bell peppers and cook, stirring occasionally, until the onions are a light golden brown, about 4 to 5 minutes. Stir in *1 tablespoon* of the seasoning mix and cook 1 minute. Push the vegetables to one side of the skillet and add the ground pork to the cleared space. Sprinkle *2 tablespoons* of the seasoning mix over the pork and cook, stirring, 3 to 4 minutes. Stir the pork into the vegetables, breaking up any lumps of meat, and cook until the pork is a rich dark brown and a crust has formed on the bottom of the skillet, about 3 to 5 minutes. Add the reserved tomato pulp and scrape up the crust on the skillet bottom. Cook, stirring occasionally, until most of the liquid has evaporated but the mixture isn't sticking to the skillet, about 30 minutes. (The time will vary depending on the juiciness of the tomatoes.) Stir in the mushrooms, brown sugar, and garlic and cook 2 to 3 minutes. Add the puréed chicken livers and the *remaining* seasoning mix, stir well, and cook 1 minute. Do not overcook the livers, or they will become bitter. Remove from the heat and stir in *½ cup* of the Parmesan and the Monterey Jack. Makes about 7 cups.

Place the tomatoes in a baking pan. Stuff each tomato with about ¾ cup of the pork mixture and top each with *½ teaspoon of the remaining* Parmesan cheese. (You can bake any remaining stuffing mixture in a cake pan, with additional Parmesan cheese sprinkled on top.) Bake until brown, about 12 minutes.

Serve immediately.

NOTE: These are the ground chile peppers we used. You can use whatever is available in your area, but be sure to buy pure ground chile peppers, not commercial chili powder.

# Stuffed Eggplant

MAKES 10 SERVINGS

*Color photograph 22*

★

It is believed that Thomas Jefferson introduced eggplant to America. This shiny purple wonder has enjoyed only mild popularity, usually in the form of eggplant parmigiana and eggplant sticks. But Americans love to stuff foods with other foods, and the eggplant makes a wonderful container for such delicacies as shrimp and mushrooms, as this recipe demonstrates. Depending on the time of year, your eggplant may taste a little bitter, but you can adjust the amount of brown sugar in the recipe accordingly. Be sparing, though, so the sugar doesn't overtake and swallow the wonderful medley of flavors in the stuffing.

SEASONING MIX
1 tablespoon paprika
2 teaspoons salt
1 teaspoon white pepper
1 teaspoon black pepper
1 teaspoon onion powder
1 teaspoon garlic powder
1 teaspoon dried tarragon leaves
1 teaspoon dried thyme leaves
¾ teaspoon dried oregano leaves
½ teaspoon dried marjoram leaves
½ teaspoon ground nutmeg

☆

5 medium eggplants (about 1 pound each)
½ cup plus 2 tablespoons bread crumbs

½ cup plus 2 tablespoons freshly grated Parmesan cheese
3 tablespoons olive oil
2 cups chopped onions, in all
1½ cups chopped green bell peppers, in all
1 cup chopped celery
3 whole bay leaves
3 cups sliced fresh mushrooms, in all
4 tablespoons unsalted butter
2 cups seafood stock, (see page 11), in all
3 tablespoons light brown sugar
¼ cup chopped fresh parsley
1 pound peeled shrimp (about 1½ pounds unpeeled shrimp)

Preheat the oven to 350°.

Combine the seasoning mix ingredients thoroughly in a small bowl. Makes ¼ cup plus ¾ teaspoon.

Place the eggplants on a baking sheet and bake 45 minutes. Remove from the oven and let cool a few minutes. (Do not turn off the oven.)

Cut the eggplants in half lengthwise. Spoon out and reserve the flesh from the centers, leaving shells about ¼ inch thick.

Combine the bread crumbs and Parmesan cheese in a small bowl. Set aside.

Heat the oil in a 10-inch skillet over high heat. When the oil is very hot, about 4 minutes, add *1 cup* of the onions, *1 cup* of the bell peppers, and the celery. Stir once and cook 2 minutes. Stir in the reserved eggplant flesh and cook 4 minutes. Add the bay leaves and *2 tablespoons* of the seasoning mix and cook 4 minutes. Add *1 cup* of the mushrooms, scrape the bottom of the skillet and cook until the mixture is sticking hard to the bottom of the skillet, about 1 minute. Add *½ cup* of the onions, scrape the *skillet* bottom, and cook 3 minutes. Stir in the butter and *2 teaspoons* of the seasoning mix and scrape the bottom of the skillet. Cook, scraping occasionally, about 8 minutes. Add *½ cup* of the seafood stock and the *remaining ½ cup* each onions and bell peppers. Scrape the bottom of the skillet clean and cook 3 minutes. Stir in the sugar and cook, scraping occasionally, about 4 minutes. Add *½ cup* more seafood stock, scrape the skillet, and cook 2 minutes. Sprinkle on the parsley and scrape the bottom of the skillet. The mixture should be a nice, dark brown. Cook 4 to 5 minutes more, stir in the *remaining 1 cup* seafood stock, and cook 3 minutes. Remove the bay leaves. Stir in the shrimp, the *remaining 2 cups* mushrooms, and the *remaining* seasoning mix and remove from the heat.

Place the eggplant shells in a shallow baking pan, fill each with about ½ cup stuffing, and sprinkle the top of each shell with about 2 tablespoons of the bread crumb/Parmesan mixture. Bake 15 minutes; then turn on the broiler.

Place the eggplants under the broiler and broil 2 minutes; turn the pan around and broil until browned on top, about 1 or 2 minutes.

Serve 1 stuffed eggplant half per person.

# Indiana Dutch Cabbage Rolls

MAKES 7 SERVINGS

*Color photograph 23*

★

This is a classic dish in many parts of the country and it has its origins in a number of different cultures. We chose a version from northern Indiana, where the Amish people often make their cabbage rolls with a crushed gingersnap topping. We omitted the topping but put ground ginger in our seasoning mix. Keep in mind that the baking time may vary depending on the tenderness of the cabbage and the meat. Remember that our instructions are always intended as a guide—test all results as you proceed, and use your own very good judgment.

**SEASONING MIX**

1 tablespoon salt

2 teaspoons dry mustard

2 teaspoons dried cilantro leaves
   or parsley flakes

1½ teaspoons black pepper

1½ teaspoons onion powder

1 teaspoon garlic powder

1 teaspoon white pepper

1 teaspoon ground ginger

1 teaspoon ground savory

1 teaspoon dried thyme leaves

¾ teaspoon ground sage

½ teaspoon ground allspice

☆

**SAUCE**

1 (28-ounce) can whole
   tomatoes

¼ cup vegetable oil

2 cups chopped onions

1 cup chopped celery

2 tablespoons Seasoning Mix (see
   above)

3 small bay leaves

1 teaspoon minced fresh garlic

1 cup beef stock (see page 11)

3 tablespoons dark brown sugar

**FILLING**

1 pound ground pork

1 pound ground beef

2 cups chopped onions

1 cup chopped celery

3 tablespoons plus 1¼ teaspoons
   Seasoning Mix (see above)

2 teaspoons minced fresh garlic

3 cups beef stock (see page 11),
   in all

1 cup uncooked converted rice

**FINISH**

1 large head green cabbage

Combine the seasoning mix ingredients thoroughly in a small bowl. Makes 5 tablespoons plus 1¼ teaspoons.

**FOR THE SAUCE,** pour the tomatoes into a large bowl or container and break them up with your hands.

Heat the oil in a 12-inch skillet over high heat. When the oil is hot, add the onions, celery, seasoning mix, and bay leaves. Cook, stirring once or twice, until the vegetables are caramelized, golden brown, and sticking hard to the bottom of the skillet, about 6 to 8 minutes. Stir in the garlic and beef stock and scrape up the crust on the bottom of the skillet. Cook, stirring occasionally, until most of the liquid in the skillet has evaporated, about 11 to 12 minutes. Add the tomatoes and their juices, scrape the bottom of the skillet, and bring to a boil. Stir in the brown sugar and stir until it has dissolved. Reduce the heat to low and simmer 3 to 4 minutes. Remove from the heat and set aside. Makes about 4 cups.

**FOR THE FILLING,** place a 12-inch skillet over high heat and when the skillet is hot, add the meat. Break up any lumps of meat with a spoon and cook until browned, about 4 to 5 minutes. Stir in the onions, celery, and seasoning mix and cook, stirring occasionally, about 8 to 9 minutes. Stir in the garlic and cook, scraping the bottom of the skillet occasionally, until the mixture is brown and sticking hard to the skillet bottom (but not burning!), about 8 to 10 minutes. Stir in *2 cups* of the stock, scraping the crust from the bottom of the skillet, and bring to a simmer. Stir in the *remaining 1 cup* stock and the rice and cook 10 to 12 minutes, or until most of the liquid has been absorbed. Remove from the heat. Makes about 7 cups.

Preheat the oven to 350°.

**TO FINISH,** set the cabbage on a flat surface, core side up, and dig out the core with a small, sharp knife, making a cone-shaped hole about 3 inches deep. Then, holding the cabbage under lukewarm water, let the water run into the hole and around the edge of each leaf and gently peel off the leaves one at a time until you have 14 untorn leaves. (You may have to trim the core further to remove enough leaves.)

Meanwhile, bring a large pot of water to a boil over high heat.

Place 3 or 4 cabbage leaves at a time in the boiling water and blanch until the leaves are soft, about 30 seconds. Remove the leaves with tongs to a bowl.

Place a scant ½ cup meat filling (or slightly more or less depending on the size of the leaf) on one end of each cabbage leaf. Roll each leaf into an oblong roll, tucking in the sides. Arrange the rolls in a large baking pan, pour the sauce over them, cover, and bake 30 minutes. Uncover and bake until the cabbage leaves and meat are tender, another 30 to 45 minutes.

Allow 2 cabbage rolls, covered with sauce, per serving.

# Bayou Fried Catfish

## MAKES 6 SERVINGS

This is the way folks down here used to fry their catfish—just dip them in a little bit of batter and fry until real crunchy. The result is the best, melt-in-your-mouth catfish you've ever eaten. If you've never eaten catfish, do yourself a favor and cook some up this way.

SEASONING MIX
2 tsp
~~1 tablespoon~~ salt
2 teaspoons paprika
1½ teaspoons onion powder
1½ teaspoons garlic powder
1½ teaspoons dried sweet basil
  leaves
1 teaspoon dried thyme leaves
1 teaspoon black pepper
¾ teaspoon dried oregano leaves
½ teaspoon white pepper

6 catfish fillets, 5 to 6 ounces
  each
½ cup yellow cornmeal, *fine grind*
½ cup corn flour (see Note)
½ cup all-purpose flour
1 cup vegetable oil *(use ½ cup for ½ batch)*

Combine the seasoning mix ingredients thoroughly in a small bowl. Makes ¼ cup plus ¾ teaspoon.

Sprinkle the catfish fillets lightly with about 2 *teaspoons* of the seasoning mix, and rub it in well with your hands.

In a shallow pan combine the cornmeal, corn flour, all-purpose flour, and *remaining* 1 tablespoon plus 2 teaspoons of the seasoning mix. Heat the oil in a 12-inch skillet over high heat. While the oil is heating, dredge 3 of the catfish fillets one at a time in the cornmeal mixture, pressing the fish into the mixture to make it stick. *keep heat on high*

When the oil is very hot, add the fillets to the skillet and fry, turning 4 or 5 times, until the fish is brown and very crispy on both sides, about 6 to 7 minutes. Remove and drain on paper towels. Dredge the remaining fish in the cornmeal mixture, let the oil get very hot again, and repeat the procedure.

Serve immediately.

NOTE: If you can't find corn flour, increase both the white flour and cornmeal by ¼ cup.

# Louisiana Crawfish Boil

MAKES 4 TO 6 SERVINGS

★

Live crawfish are shipped to various markets around the country, and your fish market may be able to get them for you if you put in an order. Of course, in Louisiana they're available almost everywhere from about November through June or July. To eat the crawfish when they're cooked, twist the tail from the "head" (which is really the body), and suck out the juices from the head. Then remove the top ring of shell from the tail, and pinch the very end of the tail while pulling the meat out with your teeth. Don't serve these on a first date. Do make sure everyone has enough paper towels or napkins, and have fun!

10 pounds live crawfish
4 unpeeled onions
¼ cup cayenne pepper
½ cup salt
½ cup sugar

1 pound smoked sausage
20 unpeeled new potatoes
2 unpeeled garlic cloves
6 ears fresh corn, husked

Place the crawfish in the kitchen sink. Rinse once or twice in lukewarm water (make sure the water isn't hot, or it will kill the crawfish) and wash the mud off them. Remove and discard any dead crawfish. Fill the sink with fresh water to cover the crawfish and leave them there until you're ready to cook them.

Bring 3 gallons of water to a boil in a covered 6-gallon pot over high heat. When the water is boiling, add the onions, cayenne pepper, salt, and sugar. Cover the pot, bring back to a boil, and cook 15 minutes. Add the sausage and potatoes, cover, and cook 6 minutes. Add the garlic, cover, and cook 6 minutes.

Remove the onions, garlic, potatoes, and sausage and place in a large bowl. Cover the bowl tightly with aluminum foil and set aside to steam.

Add the corn to the pot of boiling water, cover, and cook 4 minutes.

Meanwhile, remove the crawfish from the sink and drain in a large colander.

Add the crawfish to the pot of corn and cook 8 minutes.

Transfer the corn to the bowl with the potatoes and cover tightly. Remove the crawfish from the water, place in another large pot, cover tightly, and set aside to steam for 10 minutes.

The best way to serve a crawfish boil is to spread newspapers on a big table, throw all the food on top, provide lots of paper towels or napkins and trash receptacles, and let the eaters dig in! This looks wonderful with the vegetables mixed right in with the crawfish; it's colorful and tastes fantastic.

# Louisiana
# Fried Catfish with
# Crabmeat Topping

MAKES 6 SERVINGS

*Color photograph 24*

**SEASONING MIX**

*1 tablespoon salt*

*2 teaspoons paprika*

*1 1/2 teaspoons garlic powder*

*1 1/2 teaspoons onion powder*

*1 1/2 teaspoons dried sweet basil
leaves*

*1 teaspoon dried thyme leaves*

*1 teaspoon black pepper*

*3/4 teaspoon dried oregano leaves*

*1/2 teaspoon white pepper*

☆

*6 catfish fillets, 5 to 6 ounces
each*

*1 cup milk*

*1 tablespoon plus 1 teaspoon
prepared Dijon mustard*

*1 egg*

**CRABMEAT TOPPING**

*5 tablespoons unsalted butter,
in all*

*2 tablespoons Seasoning Mix
(see above)*

*1/2 cup chopped green onion
tops*

*1/4 cup chopped fresh parsley*

*1 teaspoon minced fresh garlic*

*1/2 pound lump crabmeat,
picked over for shells and
cartilage*

*1 cup heavy cream*

**FINISH**

*1 1/2 cups all-purpose flour*

*1 cup vegetable oil*

**DAY 1:** Combine the seasoning mix ingredients thoroughly in a small bowl. Makes 1/4 cup plus 3/4 teaspoon.

Sprinkle the catfish fillets on both sides with a total of *2 teaspoons* of the seasoning mix, and rub it in with your hands.

Combine the milk, mustard, egg, and *1 tablespoon* of the seasoning mix in a bowl large enough to hold all the fillets. Blend well with a spoon, add the fillets, and marinate overnight in the refrigerator.

**DAY 2:** For the topping, place *2 tablespoons* of the butter in a 10-inch skillet over high heat and sprinkle the seasoning mix directly on top of the butter so it will brown lightly as the butter melts. When the butter has melted, add the green onions, parsley, garlic, and the *remaining 3 tablespoons* butter. Stir well and heat until the butter melts. Add the crabmeat and cook, stirring gently, 1 minute. Add the cream, stir gently, and bring to a rolling boil. Remove from the heat. Makes about 2¼ cups.

**TO FINISH,** combine the flour and the *remaining* seasoning mix in a shallow pan. Remove the fish from the refrigerator.

Heat the oil in a 12-inch skillet over high heat. While the oil is heating, remove 3 fillets from the marinade and dredge in the seasoned flour, one at a time. When the oil is very hot, add the floured fillets to the skillet. Fry, turning several times, until brown and very crispy on both sides, about 8 to 10 minutes. Remove the fillets and drain on paper towels. Repeat with the remaining catfish, making sure the oil is very hot before adding the fish to the skillet.

Warm the sauce for serving. Allow 1 catfish fillet topped with a generous ⅓ cup sauce per person.

# Fish en Papillote

## MAKES 6 SERVINGS

The long-famous Antoine's restaurant in New Orleans is credited with inventing Pompano en Papillote, created in honor of a celebrated balloonist who was visiting the city. The parchment paper used in the dish was intended to represent a balloon, but it also seals in all the juices and their flavor. In our recipe, the seasonings in the juices magnify the flavors even more. This makes a pretty presentation, and you'll be proud to serve it for company.

SEASONING MIX
1 tablespoon salt
1 tablespoon paprika
2 teaspoons dried sweet basil
 leaves
1½ teaspoons dried thyme leaves
1½ teaspoons onion powder
1½ teaspoons garlic powder
1½ teaspoons black pepper
1½ teaspoons white pepper
1¼ teaspoons dried oregano
 leaves
½ teaspoon ground nutmeg

☆

10 tablespoons (1¼ sticks)
 unsalted butter, in all
¼ cup all-purpose flour
6 ounces bacon, diced
1 cup diced ham (about 4
 ounces)

2 cups chopped onions
2 cups chopped green bell
 peppers
1 cup chopped celery
3 cups sliced fresh mushrooms
1 cup seafood stock (see
 page 11)
2 cups heavy cream
½ pound lump crabmeat, picked
 over for shells and cartilage
½ pound peeled shrimp (about
 ¾ pound unpeeled shrimp)
6 fillets of any fresh fish available
 in your area, such as
 pompano, tilapia, grouper,
 sole

Parchment paper (available in
 kitchenware shops and some
 supermarkets; see Note)

Combine the seasoning mix ingredients thoroughly in a small bowl. Makes 5 tablespoons plus 2¼ teaspoons.

Make 6 hearts out of parchment paper: Cut 6 sheets of paper 18 inches square and fold them in half. Cut out the shape of a heart half in each, and open up to hearts measuring 18 inches across the widest part and 13 inches from the top "V" to the bottom point. Set aside.

Melt *6 tablespoons* of the butter in an 8-inch skillet over high heat. When the butter sizzles, add the flour and *1 teaspoon* of the seasoning mix and cook, whisking constantly with a wire whisk, until thick and thoroughly blended into a roux, about 1 minute. Remove from the heat.

Place the bacon in a 12-inch skillet over high heat and cook until lightly browned, about 6 to 7 minutes. Stir in the ham and cook, stirring occasionally, until the bacon and ham are well browned, about 4 minutes. Remove the bacon and ham with a slotted spoon and set aside.

Pour off all but 3 tablespoons of the fat and return the skillet to high heat. Add the onions, bell peppers, celery, and *1 tablespoon* of the seasoning mix. Scrape the bottom of the skillet and cook, stirring occasionally, until the onions are lightly browned, about 4 to 5 minutes. Stir in the mushrooms and *1 tablespoon* of the seasoning mix and cook, stirring occasionally, 2 minutes. Add the seafood stock and cook, stirring occasionally, about 4 minutes. Add the heavy cream, bring to a rolling boil, and cook, stirring occasionally, about 2 minutes. Then cook, whisking constantly, 1 minute. Add the reserved bacon and ham and the butter/flour roux and cook, whisking, about 2 minutes. Reduce the heat to low and simmer 1 minute. Remove from the heat and stir in the crabmeat, shrimp, and *1 tablespoon plus 1½ teaspoons* of the seasoning mix. Pour this stuffing mixture into a shallow pan and refrigerate until cold.

Preheat the oven to 450°.

Melt the *remaining 4 tablespoons* butter in a small pan. Remove from the heat.

Brush each paper heart with some of the melted butter and place a fish fillet on one half of each heart. Brush the fish with butter and sprinkle each fillet with *½ teaspoon* of the seasoning mix. Spoon 1 cup of the stuffing over each fillet. Fold over the hearts, twist the edges to seal, and brush the outside of each package with the melted butter. Place on a baking sheet and bake until the paper is puffed and lightly browned, about 15 minutes.

Use a sharp knife to cut a large "X" in the top of the parchment hearts, fold back the paper, and serve immediately.

NOTE: If you can't find parchment paper, you can use aluminum foil.

# Stuffed Rocky Mountain Trout

MAKES 8 SERVINGS

*Color photograph 25*

★

Early settlers learned to prepare trout, which for them became an everyday food, from the Indians. Today trout is prepared in many ways, and we've chosen to stuff ours as they do fresh-caught trout in the Rocky Mountains.

SEASONING MIX
*1½ teaspoons salt*
*1¼ teaspoons dried sweet basil*
  *leaves*
*¾ teaspoon dried oregano leaves*
*¾ teaspoon dried thyme leaves*
*¾ teaspoon dry mustard*
*¾ teaspoon onion powder*
*¾ teaspoon garlic powder*
*¾ teaspoon white pepper*
*¼ teaspoon black pepper*

☆

*4 whole rainbow or speckled*
  *trout, about 1¼ to 1¾ pounds*
  *each after the heads are*
  *removed and the fish scaled,*
  *gutted, and thoroughly*
  *cleaned*

*1 tablespoon plus 1 teaspoon*
  *olive oil*
*3 tablespoons bread crumbs*
*¼ pound bacon, diced*
*½ cup chopped onions*
*½ cup chopped green bell*
  *peppers*
*2 cups thickly sliced fresh*
  *mushrooms*
*10 ounces fresh spinach, rinsed*
  *and stems removed*
*3 tablespoons grated Parmesan*
  *cheese*
*½ cup grated Cheddar cheese*

Combine the seasoning mix ingredients thoroughly in a small bowl. Makes 2 tablespoons plus 1½ teaspoons.

Rinse the fish and dry with paper towels. Drizzle *1 teaspoon* of the olive oil over each fish and sprinkle each inside and out with *¾ teaspoon* of the seasoning mix, rubbing the oil and seasonings into the fish with your hands.

Toast the bread crumbs in a small skillet over medium heat until golden brown, about 4 minutes. Remove from the heat and set aside.

Fry the bacon in a 12-inch skillet over high heat until browned, about 5 to 7 minutes. Remove the bacon with a slotted spoon and set aside.

Add the onions, bell peppers, mushrooms, and the *remaining* seasoning mix to the fat in the skillet. Cook over high heat until the vegetables and seasonings have absorbed all the fat, about 1 minute. Remove from the heat.

Combine the spinach, Parmesan and Cheddar cheeses, the cooked bacon, and the toasted bread crumbs in a large bowl. Add the onion/mushroom mixture and toss thoroughly, transfer to the hot skillet, turn off the heat, and stir until the spinach just starts to wilt. Refrigerate this stuffing until cool. Makes 3 cups.

Preheat the oven to 400°.

Stuff the cavity of each fish with ¾ cup of the stuffing. Place the fish on a baking sheet and bake, uncovered, 25 to 35 minutes: The cooking time will depend on the size of your trout. To determine doneness, cut into the fish at the thickest part of the meat; if it is no longer translucent, it's done.

Remove the stuffing from the fish, and cut each fish in half lengthwise to form 2 fillets. (Remove the center bones.) To serve, place a mound of stuffing on each plate and cover with 1 fillet. Serve with lemon wedges, if desired, and watch out for wayward bones!

# Lobster Newburg

MAKES 4 TO 6 SERVINGS

★

Lobster Newburg became a signature dish at Delmonico's restaurant in New York City in the 1870s. Restaurateur Charles Delmonico originally called it "Lobster à la Wenberg," after Ben Wenberg, the sea captain who had brought the recipe to him. When Wenberg and Delmonico had a falling out, the name was changed to "Lobster à la Newburg." Its rich, full flavor, from a blend of egg yolks, cream, and in this case, cognac, accounts for the popularity of this wonderful creation. As you remove the meat from the lobsters, be sure to scrape all of the gelatinous material from the shells, since it will add incredible flavor to your dish.

SEASONING MIX
1¼ teaspoons salt
¾ teaspoon onion powder
½ teaspoon white pepper
½ teaspoon garlic powder
⅛ teaspoon cayenne pepper

☆

2 live lobsters, about 5 pounds
   total
12 tablespoons (1½ sticks)
   unsalted butter, in all

1 cup chopped onions
4 cups water, approximately,
   in all
2 bay leaves
1 teaspoon dried sweet basil
   leaves
½ teaspoon dried winter savory
   leaves
2 cups heavy cream
¼ cup cognac
8 small or 7 medium egg yolks

Combine the seasoning mix ingredients thoroughly in a small bowl. Makes 3⅛ teaspoons.

Kill the lobsters by severing the heads and the tails from the bodies. Remove all the meat and juices from the shells and reserve the shells. Throw away the greenish sacs from the heads. Cut the lobster meat into 1-inch pieces. There should be about 1½ cups of lobster meat. Sprinkle *1 teaspoon* of the seasoning mix over the lobster meat and work it in well with your hands.

Place half the lobster shells in a 10-inch skillet over high heat. Add *8 tablespoons (1 stick)* of the butter and the onions and cook, stirring occasionally, about 10 to 12 minutes. Add *2 cups* of the water, the bay leaves, basil and savory. Stir well, cover the skillet, bring to a boil, and cook about 10 to 12 minutes. Remove and discard about half of the shells from the skillet and add the remaining shells. Stir, cover the skillet, and cook, adding water if necessary, about 15 to 20 minutes. (Be careful not to let the water cook all the way down!) Uncover the skillet and bring the liquid to a strong boil. Remove from the heat, and strain and reserve the liquid; there should be about ½ cup of this lobster stock. Set aside. Discard the shells.

Place the cream in the top of a double boiler set over simmering water.

Combine the the *remaining 4 tablespoons* butter and the *remaining* seasoning mix in a 10-inch skillet and heat over high heat. When the butter sizzles, stir in the lobster pieces. Add the cognac and touch with a lit match to flame. As soon as the cognac ignites, remove the skillet from the heat and let the flame go out by itself. (If the cognac refuses to ignite, just stir the cognac thoroughly into the lobster and remove from the heat.)

Place the reserved lobster stock and the egg yolks in a blender and process until very frothy, about 15 seconds. Whisk this mixture into the cream and cook gently, whisking constantly, until the mixture resembles a thin custard, about 3 minutes. Add the lobster mixture and cook, whisking gently, until the sauce thickens to a soft custard, about 4 minutes. Do not overcook or overwhisk, or the sauce will break.

Serve immediately over rice or toast points.

# Cape Cod Mussels

MAKES 4 TO 6 SERVINGS

★

Mussels may be the most misunderstood American shellfish, although they're abundant in our coastal waters. For those unfamiliar with this tender mollusk, which comes encased in an attractive blue-black shell, the following recipe—representative of the way mussels are often eaten in New England—is a great place to start. When you've finished eating all the mussels and sopped up all the sauce, I guarantee you'll be looking for more.

SEASONING MIX

1½ teaspoons dry mustard
1 teaspoon salt
1 teaspoon dried dill weed
¾ teaspoon dried thyme leaves
¾ teaspoon white pepper
½ teaspoon garlic powder
½ teaspoon onion powder
½ teaspoon ground fennel or
　fennel seed

☆

5 pounds mussels
11 tablespoons unsalted butter,
　in all
2 cups chopped onions
1 cup chopped celery
2 bay leaves
2 tablespoons plus 2 teaspoons
　fresh lemon juice, in all
1 cup dry white wine
1 teaspoon minced fresh garlic
2 cups seafood stock (see
　page 11)
½ cup heavy cream

Combine the seasoning mix ingredients thoroughly in a small bowl. Makes 2 tablespoons plus ½ teaspoon.

To clean the mussels, remove their beards and scrub each shell with a stiff brush. Soak the mussels in a large pot of ice water for an hour. Discard any mussels that are open or whose shells are broken.

Melt *3 tablespoons* of the butter in a heavy 8-quart pot over high heat. When the butter starts to sizzle, add the onions, celery, bay leaves, and all of the seasoning mix. Cook, stirring gently once or twice, until the vegetables begin to stick to the bottom of the pot, about 5 to 6 minutes. Stir in *2 tablespoons* of the lemon juice, scrape the bottom of the pot, and cook until a light crust forms, about 3 to 4 minutes. Add the wine, scrape the pot bottom clean, and bring to a boil. Stir in the garlic and cook 3 minutes. Add the seafood stock and bring to a boil. Reduce the heat slightly and simmer, whipping occasionally with a wire whisk, about 5 minutes. Add the mussels, cover the pot, and cook, uncovering once to stir, until all the shells are open, about 5 to 6 minutes. Remove the mussels from the pot, and discard any that haven't opened. Pour the cooking liquid into a 10-inch skillet. Return the mussels to the pot, cover, and set aside. Bring the cooking liquid just to a boil over high heat. Add the *remaining 8 tablespoons (1 stick)* butter and whisk until the butter has melted, about 3 minutes. Stir in the *remaining 2 teaspoons* lemon juice, remove from the heat, and whisk in the cream until thoroughly blended.

To serve, place the mussels in a bowl, pour the sauce over, and toss.

# Seaside Stuffed Shrimp

MAKES 6 MAIN-COURSE SERVINGS OR

12 APPETIZER SERVINGS

*Color photograph 26*

★

A favorite food of many Americans—and probably the most popular of all seafoods—is shrimp. Every year, zillions of shrimp are consumed boiled, broiled, deep-fried, stir-fried—and even raw at local sushi bars. This recipe for stuffed shrimp was inspired by a dish at an inn in Connecticut. It makes a beautiful main course, but could also be served as an appetizer for 12 dinner guests.

SEASONING MIX

*2 teaspoons salt*

*2 teaspoons paprika*

*1½ teaspoons white pepper*

*1½ teaspoons dry mustard*

*1½ teaspoons dried sweet basil leaves*

*1½ teaspoons onion powder*

*1 teaspoon garlic powder*

*1 teaspoon dried thyme leaves*

*½ teaspoon ground sage*

*½ teaspoon dried oregano leaves*

☆

*36 large shrimp, peeled (except for the tails), deveined, and butterflied*

*2 tablespoons olive oil*

*¾ cup bread crumbs*

*1 cup shredded mozzarella cheese*

*¼ cup plus 3 tablespoons grated Parmesan cheese, in all*

*8 tablespoons (1 stick) unsalted butter, in all*

*2 cups chopped onions*

*1 cup chopped green bell peppers*

*1 cup chopped celery*

*1 cup grated carrots*

*2 teaspoons minced fresh garlic*

*1 pound lump crabmeat, in all, picked over for shells and cartilage*

*1½ cups seafood stock (see page 11), in all*

*Vegetable oil cooking spray*

*2 cups heavy cream*

*6 thin lemon slices*

Preheat the oven to 450°.

Combine the seasoning mix ingredients thoroughly in a small bowl. Makes ¼ cup plus 1 teaspoon.

Put the shrimp in a bowl, sprinkle *1 tablespoon* of the seasoning mix over them, and rub it in well with your hands. Trickle the olive oil over the shrimp, rub in, and set aside.

Combine the bread crumbs, mozzarella cheese, and *3 tablespoons* of the Parmesan in a large bowl and set aside.

Melt *4 tablespoons* of the butter in a 10-inch skillet over high heat. When the butter begins to sizzle, add the onions, peppers, celery, carrots, and *2 tablespoons* of the seasoning mix. Cook, stirring occasionally, about 3 minutes. Stir in the garlic and *½ cup* of the crabmeat and cook, stirring occasionally, until a crust has formed on the bottom of the skillet, about 8 to 10 minutes. Add *½ cup* of the seafood stock, scrape up the crust, and cook, stirring occasionally, about 7 to 9 minutes. Add *½ cup* more stock, the *remaining 4 tablespoons* butter, and the *remaining* seasoning mix and cook, stirring occasionally, 2 minutes. Remove from the heat and stir into the bread crumb mixture. Fold in the *remaining* crabmeat. Set aside ½ cup of this stuffing. Set the skillet aside.

Spray a baking sheet with cooking spray. Place the shrimp in rows (reserve any drippings that have accumulated in the bowl) on the baking sheet, butterflied side up, and mound 2 tablespoons of the stuffing mixture on top of each. Bake until browned about 10 minutes.

Meanwhile, pour any accumulated shrimp drippings from the bowl into the 10-inch skillet and set over high heat. Stir in the reserved stuffing and cook 2 minutes. Add the *remaining ½ cup* seafood stock and scrape the bottom and sides of the skillet clean. Bring to a boil, whisk in the cream, and cook, whisking constantly, about 7 minutes. Add the lemon slices and cook, whisking, about 2 minutes. Whisk in the *remaining ¼ cup* Parmesan cheese and remove from the heat. Makes 2½ cups.

Allow 6 shrimp with a generous ⅓ cup sauce per serving. Garnish each with a lemon slice.

# Texas Shrimp and Rice

MAKES 6 SERVINGS

*Color photograph 27*

★

Since 1900, thousands of Mexicans have crossed the border into Texas, looking for work and a better life. One of their valuable contributions to this country is their exciting food, which was quickly adopted and adapted by Southwesterners. And Tex-Mex, one of my favorite regional cuisines, was born. You can impress your friends by correctly pronouncing the name of this dish in Spanish—*camerones y arroz*—or you can just wow them by having them over for dinner next time you prepare it.

**SEASONING MIX**

1 tablespoon salt

2 teaspoons ground ancho chile pepper (see Note)

1¾ teaspoons dried oregano leaves

1½ teaspoons dried cilantro leaves

1½ teaspoons ground cumin

1 teaspoon paprika

1 teaspoon white pepper

1 teaspoon onion powder

1 teaspoon garlic powder

1 teaspoon dried sweet basil leaves

1 teaspoon ground guajillo chile pepper (see Note)

½ teaspoon cayenne pepper

☆

3 tablespoons olive oil

2 cups chopped onions

1 cup chopped green bell peppers

3 bay leaves

2 tablespoons fresh lemon juice

2 tablespoons fresh lime juice

1½ cups uncooked converted rice

1 (4-ounce) can green chiles, finely chopped

3 cups seafood stock (see page 11)

½ teaspoon minced fresh garlic

1½ pounds peeled large shrimp (about 2¼ pounds unpeeled shrimp)

½ cup chopped fresh parsley

1 cup chopped green onions

Combine the seasoning mix ingredients thoroughly in a small bowl. Makes 5 tablespoons plus 1¼ teaspoons.

Heat the oil in a large heavy pot over high heat. When the oil is very hot, about 4 to 5 minutes, add the onions, bell peppers, and *2 tablespoons* of the seasoning mix, stir, and cook 2 minutes. Add the bay leaves and cook, stirring occasionally, 5 minutes. Add the lemon and lime juices and rice and cook, stirring occasionally, until the rice is lightly browned, about 4 minutes. Stir in the chilies and *1 tablespoon plus 2 teaspoons* of the seasoning mix and cook until a light crust forms on the bottom of the pot, about 3 minutes. Add the seafood stock and scrape the bottom of the pot clean. Cook, stirring occasionally, 4 minutes. Add the garlic, stir, and cook 1 minute. Add the shrimp and *1 tablespoon* of the seasoning mix. Stir well, cover the pot, and cook 2 minutes. Stir in the parsley and green onions, cover, and cook 2 minutes. Remove from the heat and let the pot sit, covered, 15 minutes before serving.

Allow about 1½ cups rice and shrimp per serving.

NOTE: These are the ground chile peppers we used. You can use any that are available in your area. If you can't find pure ground chile pepper, roast some dried whole peppers and grind them in a food processor. Do not use commercial chili powder.

# Saucy Sausalito Stir-fry

MAKES 6 SERVINGS

*Color photograph 28*

In the mid-1800s, Chinese immigrants settled in San Francisco to work on the railroads. They brought with them foods and spices that had never before been seen in this country, as well as their very distinct style of cooking. The meats, fish, and vegetables cooked in their woks always tasted fresh, juicy, and crisp, and many Americans began stir-frying in their own kitchens. This dish tastes great served over rice, but is also wonderful over noodles.

SEASONING MIX

2 teaspoons salt

2 teaspoons grated fresh ginger
(preferred) or ½ teaspoon
ground ginger

1 teaspoon paprika

1 teaspoon white pepper

1 teaspoon ground cardamom

½ teaspoon black pepper

☆

1 pound peeled large shrimp
(about 1½ pounds unpeeled
shrimp)

1 pound bay or sea scallops

2 tablespoons cornstarch

2 cups plus 2 tablespoons
seafood stock (see page 11),
in all

2 tablespoons sesame oil

1 tablespoon peanut oil

1 tablespoon olive oil

2 cups onions, thinly sliced

1½ cups sliced celery (cut into
thin diagonal slices)

2 cups sliced green bell peppers
(cut into thin diagonal slices)

1 cup sliced red bell peppers (cut
into thin diagonal slices)

1 cup sliced green onions, both
tops and bottoms (cut into
thin diagonal slices)

1¼ cups chopped pecans (or
whatever nuts are native to
and readily available in your
area)

3 fresh jalapeños or other small
hot peppers, seeded and
slivered, optional

4 cloves garlic, slivered

1 tablespoon low-sodium or light
soy sauce

8 cups fresh spinach, rinsed,
stemmed, and shredded

Combine the seasoning mix ingredients thoroughly in a small bowl. Makes 2 tablespoons plus 1½ teaspoons if you use fresh ginger, 2 tablespoons if you use ground ginger.

Place the shrimp and scallops in a bowl, sprinkle with all of the seasoning mix, and blend it in well with your hands.

Combine the cornstarch with *2 tablespoons* of the seafood stock and set aside.

Heat the sesame, peanut, and olive oils in a 14-inch skillet or wok over high heat. When the oil is very hot, add the onions, celery, and green and red bell peppers and cook, stirring occasionally, 2 minutes. Add the green onions and cook, stirring occasionally, 2 minutes. Remove the vegetables to a bowl with a slotted spoon, leaving the skillet over high heat. When the juices in the skillet begin to smoke, add the seasoned seafood and cook just until the shrimp and scallops lose their translucence, about

1 to 2 minutes. Remove the seafood to a bowl with a slotted spoon. When the juices in the skillet begin to smoke again, add the pecans and cook, stirring and shaking the pan, until they just begin to toast, about 1 minute. Add the jalapeños, if desired, and garlic and cook, stirring occasionally, 2 minutes. Return the vegetables to the skillet, add the *remaining 2 cups* stock, and cook 1 minute. Stir in the cornstarch mixture and cook 1 minute. Add the soy sauce and cook 1 minute. Return the seafood to the skillet and add the spinach. Cook, pushing the spinach gently down into the liquid, just until it starts to wilt. Makes 8 cups.

Serve immediately over mounds of white rice.

# Chicago
# Chicken à la King

## MAKES 8 SERVINGS

Many legends surround the origins of chicken à la king. One says it was created by the chef at New York's Brighton Beach Hotel for the proprietors, Mr. and Mrs. E. Clark King III. Another asserts it was first served at Claridge's restaurant in London and named for Wall Street broker James R. Keene. Still another credits Keene's son with its creation at the original Delmonico's. Whatever the true story, chicken à la king has taken its place as standard American fare at the buffet table and in homes all across the country. Unfortunately, it has suffered a decline from elegance to mediocrity in most cases, but we found this version in Chicago, used it as a guide, and created a delicious blend of seasonings to restore its grace— not to mention its superb flavor. This would also make a great filling for crêpes.

SEASONING MIX
*1 tablespoon salt*
*1½ teaspoons dried sweet basil
  leaves*
*1 teaspoon garlic powder*
*1 teaspoon onion powder*
*1 teaspoon white pepper*
*1 teaspoon paprika*
*1 teaspoon dry mustard*
*½ teaspoon ground savory*
*½ teaspoon ground nutmeg*

☆

*2 pounds boneless, skinless chicken
  breasts, cut into 1-inch cubes*
*8 tablespoons (1 stick) unsalted
  butter, softened, plus 5
  tablespoons unsalted butter,
  cut into pats*
*¼ cup all-purpose flour*
*6 tablespoons dry sherry, in all*
*1 cup chopped onions*
*1 cup chopped red bell peppers*
*1 cup chopped green bell peppers*
*2 cups thinly sliced fresh
  mushrooms*
*2½ cups heavy cream, in all*

Combine the seasoning mix ingredients thoroughly in a small bowl. Makes 3 tablespoons plus 1½ teaspoons.

Sprinkle *1 tablespoon plus 1 teaspoon* of the seasoning mix over the chicken and rub it in well with your hands.

Combine the *8 tablespoons* soft butter with the flour, and mash together until the flour disappears. Set aside.

Place a 5-quart pot over high heat. When the pot is hot, about 5 minutes, add the chicken and dot the *remaining 5 tablespoons* butter evenly over the top of the chicken. Cover the pot and cook, without stirring, until the chicken can be easily unstuck from the bottom of the pot, about 5 to 6 minutes. Stir, cover the pot, and cook 5 minutes. Add *¼ cup* of the sherry, the onions, red and green peppers, mushrooms, and the *remaining* seasoning mix. Stir well, cover, and cook 5 minutes. Uncover the pot and add the butter/flour mixture a spoonful at a time, stirring constantly as the mixture dissolves and the sauce thickens. Stir in *2 cups* of the cream and heat until "small volcanoes" begin to erupt in the sauce—but don't allow the sauce to come to a rolling boil. Let the "volcanoes" erupt 3 times, stirring after each eruption. Add the *remaining ½ cup* cream and heat until another group of small "volcanoes" erupts, about 1 minute. Remove from the heat and stir in the *remaining 2 tablespoons* sherry. Makes about 8 cups.

Serve in patty shells or crêpes, or over pasta or croissants.

# Atchafalaya
# Roast Boneless Chicken

MAKES 4 SERVINGS

*Color photograph 29*

★

In my family, a roast chicken always meant a special occasion; our usual chicken dishes consisted of tough old hens that were potted or smothered and cleverly stretched to serve fifteen hungry people. This little roaster is stuffed and slow-cooked the old-fashioned way, and the result is the most tender, delicious chicken you've ever tasted. It seems so ordinary, but just try it!

SEASONING MIX

*1 tablespoon salt*

*2 teaspoons paprika*

*1½ teaspoons onion powder*

*1½ teaspoons garlic powder*

*1½ teaspoons dried sweet basil leaves*

*1 teaspoon dry mustard*

*1 teaspoon ground cumin*

*1 teaspoon black pepper*

*¾ teaspoon white pepper*

*½ teaspoon dried thyme leaves*

*½ teaspoon ground savory*

*2 tablespoons unsalted butter*

*2 cups chopped onions*

*1 cup chopped green bell peppers*

*1 (3½- to 4-pound) roasting chicken*

*¼ cup all-purpose flour*

*2 cups chicken stock (see page 11)*

☆

Preheat the oven to 250°.

Combine the seasoning mix ingredients thoroughly in a small bowl. Makes ¼ cup plus 2¼ teaspoons.

Melt the butter in an 8-inch skillet over high heat. When the butter starts to sizzle, add the onions, bell peppers, and *3 tablespoons* of the seasoning mix. Cook, flipping and stirring the onions and peppers occasionally, until the onions are golden brown, about 6 minutes. Transfer to a bowl, scraping all of the seasonings from the skillet into the bowl, and let cool.

Remove the giblets from the chicken and clean out the cavity. Stuff the cavity with the cooled vegetables and fold the skin flaps over the stuffing to keep it in. Sprinkle *1 tablespoon* of the seasoning mix all over the outside of the chicken, and rub it in well with your hands.

Place the chicken in a large baking pan and bake until tender, about 3 hours. Remove from the oven and set aside until the chicken is cool enough to handle.

Remove the stuffing from the chicken, and put the stuffing and any juices that have accumulated in the cavity of the chicken in the baking pan.

Cut the chicken in half lengthwise along the breastbone and backbone and carefully remove the bones, pulling out the breastbone first. The bones will come out easily if you take your time.

Place the baking pan over high heat and whisk the flour into the stuffing until it's completely absorbed. Whisk in the chicken stock and cook, whisking until thoroughly blended, about 1 to 2 minutes. Cook the gravy 2 minutes more, and remove from the heat. Makes 3 cups.

Serve the chicken with the gravy over rice or mashed potatoes.

★ To make this into an elegant dish, remove the skin from the chicken breasts and thighs, taking care not to tear it. Turn the oven heat up to 400°. Pour about 1 teaspoon chicken stock into an 8-inch cake pan. Place the breasts and thighs on one side of the pan and cover with foil. Place the skin on the other side of the pan, and leave uncovered. Roast until the skin is crackling-crisp, about 8 to 10 minutes. To serve, spoon some of the gravy onto each plate, add a portion of chicken, and place some of the crisp skin on top.

# Chicken Florentine

MAKES 8 SERVINGS

*Color photograph 30*

★

Most Americans know that when a recipe is designated "Florentine," it's a sure tip-off that there's going to be spinach involved. This chicken dish is juicy and delicious, with beautifully subtle flavoring. Chicken Florentine, sometimes called Chicken Gismonda, is a particular favorite on the West Coast.

SEASONING MIX
2 teaspoons salt
1½ teaspoons paprika
1 teaspoon onion powder
1 teaspoon garlic powder
1 teaspoon dry mustard
1 teaspoon dried thyme leaves
1 teaspoon dried sweet basil
   leaves
¾ teaspoon white pepper
½ teaspoon ground sage
½ teaspoon ground nutmeg
☆

8 boneless, skinless chicken
   breast halves
½ cup all-purpose flour
3 eggs
¼ cup plus 3 tablespoons half-
   and-half, in all
¾ cup bread crumbs
½ cup grated Parmesan cheese,
   in all
8 tablespoons (1 stick) unsalted
   butter, in all
1½ pounds fresh (preferred) or
   frozen spinach, thawed if
   frozen, rinsed if fresh, and
   drained and toweled dry

Combine the seasoning mix ingredients thoroughly in a small bowl. Makes 3 tablespoons plus 1¼ teaspoons.

   Place the chicken breasts on a flat surface and pound them a few times with the flat side of a cleaver or a heavy knife. Sprinkle the breasts on one side with *1 tablespoon* of the seasoning mix, patting it in with your hands. Turn the breasts and pat another *2½ teaspoons* of the seasoning mix into the second side.

Combine the flour and *1 teaspoon* of the seasoning mix in a shallow bowl. Combine the eggs, *3 tablespoons* of the half-and-half, and ¼ *teaspoon* of the seasoning mix in another shallow bowl. Beat thoroughly with a fork. Combine the bread crumbs, *2 teaspoons* of the seasoning mix, and ¼ *cup* of the Parmesan cheese in a third bowl.

Dredge the chicken breasts one at a time in the seasoned flour, dip them in the egg mixture, and then dredge them in the bread crumb mixture, shaking off any excess crumbs. Add the *remaining* ¼ *cup* half-and-half to the egg mixture, beat briefly with a fork, and set aside.

Melt *4 tablespoons* of the butter in a 12-inch skillet over high heat. As soon as the butter starts to sizzle, add the chicken breasts and brown on both sides. Remove the chicken from the skillet and set aside. Add the *remaining 4 tablespoons* butter to the pan, along with the *remaining* seasoning mix. When the butter sizzles, add the spinach, pressing it down gently, and cook until it starts to wilt, about 1 minute. Pour the reserved egg/half-and-half mixture over the spinach and stir well. Sprinkle with the *remaining* ¼ *cup* Parmesan cheese. Place the chicken breasts on top, cover, and turn the heat down to medium low. Cook until the chicken is cooked through, about 13 minutes. Serve immediately.

# New World Chicken Fricassee

MAKES 6 TO 8 SERVINGS

When the first settlers arrived in what is now New England, they had to learn to live in the wilderness and use it to stay alive. The Native Americans taught the English to gather their foods from the woods, and rabbits may have been the first game they cooked. To make them tender, they stewed them fricassee style, and eventually they came to cook chickens the same way.

SEASONING MIX

1 tablespoon salt
2 teaspoons paprika
1½ teaspoons garlic powder
1 teaspoon onion powder
1 teaspoon black pepper
1 teaspoon white pepper
1 teaspoon dry mustard
1 teaspoon marjoram
½ teaspoon dried tarragon
  leaves
¼ teaspoon ground allspice

☆

1 (3½- to 4-pound) chicken, cut
  into 8 pieces, all visible fat
  removed
1 tablespoon olive oil
1 cup chopped onions
1 cup chopped celery
2 cups sliced carrots, in all
5 small bay leaves
2 cups tiny pearl onions, peeled
3 cups small fresh mushrooms
2 teaspoons minced fresh garlic
½ cup all-purpose flour
4 cups chicken stock (see page 11)
2 cups heavy cream

Combine the seasoning mix ingredients thoroughly in a small bowl. Makes ¼ cup plus ¼ teaspoon.

Sprinkle *2 tablespoons* of the seasoning mix over the chicken and rub it in well with your hands.

Place the oil in a large heavy pot over high heat. When the oil is very hot, add the chicken pieces, skin side down, and cook, turning several times, until the chicken is a deep brown color on all sides, about 12 to 14 minutes. (You may have to cook the chicken in batches.) Remove the chicken to a bowl. Add the chopped onions, celery, *½ cup* of the carrots, the bay leaves, and *1 tablespoon* of the seasoning mix to the fat in the pot. Scrape the pot bottom, cover, and cook, uncovering the pot and scraping once or twice so the mixture doesn't stick, about 5 to 6 minutes. Stir in the pearl onions, mushrooms, garlic, and *1 teaspoon* of the seasoning mix. Add the flour and cook, stirring to keep it from turning brown and sticking to the bottom of the pot, about 1 to 2 minutes. Add the *remaining* seasoning mix and the *remaining 1½ cups* carrots, stir in the stock, and bring to a boil. As soon as the mixture begins to bubble, stir in the cream. Add the chicken and any accumulated chicken juices and bring the mixture back to a boil. Cover, reduce the heat to low, and simmer until the chicken is tender, about 25 minutes.

Serve over egg noodles for a feel-good dinner.

# Vermont Common Cracker Chicken with Cracker Custard Sauce

MAKES 4 TO 8 SERVINGS

★

Common crackers date all the way back to 1828, when they were first made in Montpelier, Vermont. New Englanders like to crumble them in milk or eat them split in half with butter and Cheddar cheese. But the uniqueness of these crackers has also led people to use them to enhance other foods they were cooking. Coating chicken breasts with crushed common cracker crumbs makes an uncommonly delicious dish. Most specialty food stores or supermarkets around the country carry common crackers, but if you have trouble finding them, use unsalted saltines instead.

**SEASONING MIX**

*½* 2 teaspoons salt, ~~Accent~~

2 teaspoons paprika

1 teaspoon garlic powder

1 teaspoon dried thyme leaves

1 teaspoon dried sweet basil
  leaves

¾ teaspoon onion powder

¾ teaspoon black pepper

½ teaspoon white pepper

½ teaspoon ground sage

☆

8 boneless, skinless chicken
  breast halves (about
  ~~1½ to~~ 2 pounds total)

1½ cups ~~fine common cracker~~
  crumbs *unsalted saltines*

~~½ cup sesame seeds~~

2 eggs

3 tablespoons milk

1 cup vegetable oil

7 tablespoons unsalted butter,
  in all

1 tablespoon sesame oil

1 tablespoon fresh lemon juice

½ cup chopped green onion tops

2 cups chicken stock (~~see page 11~~),
  in all *Campbells Chix Broth*

Combine the seasoning mix ingredients thoroughly in a small bowl. Makes 3 tablespoons plus ½ teaspoon.

Sprinkle *1 tablespoon plus ½ teaspoon* of the seasoning mix all over the chicken breasts and pat it in well with your hands.

Combine the cracker crumbs, sesame seeds, and *1 tablespoon plus 1 teaspoon* of the seasoning mix in a shallow dish. Beat the eggs and milk in a large shallow dish until frothy.

Soak the chicken breasts in the egg mixture; remove and let drain several seconds. Set aside any remaining egg mixture.

Heat the vegetable oil in a 10-inch skillet over high heat. When the oil is very hot, dip the chicken in the cracker crumb mixture (reserve the excess crumbs), and shake off any excess. Add the chicken to the skillet, cover, and reduce the heat to medium. Fry until golden brown, uncovering the skillet several times to turn the chicken, about 4 to 6 minutes. Drain the chicken on paper towels. (You may have to do this in two batches; if so, make sure the oil is very hot again before adding the second batch of chicken.)

Pour off the fat from the skillet, place the skillet over high heat, and add *3 tablespoons* of the butter, the sesame oil, lemon juice, green onions, *1 cup* of the chicken stock, the reserved cracker crumb mixture, and the *remaining* seasoning mix. Bring to a boil and cook 4 minutes. Using a wire whisk, whip in the *remaining 4 tablespoons* butter, the reserved egg mixture, and the *remaining 1 cup* stock. Cook, whisking constantly, until the sauce is just thickened and ready to boil, about 4 to 5 minutes. Remove from the heat. Makes 3 cups.

To serve 8, pour a generous ⅓ cup sauce onto each plate and top with a chicken breast. For 4 servings, allow ¾ cup sauce and 2 chicken breasts.

# Mulacalong Chicken

## MAKES 6 TO 8 SERVINGS

★

The exact origin of this dish is a mystery, but recipes for it appeared in both *The Carolina Housewife* (1847) and *200 Years of Charleston Cooking* (1930). It's possible that its soft curry flavor can be traced to the days when

Charleston was a busy trading port, and exotic spices came off the ships from India. Savannah, Georgia, has also laid claim to this recipe, but now it belongs to all of us.

SEASONING MIX
1 tablespoon salt
1½ teaspoons ground turmeric
1½ teaspoons dried cilantro leaves
1½ teaspoons crushed dried red pepper
1 teaspoon garlic powder
1 teaspoon onion powder
1 teaspoon ground coriander
1 teaspoon dry mustard
1 teaspoon curry powder
1 teaspoon dried thyme leaves
¾ teaspoon ground savory
½ teaspoon black pepper
½ teaspoon ground ginger

1 (3- to 4-pound) chicken, cut into 8 pieces, all visible fat removed
2 cups corn kernels, preferably fresh (about 4 ears)
4½ cups chicken stock (see page 11), in all
3 tablespoons vegetable oil
2 cups chopped onions
1 tablespoon grated lemon zest
Juice of 1 lemon
1 red bell pepper, cored, seeded, and cut into thin strips

☆

Combine the seasoning mix ingredients thoroughly in a small bowl. Makes 5 tablespoons plus ¼ teaspoon.

Sprinkle *3 tablespoons* of the seasoning mix all over the chicken and pat it in well with your hands.

Place the corn kernels and *½ cup* of the chicken stock in the container of a blender and purée about 2 minutes. (The mixture should be somewhat coarse, not smooth.)

Heat the oil in a large heavy pot over high heat. When the oil is very hot, add the seasoned chicken and cook, in batches if necessary, turning the pieces to brown on all sides, about 13 to 15 minutes. Remove the chicken to a bowl. Add the onions to the oil in the pot and cook 2 minutes. Add the puréed corn and scrape up any browned bits from the bottom of the pot. Cook, scraping the bottom of the pot occasionally, until the mixture resembles a thick brown roux, about 8 minutes. Add the *remaining* seasoning mix, stir, and cook 3 minutes. Stir in the lemon zest, lemon juice, and the *remaining 4 cups* stock and bring to a simmer. Return the chicken to the pot, along with any juices that have accumulated in the bowl. Cover and cook, uncovering the pot occasionally to stir, about 40 minutes. Add the red pepper, cover, and cook until the chicken and pepper strips are tender, about 8 to 10 minutes. Remove from the heat. Makes about 5 cups sauce, plus the chicken.

Serve immediately over mounds of rice.

# Carolina Chicken Pilau

MAKES 6 SERVINGS

Often pronounced "perloo," this dish gained popularity in the South during the years of busy spice trading with ships from India in the ports of Charleston and Savannah. There are many versions, but basically pilau is steamed rice with meat, chicken, or fish. Our pilau tastes even better the second day, so if you can, prepare it a day ahead.

**SEASONING MIX**
*1 tablespoon plus 1 teaspoon paprika*
*1 tablespoon plus 1 teaspoon dry mustard*
*1 tablespoon salt*
*2½ teaspoons onion powder*
*2½ teaspoons garlic powder*
*2½ teaspoons dried thyme leaves*
*2 teaspoons black pepper*
*1½ teaspoons white pepper*
*1 teaspoon dried tarragon leaves*

☆

*1 (3- to 3½-pound) chicken, cut into 8 pieces, all visible fat removed*
*12 slices bacon, diced*
*1 cup chopped onions*
*1 cup chopped celery*
*1 cup chopped green bell peppers*
*3 bay leaves*
*6 cups chicken stock (see page 11), in all*
*¼ cup all-purpose flour*
*1 teaspoon minced fresh garlic*
*1 cup thickly sliced carrots*
*1½ cups sliced celery (cut on the diagonal)*
*2 cups uncooked converted rice*

Preheat the oven to 350°.

Combine the seasoning mix ingredients thoroughly in a small bowl. Makes 7 tablespoons plus 1 teaspoon.

Sprinkle *1 tablespoon plus 2 teaspoons* seasoning mix all over the chicken and pat it in with your hands.

Place the bacon in a 5-quart ovenproof pot over high heat. Cook, stirring occasionally, until the bacon is brown and crisp, about 10 minutes. Remove the bacon with a slotted spoon and set aside.

Add the seasoned chicken, skin side down, to the bacon fat in the pot. Cover and cook, turning once or twice, until browned on all sides, about 7 to 9 minutes. (You'll probably have to cook the chicken in 2 batches.) Remove the chicken pieces to a bowl.

Drain off all but 3 tablespoons of the fat from the pot. Add the onions, chopped celery, and bell peppers. Cook, stirring occasionally and scraping up the crust that forms on the bottom of the pot, about 2 minutes. Stir in the bay leaves, cover the pot, and cook 3 minutes. Stir in *3 tablespoons* of the seasoning mix, cover the pot, and cook 2 to 3 minutes. Stir in the flour, and as soon as it turns a rich brown color and begins to stick to the bottom of the pot (which will be almost immediately, so have your stock ready) add *1 cup* of the chicken stock and scrape up the crust from the bottom of the pot. Cook, uncovered, stirring gently once or twice, until the mixture sticks to the bottom of the pot, about 2 minutes. Add *1 cup* more chicken stock, scrape the pot bottom again, and bring to a boil, stirring often. Add the *remaining 4 cups* stock and the garlic, scrape the pot bottom, and cook 1 minute. Add the *remaining* seasoning mix and bring to a boil, whipping constantly with a wire whisk. Boil, without whisking, 2 minutes, then add the carrots, sliced celery, rice, and the chicken pieces and any accumulated juices. Stir well, cover, and bring to a boil. Transfer the pot to the oven and bake 17 minutes.

Remove from the oven and let sit 10 minutes. Stir in the cooked bacon and serve immediately, with a light salad. (Or let the pilau come to room temperature, then refrigerate overnight. Before serving, skim off any congealed fat, bring to room temperature, and reheat, covered, either in a slow oven or over low heat on the stovetop.)

# Arroz con Pollo

MAKES 6 TO 8 SERVINGS

★

*Arroz con pollo*, literally translated, means "chicken with rice." If seasoned properly, this "poor man's paella," which was popular on the early ranches in Southern California, can be dazzling.

SEASONING MIX
1 tablespoon salt
2 teaspoons paprika
2 teaspoons ground guajillo chile pepper (see Note)
2 teaspoons ground ancho chile pepper (see Note)
1½ teaspoons dried thyme leaves
1½ teaspoons onion powder
1 teaspoon garlic powder
1 teaspoon ground pasilla chile pepper (see Note)
1 teaspoon ground New Mexico chile pepper (see Note)
1 teaspoon dried cilantro leaves
1 teaspoon dried oregano leaves
1 teaspoon ground cumin
1 teaspoon dry mustard
½ teaspoon ground savory

1 (3-pound) chicken, cut into 8 pieces, all visible fat removed
2 tablespoons vegetable oil
½ pound mild Italian sausage meat
6 ounces ham, cut into ¼-inch dice
2 cups chopped onions
2 cups chopped green bell peppers
1 cup chopped celery
1¼ cups uncooked converted rice
2 teaspoons minced fresh garlic
4 medium fresh tomatoes, peeled and chopped
½ cup dry sherry
2 cups chicken stock (see page 11)

☆

Combine the seasoning mix ingredients thoroughly in a small bowl. Makes 6 tablespoons plus 1½ teaspoons.

Sprinkle *1 tablespoon plus 1 teaspoon* of the seasoning mix all over the chicken pieces and work it in well with your hands.

Heat the oil in a large, heavy pot over high heat. When the oil begins to smoke, add the chicken pieces, skin side down, and cook, in batches if necessary, until browned on all sides, about 6 to 8 minutes. Remove the chicken and set aside. Add the sausage and ham and cook, stirring occasionally to break up the sausage, about 4 minutes. Stir in the onions, bell peppers, celery, and *2 tablespoons* of the seasoning mix. Cover and cook 10 minutes. Uncover the pot and stir in the rice, garlic, and *2 tablespoons* of the seasoning mix. Cook, uncovered, occasionally scraping the bottom of the pot, about 4 minutes. Stir in the tomatoes and their juices, the sherry, and the *remaining* seasoning mix, cover, and cook 3 minutes. Uncover, add the chicken stock, and scrape the bottom of the pot clean. Return the chicken and any accumulated juices to the pot, cover the pot, and bring to a boil. Reduce the heat to low and simmer until the chicken is tender, about 20 minutes.

Serve immediately, in shallow bowls, with a crisp salad.

NOTE: These are the ground chile peppers we used. You can use whatever is available in your area, but make sure you get pure ground chile peppers, not commercial chili powder.

# Basque Chicken and Shrimp in Wine

MAKES 4 TO 8 SERVINGS

*Color photograph 31*

The Basques who came to the mountains of America's West from the mountainous borders between Spain and France were sheepherders, and today their descendants still dominate sheepherding in that area. Most of the cooking is done by the men and is traditionally simple and filling— a cuisine shaped by their rugged lifestyle. This dish, which is known as *pollo vascongado* to the Basques, is a blend of tantalizingly subtle flavors. We've rounded out the original recipe with a complement of herbs and seasonings, and we hope you like this dish as much as we do. Serve it with crisp greens in a light olive oil dressing and you'll have a perfect Basque meal!

SEASONING MIX

1 tablespoon paprika

2 teaspoons salt

1 teaspoon white pepper

1 teaspoon black pepper

1 teaspoon onion powder

1 teaspoon garlic powder

1 teaspoon dried sweet basil
leaves

1 teaspoon dried thyme leaves

½ teaspoon dried oregano leaves

¼ teaspoon ground nutmeg

☆

1 (2½- to 3-pound) chicken, cut
into 8 pieces, all visible fat
removed

1 pound peeled shrimp (about
1½ pounds unpeeled shrimp)

2 tablespoons olive oil

2 cups diced lean ham (about ½
pound)

1½ cups chopped onions

¼ cup all-purpose flour

1¼ cups dry white wine, in all

2 cups chicken stock (see page 11)

Preheat the oven to 350°.

Combine the seasoning mix ingredients thoroughly in a small bowl. Makes 3 tablespoons plus 2¾ teaspoons.

Sprinkle *1 tablespoon* of the seasoning mix over the chicken pieces and rub it in thoroughly with your hands.

Sprinkle *1½ teaspoons* of the seasoning mix over the shrimp and rub it in well with your hands. Set aside.

Heat the oil in a heavy 12-inch skillet over high heat. When the oil is very hot, add the chicken pieces, in batches if necessary, and brown on all sides, about 8 to 10 minutes. Transfer the chicken pieces to a bowl and set aside.

Add the ham to the oil in the skillet and sauté, stirring once or twice, about 2 minutes. Add the onions and *1 tablespoon* of the seasoning mix and cook until a crust forms on the bottom of the skillet, about 8 minutes. Then cook until the onions and ham are browned, about 3 minutes. Stir in the flour and cook until the crust hardens (without letting it get out of control), about 3 minutes. Add *1 cup* of the wine and scrape the bottom of the skillet fairly clean. Cook, scraping to keep the mixture from sticking, about 1 to 2 minutes. Stir in the stock, scrape the skillet bottom, and bring to a boil. Stir in the *remaining* seasoning mix and bring to a rolling boil. With a wire whisk, whip in the *remaining* ¼ *cup* wine and cook 2 minutes. Remove from the heat.

Put the chicken and any accumulated juices in an ovenproof casserole or baking pan approximately 8 inches square by 4 inches deep. Arrange the shrimp over the chicken, and pour the sauce over all. Cover the casserole and bake until the chicken is cooked through, about 30 minutes.

Serve with salad and thick slices of peasant bread.

# Chicken Cacciatore

MAKES 4 SERVINGS

*Color photograph 32*

This hearty chicken dish gained great popularity after World War II, when it became standard fare in Italian-American restaurants. Its name means chicken "hunter's style," probably because of the mushrooms with which it's always prepared.

SEASONING MIX
*1 tablespoon salt*
*2½ teaspoons dried sweet basil leaves*
*2 teaspoons dried parsley flakes*
*2 teaspoons dried oregano leaves*
*2 teaspoons dried thyme leaves*
*1½ teaspoons onion powder*
*1½ teaspoons garlic powder*
*1 teaspoon white pepper*
*¾ teaspoon black pepper*
☆
*1 (3- to 3½-pound) chicken, cut into 8 pieces, all visible fat removed*

*2 (16-ounce) cans whole tomatoes with their liquid*
*2 tablespoons olive oil*
*1 cup chopped onions*
*1 cup chopped green bell peppers*
*1 cup chopped fresh mushrooms*
*1 cup dry red wine,* in all
*1 (6-ounce) can tomato paste*
*½ teaspoon minced fresh garlic*
*2 cups chicken stock (see page 11),* in all
*1 cup julienned onions*
*2 cups julienned green bell peppers*
*¼ cup sliced fresh garlic*
*3 tablespoons dark brown sugar*
*2 cups sliced fresh mushrooms*

Combine the seasoning mix ingredients thoroughly in a small bowl. Makes 5 tablespoons plus 1¼ teaspoons.

Sprinkle a total of *4 teaspoons* of the seasoning mix over the chicken pieces and rub it in well with your hands.

Pour the tomatoes, with their liquid, into a bowl and crush them with your hands.

Heat the oil in a heavy 8-quart pot over high heat until very hot, about 4 minutes. Add the chicken pieces, skin side down, and cook, turning the pieces once or twice, until just golden brown on all sides, about 8 to 10 minutes. (You may have to cook the chicken in batches.) Remove the chicken pieces to a bowl and set aside.

Add the chopped onions, bell peppers, and mushrooms to the oil in the pot and scrape up all the browned bits on the bottom of the pot. Cook, stirring occasionally, until the vegetables are lightly browned and beginning to stick to the bottom of the pot, about 5 minutes. Add *½ cup* of the wine and scrape the pot bottom clean. Cook, stirring occasionally, 3 to 5 minutes. Stir in the tomato paste and cook, scraping the bottom of the pot from time to time, about 4 minutes. Add *2 tablespoons* of the seasoning mix and cook, stirring, about 1 minute. Stir in the crushed tomatoes and the minced garlic, scrape the bottom of the pot clean, and bring to a bubbling boil. Add the *remaining* seasoning mix, the *remaining ½ cup* wine, and *1 cup* of the chicken stock. Stir in the julienned onions and bell peppers and the sliced garlic and cook, stirring occasionally, 4 minutes. Return the chicken pieces and any accumulated juices to the pot, stir, and bring to a bubbling boil. Cover the pot, reduce the heat to medium, and simmer 2 minutes. Stir in the *remaining 1 cup* stock, cover the pot, and simmer 7 minutes. Stir in the brown sugar, cover the pot, and simmer 5 minutes. Add the sliced mushrooms and simmer 5 minutes. The sauce should be a rich, dark, reddish-brown color.

Serve 2 pieces of chicken per person with about 1 cup sauce over your favorite pasta. (You can freeze any leftover sauce for another pasta dinner.)

# Country Captain

MAKES 6 SERVINGS

★

This dish probably has its origins in India; it seems to have arrived in Savannah, Georgia, in the nineteenth century, and it first appeared in print in this country in 1857, in *Miss Leslie's New Cookery Book.* Its name in all likelihood refers to a captain of the native Indian troops in the pay of England. Whatever its exotic origins, it is, according to James Beard, probably the most important chicken dish we ever inherited, aside from Southern fried chicken.

SEASONING MIX

*1 tablespoon plus 1 teaspoon*
  *curry powder*
*2 teaspoons salt*
*2 teaspoons dark brown sugar*
*¾ teaspoon dried thyme leaves*
*½ teaspoon dried cilantro leaves*
*½ teaspoon dry mustard*
*½ teaspoon dried sweet basil*
  *leaves*
*½ teaspoon white pepper*
*¼ teaspoon ground cumin*
*¼ teaspoon ground cardamom*
*¼ teaspoon ground allspice*

☆

*1 (3- to 4-pound) chicken, cut*
  *into 8 pieces, all visible fat*
  *removed*
*⅓ cup all-purpose flour,* in all
*2 tablespoons olive oil*
*½ cup chopped onions*
*2 cups chopped green bell*
  *peppers,* in all
*1 cup uncooked long-grain*
  *converted rice*
*1½ teaspoons minced fresh garlic*
*2 cups chopped peeled fresh*
  *tomatoes (3 or 4 medium)*
*¼ cup sliced almonds*
*½ cup raisins*
*3 cups chicken stock (see page 11)*

Combine the seasoning mix ingredients thoroughly in a small bowl. Makes 3 tablespoons plus 2½ teaspoons.

Sprinkle *1 tablespoon plus 1 teaspoon* of the seasoning mix over the chicken, rubbing it in with your hands.

Combine the flour and *2 teaspoons* of the seasoning mix in a shallow bowl.

Heat the oil in a heavy 5-quart pot. While the oil is heating, dredge the chicken in the seasoned flour, shaking off the excess. Set aside 1 tablespoon of the seasoned flour.

When the oil is very hot, about 3 to 4 minutes, carefully add the chicken and cook, turning several times, until browned, about 7 to 9 minutes. (You may have to cook the chicken in 2 batches; if so, make sure the oil is very hot before adding the second batch.) Remove the chicken to a bowl.

Pour off all but 1 tablespoon of the fat from the pot and set the pot over high heat. Add the onions, *½ cup* of the bell peppers, and *2 teaspoons* of the seasoning mix, and cook 3 minutes. Stir in the reserved seasoned flour and the rice. Cook, stirring occasionally and scraping to keep the mixture from sticking to the pot, until the flour is no longer visible and the rice has started to brown, about 3 minutes. Stir in the garlic, tomatoes, almonds, raisins, the *remaining 1½ cups* bell peppers, and the *remaining* seasoning mix, and cook 2 minutes. Add the stock and scrape up any brown crust sticking to the bottom of the pot. Return the chicken pieces to the pot, cover, and bring to a boil. Reduce the heat to low and simmer 20 minutes. Remove from the heat and let sit, covered, 15 minutes.

Serve in shallow bowls.

# Chicken Paprika

MAKES 6 TO 8 SERVINGS

*Color photograph 33*

Around the middle of the nineteenth century, Hungarian immigrants settled in the Midwest, bringing with them the exotic flavors of their native country. Chicken *paprikash*, as it is known in Hungary, became chicken paprika, a Hungarian-American dish that is now popular in many parts of the United States.

SEASONING MIX

1 tablespoon salt

1 teaspoon onion powder

1 teaspoon dried sweet basil
  leaves

¾ teaspoon dried thyme leaves

½ teaspoon garlic powder

½ teaspoon black pepper

½ teaspoon white pepper

½ teaspoon dried dill weed

☆

1 (3- to 4-pound) chicken, cut
  into 8 pieces, all visible fat
  removed

2 tablespoons olive oil

2 cups chopped onions, in all

1 teaspoon minced fresh garlic

¼ cup sweet paprika

1 (6-ounce) can tomato paste

3½ cups chicken stock (see
  page 11)

1 (8-ounce) container sour
  cream

Combine the seasoning mix ingredients thoroughly in a small bowl. Makes 2 tablespoons plus 1¾ teaspoons.

Sprinkle *2 tablespoons* of the seasoning mix over the chicken pieces and rub it in well with your hands.

Heat the oil in a 5½-quart pot over high heat. When the oil is hot, add the chicken pieces, skin side down, and brown them, about 7 minutes on each side. Remove the chicken to a bowl. Add *1 cup* of the onions to the pot, scrape up the brown crust on the bottom of the pot, and cook 2 minutes. Add the garlic, paprika, the *remaining 1 cup* onions, and the *remaining* seasoning mix. Cook, scraping the pot bottom occasionally, until the onions are browned and a crust has formed, about 4 minutes. Stir in the tomato paste, scrape the pot bottom, and cook 2 to 3 minutes. Stir in the stock, scrape up the crust on the bottom of the pot, and bring to a boil. Return the chicken to the pot, along with any juices that have accumulated in the bowl, and bring to a boil. Cover, reduce the heat to medium low, and simmer 25 minutes.

Remove the pot from the heat and stir several tablespoons of the sauce into the sour cream, a tablespoon at a time. Then gently stir the sour cream mixture back into the sauce. Place the pot over low heat and cook, stirring constantly, just until the sour cream is incorporated and the sauce is heated through. Makes about 5½ cups sauce plus the chicken.

Serve immediately over broad noodles.

# Oklahoma Fried Chicken and Biscuits

MAKES 6 TO 8 SERVINGS

★

Every part of the country has its own nuances when it comes to frying chicken, but sometimes it's difficult to recognize the subtle differences. We enhanced this rendition from Oklahoma with not-so-subtle seasonings. Although it isn't a "hot" dish, it's sure to get everyone's attention. It's pure and simple American comfort food.

SEASONING MIX
1 tablespoon plus 1 teaspoon salt
2 teaspoons paprika
1½ teaspoons onion powder
1 teaspoon garlic powder
1 teaspoon dry mustard
1 teaspoon dried sweet basil
   leaves
½ teaspoon black pepper
½ teaspoon white pepper
¼ teaspoon ground cumin

☆

1 (3- to 4-pound) frying chicken,
   cut into 8 pieces, all visible fat
   removed

1 quart buttermilk
1½ cups all-purpose flour
1½ cups vegetable oil

BISCUIT DOUGH
1½ cups all-purpose flour
1 tablespoon plus 1 teaspoon
   baking powder
1 tablespoon plus 2 teaspoons
   sugar
2 teaspoons Seasoning Mix (see
   above)
4 tablespoons unsalted butter,
   softened, cut into 8 pats
1 cup reserved buttermilk (see
   above)

Combine the seasoning mix ingredients thoroughly in a small bowl. Makes 3 tablespoons plus 2¾ teaspoons.

Place the chicken pieces in a pan or shallow bowl, pour the buttermilk over, and let marinate 1 hour at room temperature. Pour off the buttermilk add reserve 1 cup. Sprinkle *2 tablespoons* of the seasoning mix all over the chicken pieces and pat it in well with your hands.

Combine the flour and *2½ teaspoons* of the seasoning mix in a shallow bowl.

Heat the oil in a 12-inch skillet over high heat until very hot. Dredge the chicken in the seasoned flour, shaking off the excess, and add to the oil, skin side down, in a single layer. Cover the skillet, reduce the heat to medium, and fry, checking occasionally to make sure the chicken is not burning, until browned on one side, about 5 to 6 minutes. (If the chicken seems to be browning too quickly, turn down the heat.) Turn the chicken pieces over, cover, and fry, checking occasionally, until a rich, golden brown. Remove from the skillet and drain on paper towels. Set the skillet, with the oil, aside.

**FOR THE BISCUIT DOUGH,** combine the flour, baking powder, sugar, and seasoning mix in the bowl of a food processor and pulse 5 or 6 times. Distribute the butter pats evenly over the dry ingredients and process until well blended, about 25 or 30 seconds. With the machine running, add the reserved buttermilk in a steady stream and process until thoroughly blended, about 40 seconds.

Set the skillet over high heat and when the oil is very hot, drop in the biscuit dough by large spoonfuls. Cover tightly, reduce the heat to medium and fry until golden brown, about 1½ to 2 minutes on each side.

Serve family-style: Place the chicken and biscuits on a large platter in the center of the table and let everyone help themselves.

# Philadelphia Tomato Chicken

MAKES 6 SERVINGS

Here's a delicious chicken and tomato stew that was popular in Philadelphia in the middle of the last century. It was well seasoned for a recipe from that era, but we've brought it even more up to date with additional spices and herbs.

SEASONING MIX

1 tablespoon salt
1 tablespoon paprika
1½ teaspoons onion powder
1 teaspoon garlic powder
1 teaspoon dry mustard
1 teaspoon white pepper
1 teaspoon dried sweet basil
   leaves
¾ teaspoon dried oregano leaves
¾ teaspoon ground savory
½ teaspoon black pepper
½ teaspoon ground nutmeg
½ teaspoon ground mace

☆

5 tablespoons fresh lemon juice
1 large (5- to 5½-pound)
   roasting chicken, cut into 8
   pieces, all visible fat removed
3 tablespoons olive oil
2 cups chopped onions
1½ cups chopped green bell peppers
3 cups diced sliced ham (about
   ¾ pound)
6 cups chopped peeled fresh
   tomatoes (about 10 medium
   tomatoes)
1 (15-ounce) can tomato sauce
1 large green bell pepper, cored,
   seeded, and cut into thin strips
1 medium onion, thinly sliced
2 teaspoons minced fresh garlic

Combine the seasoning mix ingredients thoroughly in a small bowl. Makes ¼ cup plus 2½ teaspoons.

Add the lemon juice to the seasoning mix and stir until it becomes a paste, or a "slush."

Place the chicken in a bowl, add all of the seasoning slush, and rub in well with your hands. Set aside for 1½ hours, turning the chicken pieces every 30 minutes.

Drain the chicken and reserve the liquid, or marinade, that accumulated in the bowl.

Heat the oil in a heavy, 8-quart pot over high heat. When the oil is hot, add the chicken, skin side down, starting with the larger pieces, and cook the chicken in batches until browned on both sides. Remove to a bowl. Pour off all but 2 tablespoons of fat from the pot. Add the chopped onions and bell peppers and cook until lightly browned, about 6 to 7 minutes. Stir in the ham and the reserved marinade. Cover the pot and cook over high heat, uncovering to scrape the bottom of the pot from time to time, until the mixture is sticking hard to the bottom, about 15 minutes. Stir in the tomatoes and tomato sauce. Add the chicken pieces and any juices that have accumulated in the bowl. Cover the pot and bring to a boil, then reduce the heat to a fast simmer and cook until the chicken is tender, 45 minutes to 1 hour. Stir in the bell pepper strips, sliced onion, and garlic. Cover and cook over medium-low heat until the vegetables are crisp-tender, about 15 minutes.

Serve over pasta or rice.

# Tampa Bay Chicken Marengo

MAKES 4 TO 6 SERVINGS

★

This Chicken Marengo, with its Andalusian accent, comes to us from the west coast of Florida, where a treasure of a place called Tampa has been occupied at various times by the Caloosa Indians, Spanish conquistadors, Cuban cigar makers, pirates, pioneers, missionaries, and mercenaries. With a history like that, the food's bound to be interesting, and so it is. This chicken is succulent and delicious and so easy to make.

SEASONING MIX
2 teaspoons salt
2 teaspoons paprika
2 teaspoons dry mustard
1 teaspoon white pepper
1 teaspoon onion powder
1 teaspoon garlic powder
1 teaspoon dried sweet basil
   leaves
¾ teaspoon dried thyme leaves
½ teaspoon dried tarragon
   leaves
½ teaspoon ground cumin
½ teaspoon black pepper

1 (3- to 3½-pound) chicken, cut
   into 8 pieces, all visible fat
   removed
3 tablespoons olive oil
2 cups chopped onions
1 cup chopped green bell peppers
5 cups small fresh mushrooms
   (about 1 pound)
1 (15-ounce) can tomato sauce
¾ cup dry white wine

Combine the seasoning mix ingredients thoroughly in a small bowl. Makes ¼ cup plus ¼ teaspoon.

Sprinkle *2 tablespoons plus 2 teaspoons* of the seasoning mix over the chicken pieces and rub it in well with your hands.

Heat the olive oil in a 12-inch skillet over high heat. When the oil is very hot, add the chicken pieces, skin side down (if necessary, cook the chicken in 2 batches), and brown on all sides, about 10 to 12 minutes. Remove the chicken and drain on paper towels.

Pour off all but 3 tablespoons of the fat from the skillet. Add the onions and bell peppers to the skillet and cook over high heat until lightly browned, about 5 to 6 minutes. Add the *remaining* seasoning mix and cook 3 minutes. Add the mushrooms and cook, scraping the bottom of the skillet from time to time, about 2 minutes. Stir in the tomato sauce and wine and bring to a simmer. Return the chicken pieces to the skillet, pushing them under the sauce. Reduce the heat to low, cover, and simmer until the chicken is cooked through and tender, about 20 minutes.

Serve the chicken over rice, if desired. Spoon the sauce and mushrooms on top.

# Chicken Stoltzfus

## MAKES 8 SERVINGS

When we talked to people in Lancaster County, Pennsylvania, trying to find out all about Pennsylvania Dutch cooking, we were told over and over again that Betty Groff is the foremost expert on the subject. A tenth-generation Mennonite who grew up in the heart of Pennsylvania Dutch country, Betty has authored four cookbooks and owns an award-winning restaurant as well. This recipe is considered her trademark. We've taken a few liberties with seasonings, but the original goodness is there.

1 tablespoon plus ¾ teaspoon
  salt
2½ teaspoons paprika
2½ teaspoons dry mustard
2½ teaspoons dried winter
  savory leaves
1¼ teaspoons black pepper
1¼ teaspoons white pepper
1¼ teaspoons onion powder
1¼ teaspoons garlic powder
1¼ teaspoons dried sweet basil
  leaves
1 teaspoon ground nutmeg

☆

1 (6- to 7-pound) stewing hen,
  cut into 8 pieces, all visible fat
  removed
3 tablespoons vegetable oil

3 cups chopped onions
2 cups chopped celery
6 cups chicken stock
4 tablespoons unsalted butter
3 tablespoons all-purpose flour
Pinch of saffron

DOUGH

8 tablespoons (1 stick) cold
  butter, cut into about 12 pats
1 tablespoon plus ½ teaspoon
  Seasoning Mix (see above)
2 tablespoons dark brown sugar
1 egg
2 cups all-purpose flour
½ cup milk

FINISH

All-purpose flour

Combine the seasoning mix ingredients thoroughly in a small bowl. Makes 6 tablespoons plus ½ teaspoon.

Sprinkle *2 tablespoons* of the seasoning mix all over the hen and rub it in well with your hands.

Heat the oil in a large heavy pot over high heat. When the oil is very hot, cook the hen in batches, adding the large pieces first, skin side down, until brown on all sides, about 14 minutes. Remove the hen pieces from the pot and pour off all but 1 tablespoon of the fat from the pot. Heat the fat over high heat and add the onions and celery. Place the hen pieces on top, cover the pot, and cook, uncovering occasionally to stir, until the vegetables are golden brown, about 20 minutes. Add the chicken stock and *1 tablespoon* of the seasoning mix, cover, and bring to a boil. Reduce the heat to low and simmer, uncovering occasionally to stir, until the hen is tender, about 1 hour and 15 minutes. Remove the hen pieces to a bowl and set aside. Turn up the heat to high and cook 2 minutes. Transfer the stock and vegetables to a bowl and set aside.

Place the pot over high heat and add the butter, flour, saffron, and *2 tablespoons* of the seasoning mix. Cook, whipping with a wire whisk, until the mixture forms a paste that separates into little balls, about 4 minutes. Return the stock and vegetables to the pot and bring to a rolling boil, whipping constantly. Remove from the heat.

**FOR THE DOUGH,** place the butter, seasoning mix, brown sugar, egg, and flour in the bowl of a food processor and process in 5 long pulses until the mixture looks like coarse cornmeal. With the machine running, add the milk in a thin stream and process until thoroughly blended, about 20 seconds. Refrigerate the dough until ready to use.

Preheat the oven to 350°.

**TO FINISH,** skin the hen pieces and, using your fingers, shred all the meat from the bones. Add the sauce in the pot. There should be about 8 cups sauce and chicken. Keep warm.

Remove the dough from the refrigerator. Sprinkle a clean surface with flour and roll out the dough to a thickness of about ¼ inch. The dough will be soft. Cut the dough into 2- by 4-inch rectangles; you should get about 18 to 24 pieces. Place on a baking sheet and bake until golden brown, about 25 minutes.

To serve, place 2 or 3 pieces of pastry on each plate and top with about 1 cup chicken and sauce.

# West Coast Chicken Tetrazzini

MAKES 8 TO 10 SERVINGS

Luisa Tetrazzini was a talented coloratura soprano who spent a lot of time in San Francisco, both singing and eating. The recipe for the chicken dish named after her didn't appear in print until 1951, eleven years after her death, but it's more than likely that it was created in San Francisco. Be sure the hen you buy isn't preserved with salt, or it will make the dish too salty.

SEASONING MIX

1 tablespoon plus 1 teaspoon salt

2½ teaspoons dry mustard

2½ teaspoons dried sweet basil
  leaves

2½ teaspoons dried thyme leaves

2½ teaspoons onion powder

2 teaspoons garlic powder

2 teaspoons dried oregano leaves

2 teaspoons paprika

1½ teaspoons white pepper

1½ teaspoons black pepper

1¼ teaspoons ground savory

½ teaspoon ground allspice

☆

1 gallon chicken stock (preferred)
  (see page 11) or water

3 unpeeled carrots

1 large onion, cut into quarters

4 celery stalks, with their leaves,
  cut into chunks

4 bay leaves

1 (5- to 5½-pound) stewing hen,
  all visible fat removed

1 pound uncooked spaghetti

3 tablespoons plus 1 teaspoon
  olive oil, in all

2 cups chopped onions

1 cup chopped celery

8 tablespoons (1 stick) unsalted
  butter

4 cups thinly sliced fresh
  mushrooms

½ cup dry sherry

¼ cup plus 2 tablespoons all-
  purpose flour

2 cups heavy cream

½ cup chopped fresh parsley

½ cup grated Parmesan cheese

Combine the seasoning mix ingredients thoroughly in a small bowl. Makes
½ cup plus ¾ teaspoon.

Place a large heavy pot over high heat and add the chicken stock,
carrots, onion quarters, celery chunks, bay leaves, and *2 tablespoons* of
the seasoning mix. Add the hen and bring to a boil. Cover, reduce the
heat to low, and simmer until the hen is tender, about 1½ to 2 hours.
Remove the hen from the pot and let cool.

Skim the fat from the stock in the pot, strain the stock, and return it
to the pot. Reduce over high heat to 5 cups. Remove from the heat and
set aside.

Remove the meat from the hen and discard the skin and bones. Tear
the meat into bite-size pieces.

Cook the spaghetti *al dente* according to the package directions. Drain
the spaghetti, rinse it under hot water, then cold, and drain again. Pour *1
teaspoon* olive oil onto your hands and work them thoroughly through

the spaghetti to coat it lightly and prevent it from sticking together. Set aside.

Preheat the broiler.

Heat the *remaining 3 tablespoons* oil in a heavy pot over high heat. When the oil is very hot, add the chopped onions and celery and *1 tablespoon* of the seasoning mix. Cook, stirring occasionally, until a light crust forms on the bottom of the pot, about 6 minutes. Add the butter, *2¾ tablespoons* of the seasoning mix, and the mushrooms and cook, stirring occasionally, 4 minutes. Stir in the sherry and cook 2 minutes. Using a wire whisk, whisk in the flour. Add the reserved chicken meat, the reserved 5 cups stock, and the *remaining* seasoning mix and scrape the bottom of the pot with a metal spoon. Bring to a boil, reduce the heat to low, and simmer, stirring occasionally, until thick and bubbly, about 6 to 7 minutes. Stir in the cream and simmer, stirring occasionally, 7 minutes. Add the parsley, stir well, and remove from the heat.

Spread the spaghetti in a large oven proof casserole about 10 by 14 by 2 inches deep. Cover the spaghetti with the chicken mixture. Sprinkle with the Parmesan cheese and broil, until brown and bubbly, about 3 to 5 minutes.

# Iowa Chicken and Corn Pot Pie

MAKES 4 TO 6 SERVINGS

*Color photograph 34*

★

Pot pies are all-American, popular in this country since the eighteenth century. They are traditionally filled with poultry or meat and vegetables, and the crust is often indicative of the region the recipe is from. This one's from Iowa, and it has a cornmeal crust to complement the corn in the filling.

**SEASONING MIX**

1 tablespoon salt

1 teaspoon white pepper

1 teaspoon paprika

1 teaspoon garlic powder

¾ teaspoon onion powder

¾ teaspoon dry mustard

¾ teaspoon dried thyme leaves

½ teaspoon ground cardamom

½ teaspoon black pepper

½ teaspoon ground savory

☆

**DOUGH**

2 cups all-purpose flour

¾ cup toasted cornmeal (see
Note)

1 tablespoon Seasoning Mix (see
above)

½ pound (2 sticks) unsalted
butter, cut into pats

½ cup chilled chicken stock
(see page 11)

**FILLING**

2 tablespoons plus ¾ teaspoon
Seasoning Mix (see above), in all

2 pounds boneless, skinless
chicken breasts

8 slices bacon, diced

2 cups chopped onions

1 cup chopped green bell peppers

1½ cups chopped celery

1 cup fresh corn kernels (about 2
ears)

4 cups chicken stock (see page 11),
in all

3 cloves

¼ cup toasted cornmeal (see Note)

1 cup tiny pearl onions, peeled

3 tablespoons chopped fresh parsley

2 cups sliced carrots

**FINISH**

All-purpose flour

Vegetable oil cooking spray

Combine the seasoning mix ingredients thoroughly in a small bowl. Makes
3 tablespoons plus ¾ teaspoon.

**FOR THE DOUGH,** combine the flour, toasted cornmeal, and seasoning mix
in the bowl of a food processor and pulse until blended, about 5 or 6
times. Distribute the butter over the dry ingredients and process until
blended, 25 to 30 seconds. With the machine running, add the chilled
stock in a thin stream, and process until thoroughly blended, about 40
seconds. Form the dough into a ball and refrigerate at least 30 minutes.

**FOR THE FILLING,** sprinkle *1 tablespoon* of the seasoning mix all over the
chicken and pat it in well with your hands.

Place the bacon in a 12-inch skillet and fry over high heat until crisp
and brown, about 8 to 9 minutes. Remove the bacon from the skillet with
a slotted spoon, and drain on paper towels.

Heat the bacon fat remaining in the skillet over high heat, add the chicken, and fry, turning several times, until lightly browned, about 7 to 10 minutes. Remove the chicken to a bowl.

Add the chopped onions, bell peppers, celery, corn, and *1 tablespoon* of the seasoning mix to the fat in the skillet. Cook, scraping the bottom of the skillet occasionally as the mixture forms crusts, about 5 minutes. Pour any chicken juices that have accumulated in the bowl plus *½ cup* of the stock into the skillet and scrape up any crust on the bottom. Add the cloves and simmer until the mixture begins to stick again, about 6 minutes. Add another *½ cup* stock, scrape the bottom of the skillet, and simmer until most of the liquid has evaporated, about 6 to 8 minutes. Stir in the toasted cornmeal and cook until the cornmeal is sticking hard to the bottom of the skillet but not burning, about 2 to 3 minutes. Add *1 cup* more stock, scrape the bottom of the skillet, and bring the mixture to a simmer. Add the pearl onions, parsley, carrots, the fried bacon, the *remaining 2 cups* stock, and the *remaining ¾ teaspoon* seasoning mix. Scrape the bottom and sides of the skillet and bring to a boil, reduce heat to low, and simmer until the mixture has thickened somewhat and the vegetables are barely tender, about 8 to 10 minutes. Remove from the heat.

Dice the cooled chicken breasts into ½-inch pieces. Stir the chicken into the skillet and then pour the mixture into a shallow pan. Refrigerate about 30 minutes.

Preheat the oven to 350°.

**TO FINISH,** carefully divide the dough in half with the side of your hand. Sprinkle a clean surface lightly with flour. Flatten one piece of the dough with your hand and roll out the dough to a circle about ⅛ inch thick. Coat a deep pie or cake pan with cooking spray and line with the rolled-out dough. Roll out the remaining dough the same way.

Fill the pie bottom with the cooled filling mixture, cover with the second round of dough, and seal the edges with the tines of a fork. Pierce the center of the top crust and bake until golden brown, 50 minutes to 1 hour. Cool 15 to 20 minutes. Cut into wedges; serve warm.

NOTE: To toast cornmeal place the cornmeal (you need a total of 1 cup toasted yellow cornmeal for this recipe) in a small skillet over medium-high heat. Shake the pan and flip the cornmeal constantly until a light golden brown, about 4 minutes. Remove from the heat.

# Tex-Mex Chicken Mole Tostadas

MAKES 10 SERVINGS

*Color photograph 35*

★

The word *tostada* means "toasted," and here it refers to the toasted tortillas that surround tender pieces of chicken in a dark, deliciously mysterious sauce. The blend of unusual tastes and textures and a seasoning mix that evokes the Southwest will make this Tex-Mex treat a favorite of your repertoire. Don't tell your guests—until after they've eaten and loved it —about the chocolate (and the peanut butter) in the sauce.

SEASONING MIX

*2 tablespoons plus 1 teaspoon*
  *ground New Mexico chile*
  *pepper (see Note)*
*2 tablespoons ground guajillo*
  *chile pepper (see Note)*
*2 teaspoons salt*
*1½ teaspoons ground cumin*
*1 teaspoon ground coriander*

☆

*2¾ cups finely chopped onions,*
  *in all*
*¼ cup apple cider vinegar*
*1 (4-pound) chicken, cut into 6*
  *pieces*
*6 cups chicken stock (see page 11)*
*3 unpeeled carrots, halved*
*2 unpeeled onions, halved*

*1 whole garlic bulb, sliced*
  *crosswise in half*
*1 bunch celery, tough outer*
  *stalks discarded*
*3 tablespoons unsalted butter*
*2 cups chopped green bell peppers*
*3 tablespoons dark brown sugar,*
  *in all*
*2 ounces unsweetened baking*
  *chocolate, cut into 4 pieces*
*¼ cup chunky peanut butter*
*1 (8-¼ ounce) bottle green mole*
  *sauce (available in specialty*
  *groceries and gourmet shops;*
  *see Note)*
*20 corn tortillas*
*1½ cups shredded Monterey Jack*
  *cheese*

Combine the seasoning mix ingredients thoroughly in a small bowl. Makes 5 tablespoons plus 2½ teaspoons.

Combine ¾ *cup* of the chopped onions with the vinegar and set aside.

Put the chicken, stock, carrots, halved onions, garlic, and celery in a large heavy pot over high heat, cover, and bring to a boil. Reduce the heat to low and simmer until the chicken is tender, about 40 minutes. Remove from the heat and remove the chicken from the stock. When the chicken is cool enough to handle, remove the skin and bones and discard them. Shred the chicken meat, place it in a bowl, and set aside.

Strain the cooking stock from the pot and skim off all the fat. Measure out 5 cups stock, and reserve the rest (you can freeze it) for other recipes that call for extra-rich chicken stock.

To make the sauce, melt the butter in a 12-inch skillet over high heat. When the butter sizzles, add the *remaining 2 cups* chopped onions and the bell peppers, and cook 2 minutes without stirring. Stir in *3 tablespoons* of the seasoning mix and cook, stirring occasionally, 5 to 6 minutes. Add ½ cup of the chicken cooking stock and *1 tablespoon* of the brown sugar. Cook, stirring occasionally, until the mixture begins to stick to the bottom of the skillet, about 4 minutes. Add another ½ cup stock and scrape up the crust on the skillet bottom. Stir in the chocolate, peanut butter, and green mole sauce and cook, stirring occasionally, about 3 minutes. Add the *remaining 4 cups* stock and the *remaining* seasoning mix and *2 tablespoons* brown sugar. Bring to a boil and cook, stirring occasionally, about 4 minutes. Then whip the sauce with a wire whisk and cook, whisking, until it thickens, turns dark brown, and comes to a bubbling boil. Reduce the heat to low and cook, whisking, about 1 minute. Remove from the heat and let cool.

Preheat the broiler.

Pour 1 cup of the cooled sauce over the shredded chicken and work it in well with your hands.

Drain the vinegar from the chopped onions.

Assemble the tostados in 2 batches: Arrange *10* of the tortillas on a baking sheet and place under the broiler until the tortillas are firm, about 1 to 2 minutes. Remove from the broiler and spread 2 tablespoons of the sauce over each of 5 tortillas. Spread ½ cup chicken meat over the sauce on each tortilla, sprinkle 1 tablespoon of the drained chopped onions over the chicken, and spread another 1 tablespoon sauce over the onions. Place a tortilla on top of each and sprinkle *2 tablespoons* of the shredded cheese over each tostada. Place under the broiler 2 minutes, turn the baking sheet around, and broil until browned and bubbly on top, about 2 minutes more. Repeat the process to make 5 more tostadas.

Serve immediately, with sour cream if desired.

NOTE: These are the chile peppers we used. You can use whatever is available in your area, but be sure to use only pure ground chile peppers, not commercial chili powder.

If you can't find bottled mole sauce, see the two easy recipes below for making your own.

## MOLE SAUCE 1

★

*¹/₃ cup pumpkin seeds, finely pulverized in a grinder*

*1 (8-ounce) can salsa verde*

Combine the pumpkin seeds and salsa verde in a small saucepan over medium-high heat. Cook, stirring often, until thickened and thoroughly blended, about 15 minutes.

## MOLE SAUCE 2

★

*¹/₃ cup pumpkin seeds*
*1 tablespoon dried cilantro leaves*

*2 fresh chile peppers (preferably jalapeños or serranos)*
*8 tomatillos*
*1 small onion, coarsely chopped*

Combine all of the ingredients in the bowl of a food processor and process until finely chopped and thoroughly blended. Pour into a saucepan and cook over medium-high heat, stirring often, until thickened, about 15 minutes.

# Turkey Hash

MAKES 6 TO 8 SERVINGS

★

Hash is so all-American, it's hard to say where in this country it originated. The name is derived from the French word *hacher*, which means "to chop." Hash can evoke an immediate groan when discovered on the dinner table. Or it can become a family—even a company—favorite, if it's seasoned as deliciously as this one.

SEASONING MIX
1 tablespoon salt
1½ teaspoons onion powder
1¼ teaspoons garlic powder
1 teaspoon paprika
1 teaspoon white pepper
1 teaspoon black pepper
1 teaspoon dried oregano leaves
¾ teaspoon dry mustard
½ teaspoon ground sage
½ teaspoon dried rosemary
  leaves
¼ teaspoon ground savory
¼ teaspoon ground mace
¼ teaspoon ground nutmeg

2 pounds ground turkey
12 ounces turkey or chicken
  gizzards, finely chopped
2 tablespoons olive oil
2½ cups chopped onions, in all
1½ cups chopped green bell
  peppers, in all
3¼ cups chicken stock
  (see page 11) in all
1 tablespoon unsalted butter
1½ cups uncooked converted
  rice
1 cup chopped red bell peppers

☆

Preheat the oven to 375°.

Combine the seasoning mix ingredients thoroughly in a small bowl. Makes ¼ cup plus ¼ teaspoon.

Sprinkle *1 tablespoon* of the seasoning mix over the ground turkey and blend it in well with your hands.

Heat the oil in a large ovenproof pot over high heat. Add *1½ cups* of the onions, *1 cup* of the green bell peppers, and the gizzards. Add *2 tablespoons* of the seasoning mix, stir once, and cook until a crust forms on the bottom of the pot, about 5 minutes. Add *½ cup* of the stock, scrape up the crust on the bottom of the pot, and cook 6 minutes. Add ¼ *cup* more stock, scrape the pot bottom, and push the vegetables and gizzards to one side of the pot. Put the butter in the cleared space and let it melt, then add the seasoned turkey to the butter. Cook, stirring and breaking up any lumps of meat with a large wooden spoon or spatula, until browned, about 3 to 5 minutes. Stir the vegetables into the turkey, scrape up the crust on the bottom and sides of the pot, and cook 1 minute. Stir in the rice and cook, scraping the pot bottom occasionally, about 2 minutes. Stir in the red peppers, the *remaining 1 cup* onions and ½ *cup* green peppers, the *remaining* seasoning mix, and 1¼ *cups* of the stock and cook, scraping the bottom and sides of the pot, about 1 minute. Add the *remaining 1¼ cups* stock and bring to a rolling boil. Cover the pot, transfer to the oven, and cook 17 minutes.

Remove from the oven and let sit 10 minutes. Serve as a light meal with a salad.

# Frontier Chicken-Fried Steak with Pan Gravy

MAKES 4 SERVINGS

*Color photograph 36*

Chicken-fried steak has nothing to do with chicken except as it refers to the method of frying. This dish is a big favorite in the South, but cowboys have been known to kill for a chicken-fried steak with its rich pan gravy. Although it's usually made with a tough piece of low-grade beef, we feel we haven't spoiled our version by using a better cut; the result is melt-in-your-mouth delicious. Our frying time produces medium-rare steak; if you prefer your steaks well done (the way Texans do), fry them about a minute longer on each side.

SEASONING MIX

2 teaspoons salt

1 teaspoon paprika

1 teaspoon ground guajillo chile
   pepper (see Note)

1 teaspoon ground arbol chile
   pepper (see Note)

1 teaspoon ground New Mexico
   chile pepper (see Note)

1 teaspoon garlic powder

1/2 teaspoon onion powder

1/2 teaspoon black pepper

1/2 teaspoon white pepper

1/2 teaspoon ground cumin

☆

1 pound boneless beef tenderloin
   steak, filet, or other tender cut
   of beef steak, cut into 4 equal
   steaks

3/4 cup plus 3 tablespoons all-
   purpose flour, in all

1 egg

1/4 cup milk

2 cups vegetable oil

1/2 cup chopped onions

1 1/2 cups chicken stock (see
   page 11)

1 cup heavy cream

2 tablespoons chopped fresh
   parsley

Combine the seasoning mix ingredients thoroughly in a small bowl. Makes 3 tablespoons.

Put the meat on a flat surface and pound each steak with a meat mallet or the side of a saucer, turning the meat as you pound it, until approximately 1/4 inch thick. Sprinkle 1/2 *teaspoon* of the seasoning mix on each side of each steak, and rub it in well with your hands or pound in with the mallet.

Combine 3/4 *cup* of the flour with *1 1/2 teaspoons* of the seasoning mix in a shallow bowl. Whisk together the egg and milk in a shallow bowl, until very frothy and pale yellow.

Heat the oil in a heavy 12-inch skillet over high heat until very hot. While the oil is heating, dredge the steaks one at a time in the seasoned flour, then let them soak a minute or two in the egg mixture. Dredge them in the flour again, pressing the steaks into the flour to coat them thoroughly. Immediately place the steaks in the hot oil and fry until browned, about 2 to 3 minutes on each side. Remove the steaks and set aside.

Pour off all but 1 tablespoon of the oil from the skillet, leaving the residue of juices from the meat and any brown crust remaining on the bottom. Heat over high heat and when the oil sizzles, add the onions and cook until light golden brown, about 3 minutes. Stir in the *remaining 3 tablespoons* flour and gradually add the chicken stock, whisking constantly with a wire whisk. Add the *remaining* seasoning mix and continue whisking until the gravy comes to a boil, about 2 minutes. Add the cream and parsley and cook 1 minute, whisking constantly.

Serve immediately, allowing a generous ½ cup gravy for each steak. Sensational with mashed potatoes, corn bread, biscuits, or polenta.

NOTE: These are the ground chile peppers we used. You can use whatever is available in your area, but be sure to buy pure ground chile peppers, not commercial chili powder.

# New Orleans Beef Short Ribs Etouffée

MAKES 4 SERVINGS

The word *etouffée* means "smothered," and in the world of Louisiana food, that means smothered in a sauce. In my family, an *etouffée* sauce always contained a cooked roux. Here's a wonderful way to smother short ribs in the style of Louisiana cooking. It's an easy dish to prepare and one your whole family will love. If you have any Cajun cousins, even they will be impressed.

SEASONING MIX
*1 tablespoon salt*
*1 tablespoon paprika*
*2 teaspoons onion powder*
*2 teaspoons garlic powder*
*1 teaspoon white pepper*
*1 teaspoon black pepper*
*1 teaspoon ground cumin*
☆

*4 pounds good-quality beef short ribs (about 8 ribs), excess fat removed and cut into individual ribs*
*¼ cup vegetable oil*
*6 tablespoons all-purpose flour, in all*
*3 cups chopped onions*
*2 cups chopped green bell peppers*
*1 cup chopped celery*
*3 cups beef stock (see page 11), in all*

Preheat the oven to 250°.

Combine the seasoning mix ingredients thoroughly in a small bowl. Makes ¼ cup plus 1 teaspoon.

Sprinkle the ribs on all over with *1 tablespoon plus 1 teaspoon* of the seasoning mix, and rub it in well with your hands.

Heat a 12-inch skillet, preferably cast iron, over high heat until very hot, about 6 minutes. Place the seasoned ribs in the skillet and brown, turning once or twice, about 4 minutes. Pour the oil between the ribs into the middle of the skillet and cook the ribs 3 minutes more. Remove the ribs with tongs and set aside. Whisk *¼ cup* of the flour into the oil and cook, whisking and scraping the bottom of the skillet clean, until this roux just starts to brown, about 1 minute. Whisk in the *remaining 2 tablespoons* flour and cook, whisking and scraping, until the roux is the color of light milk chocolate. Stir in the onions, bell peppers, celery, and *2 tablespoons* of the seasoning mix. Cook, whisking constantly and scraping the bottom of the skillet, until the vegetables are browned and the roux is thick, about 4 to 5 minutes. Stir in *2 cups* of the stock, scrape the bottom of the skillet clean, and bring the sauce to a rolling boil. Whisk in the *remaining* seasoning mix and the remaining *1 cup* stock, scrape the bottom of the skillet, and bring back to a boil, whisking occasionally. Whisk again and remove from the heat.

Place the ribs bone side down in a baking pan approximately 15 by 11 inches. Pour the sauce over the ribs, cover tightly with foil, and bake until the meat is very tender and almost falling off the bones, about 2½ to 3 hours.

Remove the pan from the oven and let cool a few minutes. Pour the sauce and juices into a container and skim off the excess fat. There should be about 4 cups sauce after skimming off the fat.

Serve about 1 cup sauce plus 2 ribs per person.

28.

## Saucy Sausalito Stir-fry

*page 140*

29.

## Atchafalaya Roast Boneless Chicken

*page 144*

30.

# Chicken Florentine

*page 146*

31.

# Basque Chicken and Shrimp in Wine

*page 155*

32.

# Chicken Cacciatore

*page 157*

33.

# Chicken Paprika

*page 160*

34.

# Iowa Chicken and Corn Pot Pie

*page 170*

35.

# Tex-Mex Chicken Mole Tostadas

*page 173*

36.

## Frontier Chicken-Fried Steak with Pan Gravy

*page 177*

37.

# West Virginia Sweet and Sour Short Ribs

*page 181*

38.

# New England Boiled Dinner

*page 182*

39.

## Polenta with Meat Sauce

*page 194*

40.

# Texas Chili (Texas Red)

*page 196*

41.

# Michigan Miner's Pasties

*page 202*

**42.**

# Iowa Stuffed Pork Chops

*page 204*

43.

## Navajo Tacos

*page 214*

# West Virginia
# Sweet and Sour Short Ribs

MAKES 4 SERVINGS

*Color photograph 37*

★

In the hills of West Virginia, as almost everywhere else in this country, short ribs came into their own early in this century. They were boiled, broiled, barbecued, and stewed, but sweet and sour stands out as a big favorite of the West Virginians. Of mine, too. I promise you'll lick your fingers.

**SEASONING MIX**
*2 teaspoons salt*
*2 teaspoons paprika*
*1½ teaspoons onion powder*
*1 teaspoon garlic powder*
*1 teaspoon dry mustard*
*1 teaspoon dried thyme leaves*
*1 teaspoon turmeric*
*1 teaspoon black pepper*
*1 teaspoon white pepper*
*1 teaspoon ground cumin*

☆

*2 cups chopped onions*
*1½ cups chopped green bell peppers*
*1 cup chopped celery*
*4 pounds good-quality beef short ribs (about 8 ribs), excess fat removed and cut into individual ribs*
*1 (15-ounce) can tomato sauce*
*¼ cup honey*
*¼ cup distilled white vinegar*
*½ cup bottled chili sauce*
*1 cup beef stock (see page 11)*

Preheat the oven to 300°.

Combine the seasoning mix ingredients thoroughly in a small bowl. Makes ¼ cup plus ½ teaspoon.

Combine the onions, bell peppers, and celery in a large baking pan. Sprinkle with *1 tablespoon* of the seasoning mix and rub it in well with your hands. Place the short ribs on top of the vegetables in a single layer. Sprinkle the ribs all over with *2 tablespoons* of the seasoning mix and rub it in well with your hands. Cover the pan tightly with foil and bake 1 hour. Remove the foil and bake 1 more hour.

Remove the ribs from the baking pan and drain off all the fat. Add the tomato sauce to the pan and stir in the honey. Using a wire whisk, whip in the vinegar, chili sauce, beef stock, and the *remaining* seasoning mix. Return the ribs to the pan, meat side down, and baste with the sauce. Bake, uncovered, until the meat is tender, about 1 hour.

Serve 2 ribs per portion, topped with sauce.

# New England Boiled Dinner

MAKES 4 TO 6 SERVINGS

*Color photograph 38*

An old New England favorite, this is a popular dinner all over America. The early settlers salted, or "corned" their beef with rock salt, to preserve its freshness; we use corned beef in this dish just because it tastes so good. The meat will probably shrink quite a bit, so if you have a lot of gravy left over, freeze it and use it later to make vegetable soup. If you have trouble finding parsnips, double the amount of carrots.

**SEASONING MIX 1**

*2 teaspoons salt*
*1 teaspoon white pepper*
*1 teaspoon onion powder*
*1 teaspoon garlic powder*
*½ teaspoon black pepper*
*½ teaspoon ground mace*
*¼ teaspoon ground nutmeg*

☆

*1 (approximately 3-pound) corned beef brisket, trimmed of all visible fat*

**SEASONING MIX 2**

*12 black peppercorns*
*6 allspice berries*
*4 cloves*
*4 small bay leaves*
*1 teaspoon dried dill weed*
*1 teaspoon mustard seed*

☆

*8 cups beef stock (see page 11)*
*1 cup chopped onions*
*6 unpeeled garlic cloves*
*18 small new potatoes*

*1 medium green cabbage, cut into 6 wedges, with a sliver of core left in to hold each wedge together*

*3 cups bite-size pieces peeled rutabagas or turnips (about 1 or 2 large)*

*2 small onions, cut into 8 wedges each*

*4½ cups bite-size pieces peeled parsnips (8 very small or 6 medium)*

*6 large carrots, cut in half crosswise and then lengthwise*

**DAY 1:** Thoroughly combine the ingredients for Seasoning Mix 1 in a small bowl. Makes 2 tablespoons plus ¼ teaspoon.

Sprinkle the seasoning mix all over the brisket, and rub it in well with your hands. Place the beef in a bowl and refrigerate overnight.

**DAY 2:** Remove the brisket from the refrigerator and let it come to room temperature.

Thoroughly combine the ingredients for Seasoning Mix 2 in a small bowl.

Bring the stock to a boil in a large heavy pot over high heat. Add all of Seasoning Mix 2, the chopped onions, and the brisket. Bring the stock back to a boil, reduce the heat to low and cover. Simmer, turning the meat once or twice, until the brisket is tender but not falling apart, about 2 to 2½ hours.

Add the garlic and potatoes and return to a boil. Cover the pot, reduce the heat to low, and simmer 10 minutes. Turn the heat up to high and add the cabbage, pushing it under the meat. Bring back to a boil, reduce the heat to low, cover the pot, and simmer 10 minutes. Turn the heat to high, add all the remaining vegetables, and push them under the meat. Bring to a boil, reduce the heat to low, cover the pot, and simmer 5 minutes. Turn off heat and let the pot sit, covered, another 5 minutes.

Serve immediately, with mustard or horseradish.

# Sauerbraten

MAKES 8 TO 10 SERVINGS

★

Lots of recipes for plain, good food accompanied the German immigrants wherever they settled in this country. Sauerbraten is one of those recipes, most often identified with Pennsylvania Dutch country. The main characteristic of this dish is the play of sweet against sour, a common taste sensation in food from "Dutch Country." The trick is to balance the two well. The addition of a fairly sophisticated seasoning mix creates a "roundness" with the flavor of the marinated beef.

SEASONING MIX
1 tablespoon salt
1 tablespoon sugar
1½ teaspoons white pepper
1½ teaspoons dry mustard
1½ teaspoons onion powder
1 teaspoon garlic powder
1 teaspoon ground ginger
1 teaspoon dried sweet basil
   leaves
¾ teaspoon black pepper
½ teaspoon ground coriander

☆

1 (4-pound) beef roast, such as
   boneless sirloin tip
10 cloves

2 cups chopped onions, in all
3 bay leaves
2 cups apple cider vinegar
2 cups dry white wine
2 cups grated carrots
1 cup chopped celery
1 teaspoon grated fresh ginger
6 cups beef stock (see page 11),
   in all
2 cups sliced carrots
2 cups sliced onions
12 nongourmet gingersnaps,
   pulverized in a food processor
   (about ½ cup)
1 tablespoon dry sherry, optional

**DAY 1:** Combine the seasoning mix ingredients thoroughly in a small bowl. Makes ¼ cup plus 2¾ teaspoons.

Place the roast on a flat surface and, with a small, sharp knife, poke about 10 holes in the top of the meat, approximately 1½ inches apart. Fill each of the holes with about ½ *teaspoon* of the seasoning mix, pushing the seasoning in with your finger. Rub some additional seasoning mix over the entire surface of the meat with your hands. Stick a clove in each hole. Place the roast in a large, deep casserole dish. Add *1 cup* of the chopped onions, the bay leaves, vinegar, and wine and cover the casserole. Place in the refrigerator and allow to marinate for 2 days, turning twice.

**DAY 3:** Remove the meat from the refrigerator and bring to room temperature.

Remove the meat from the marinade, allowing the marinade to drip back into the casserole.

Using a slotted spoon, remove the onions from the marinade and set aside; reserve the bay leaves separately. Reserve 1 cup of the marinade and discard the remainder.

Heat a large cast-iron pot over high heat until smoking hot, about 6 to 8 minutes. Place the roast, holes side up, in the pot and brown on all sides, about 8 minutes total. As the last side is browning, add the reserved onions from the marinade, the *remaining 1 cup* chopped onions, the grated carrots, celery, and ginger. Lift up the meat with a long fork, stir the vegetables, and replace the meat on top. Cover and cook 4 to 5 minutes, watching to be sure the vegetables don't burn. Lift up the meat and stir in the *remaining* seasoning mix, the reserved marinade, and the reserved bay leaves. Replace the meat, cover, and cook 10 minutes. Lift up the meat, add *3 cups* of the beef stock, scrape the pot bottom, and replace the meat, holes side up. Cover and bring to a boil, reduce the heat to low, and simmer, uncovering the pot once to scrape the bottom, about 20 minutes. Turn up the heat to high, add *2 cups* more stock and scrape the pot. Cover and bring to a boil, then lower the heat and simmer, uncovering to stir and scrape once or twice, about 1½ hours.

Remove the meat, let cool 10 minutes, then slice it against the grain into thin slices. Add the sliced carrots and onions to the sauce in the pot and stir. Return the sliced meat to the pot and bring to a boil. Reduce the heat to low, cover, and simmer until the carrots are tender, about 20 minutes.

Remove the meat from the sauce and arrange it on a serving platter. Turn up the heat under the sauce and whisk in the gingersnap crumbs and the *remaining 1 cup* stock. Simmer 7 minutes. Add the sherry, if desired.

Pour the sauce over the meat and serve immediately with noodles or potatoes.

# Wyoming Brisket Barbecue

## MAKES 8 SERVINGS

★

This is a Western barbecue, as opposed to a Texas barbecue, but you don't have to get out your grill, because the meat is cooked right in your kitchen. Remember that every piece of meat is different and cooks differently, and the shape of a brisket makes the timing even trickier, because it's thicker in the middle and tapers at the ends. While the whole brisket is cooking, you can judge its tenderness with a fork. After the meat has been sliced and returned to simmer in the gravy, cut into a piece several times near the end of the cooking to find the right moment when the meat turns perfectly tender. The result will be delicious meat and a deep, rich gravy that can be spooned over French bread, corn bread, or potatoes. You can even feel justified spooning it right out of the pot.

SEASONING MIX
1 tablespoon salt
2 teaspoons ground guajillo chile pepper (see Note)
2 teaspoons ground arbol chile pepper (see Note)
1½ teaspoons dry mustard
1 teaspoon garlic powder
1 teaspoon onion powder
1 teaspoon black pepper
1 teaspoon crushed bay leaves
1 teaspoon dried sweet basil leaves
1 teaspoon mustard seeds
½ teaspoon white pepper
½ teaspoon ground cumin
½ teaspoon dried thyme leaves
½ teaspoon ground savory
½ teaspoon ground coriander

1 (4- to 4½-pound) beef brisket
3½ to 4 cups beef stock (see page 11), in all
2 cups chopped onions
1 cup chopped green bell peppers
1½ cups chopped celery
2 cups canned tomato sauce
5 tablespoons apple cider vinegar
4 bay leaves
¼ cup packed dark brown sugar
½ cup honey, in all

☆

**DAY 1:** Combine the seasoning mix ingredients thoroughly in a small bowl. Makes 5 tablespoons plus 2 teaspoons.

Sprinkle *3 tablespoons plus 1 teaspoon* of the seasoning mix all over the brisket, working it in well with your hands. Cover and refrigerate overnight.

**DAY 2:** Remove the brisket from the refrigerator and let it come to room temperature.

Preheat the oven to 425°.

Place the brisket in a large roasting pan and roast, uncovered, 30 minutes. Turn the meat over, add *½ cup* of the beef stock, and cook until the meat is fairly tender, checking now and then to be sure it doesn't burn, about 1 hour. If the meat starts to stick hard to the pot, add another *½ cup* of the stock.

Remove the pan from the oven and turn the oven heat down to 350°. Remove the meat and place the roasting pan over high heat on top of the stove. Stir in the onions, bell peppers, celery, *2 tablespoons* of the seasoning mix, the tomato sauce, vinegar, bay leaves, and brown sugar, scrape the bottom of the pan, and cook 6 minutes. Stir in *3 cups* of the stock and *¼ cup* of the honey, scrape the pan bottom, and bring to a simmer. Return the brisket to the pan and bake, until tender, turning the meat once or twice, about 1 to 1½ hours.

Remove the pan from the oven and place over high heat on top of the stove. Remove the meat and cut it against the grain into thin slices. Return the slices to the gravy in the pan. Turn down the heat and simmer until the meat is very tender and the sauce has thickened and darkened to a dark red-brown, about 45 minutes to 1 hour. Stir in the *remaining ¼ cup* honey and remove from the heat.

Serve immediately over French bread or with potato salad.

**NOTE:** These are the ground chile peppers we used. You can use whatever is available in your area, but be sure you buy pure ground chile peppers, not commercial chili powder.

# Bogue Falaya
# Beef and Oyster
# Jambalaya

MAKES 16 "CITY FOLK" SERVINGS
OR 8 CAJUN SERVINGS

★

Jambalaya is a dish of rice with ham, shrimp, oysters, crawfish, sausage, chicken, or beef—or all of the above. A highly seasoned Cajun-Creole specialty, the name comes from the French *jambon*, which means "ham," and the African *ya*, meaning "rice." The French words *á là* mean "in the manner of" or "on top of," which gives you all that good stuff on top of your rice. You may be surprised to see cream in this recipe—something you've probably never seen in a jambalaya before. But this unusual version is a good example of how versatile all of our regional cooking is, and how dishes can evolve without losing their original character.

SEASONING MIX
*2 tablespoons dried parsley flakes*
*2½ teaspoons black pepper*
*2 teaspoons salt*
*2 teaspoons paprika*
*2 teaspoons dried sweet basil leaves*
*2 teaspoons dried cilantro leaves*
*1½ teaspoons dried thyme leaves*
*1½ teaspoons white pepper*
*1½ teaspoons onion powder*
*1 teaspoon garlic powder*

☆

*1 pound beef stew meat, cut into ¾-inch cubes*
*3 bay leaves*
*4 cups chopped onions, in all*

*3 cups chopped green bell peppers, in all*
*1½ cups chopped celery, in all*
*1 tablespoon minced fresh garlic*
*6 ounces smoked beef sausage*
*3 cups chopped tomatoes*
*8 tablespoons (1 stick) unsalted butter*
*10 ounces smoked pork sausage, cut into ½-inch rounds*
*1 cup seafood stock (see page 11)*
*2 cups beef stock (see page 11)*
*1½ cups heavy cream*
*3½ cups uncooked converted rice*
*1 pint shucked oysters, with their liquid*

Preheat the oven to 350°.

Combine the seasoning mix ingredients thoroughly in a small bowl. Makes 7 tablespoons plus 1 teaspoon.

Heat a large heavy ovenproof pot over high heat, about 3 minutes. Add the stew meat and cook, turning once to brown, about 2 minutes. Add the bay leaves, *3 tablespoons* of the seasoning mix, *3 cups* of the onions, *2 cups* of the bell peppers, *1 cup* of the celery, the garlic, and beef sausage and stir well. Cover the pot and cook, uncovering occasionally to stir, about 12 minutes. Uncover the pot and cook, stirring and scraping occasionally, until a hard crust forms on the bottom of the pot, about 3 minutes. Add the tomatoes, butter, and the *remaining 1 cup* each onions and bell peppers and *½ cup* celery. Stir well, cover, and cook until a crust forms on the pot bottom, about 9 to 10 minutes. Uncover and scrape the bottom of the pot clean. Stir in the pork sausage, seafood and beef stocks, cream, rice, oysters, and the *remaining* seasoning mix. Cover the pot, place in the oven, and bake 25 minutes.

Turn off the heat and leave the pot in the oven for another 15 minutes. Makes 16 cups.

Serve immediately, in bowls.

# Albuquerque Burritos

MAKES 15 BURRITOS

In the early part of the nineteenth century, the practice of making tortillas with wheat flour spread from the northern Mexican state of Sonora to the American Southwest. These flour tortillas, larger than their corny cousins, are traditionally filled with anything from refried beans to cheese to poultry or meat and known as "burritos," or little donkeys. We like to make ours with steak.

SEASONING MIX

1 tablespoon plus 1 teaspoon salt

2 teaspoons dry mustard

2 teaspoons dried cilantro leaves

2 teaspoons crushed dried dark-roasted ancho chiles (see Note)

1½ teaspoons crushed dried guajillo chiles (see Note)

1½ teaspoons garlic powder

1½ teaspoons ground cumin

1¼ teaspoons white pepper

1 teaspoon onion powder

1 teaspoon ground New Mexico chile pepper (see Note)

1 teaspoon dried thyme leaves

¾ teaspoon black pepper

½ teaspoon ground nutmeg

☆

3 pounds beef flank steak (2 steaks, about ½ inch thick, chilled)

¼ cup fresh lime juice

6 tablespoons fresh lemon juice

2 tablespoons apple cider vinegar

2 medium green bell peppers, cored, seeded, and cut into thin strips

3 medium red bell peppers, cored, seeded, and cut into thin strips

1½ large yellow onions, cut into julienne strips

½ cup vegetable oil, in all

15 flour tortillas

Guacamole (recipe follows)

Combine the seasoning mix ingredients thoroughly in a small bowl. Makes 6 tablespoons plus 2 teaspoons.

Slice the steaks (cold meat is easier to slice) into strips about 4 inches long by ¼ inch thick.

Place the meat in a large bowl and add *3 tablespoons* of the seasoning mix, the lime juice, lemon juice, and vinegar, and mix thoroughly with your hands. Cover the bowl and allow the meat to marinate at room temperature about 2½ hours.

Combine the green and red bell peppers and onions in another bowl. Strain the marinade from the beef into the vegetables. Stir in *¼ cup* of the oil and *1 tablespoon plus 1 teaspoon* of the seasoning mix. Mix thoroughly with your hands.

Add another *1 tablespoon* of the seasoning mix and the *remaining ¼ cup* oil to the meat and rub in well with your hands.

Heat a 12-inch cast iron skillet over high heat until very hot and smoking, about 8 to 9 minutes. Using tongs, add the meat to the skillet in batches and cook until browned on both sides, about 2 to 3 minutes. (Be sure to allow the skillet to get very hot before adding each new batch of meat.) Remove the meat to a bowl.

Let the skillet get very hot again, add the vegetables using a slotted spoon, and cook, tossing often with the spoon, until crisp-tender, about 4 to 5 minutes. Remove the peppers and onions from the pan with a slotted spoon or tongs, leaving the liquid in the skillet, and add to the meat. Toss to mix.

Add any liquid remaining in the marinating bowls to the skillet and cook over high heat, stirring and scraping the bottom of the skillet, until thickened. Pour over the meat and vegetables and toss to coat.

Meanwhile, heat the tortillas according to the package directions or wrap in foil and place in a 350° oven for about 3 minutes.

Top each tortilla with ½ cup of the meat mixture and ¼ cup of the Guacamole and roll up. Top each burrito with another 2 tablespoons of the Guacamole and serve immediately.

NOTE: These are the ground chile peppers we used. You can use whatever peppers are available in your area, but try to use a variety of heats for a "round" flavor. Don't use commercial chili powder.

## GUACAMOLE

### MAKES ABOUT 6 CUPS

*5 very ripe avocados (preferably California avocados, or Calavos), peeled and cut into chunks*
*1 cup chopped onions*
*2 cups chopped peeled fresh tomatoes*
*1 teaspoon minced fresh garlic*

*3 tablespoons fresh lime juice*
*2 tablespoons chopped fresh jalapeños*
*1½ teaspoons salt*
*1 teaspoon ground cumin*
*2 tablespoons chopped fresh cilantro, optional*

Place all the ingredients in the bowl of a food processor and pulse until coarsely puréed; the mixture should still be somewhat chunky.

# Beef Noodle Casserole

MAKES 8 TO 10 SERVINGS

★

In the 1930s, American homemakers were often on the lookout for in-
expensive meals to serve their families. With the hamburger's rise in
popularity, many found chopped meat the answer and the variations concocted were numerous and sometimes mind-boggling. This, however, is
a lick-the-spoon casserole that combines *two* American favorites—hamburger and pasta. Although it may at first seem a homely dish, you'll find
the seasonings both sophisticated and satisfying.

SEASONING MIX
*1 tablespoon salt*
*1¾ teaspoons onion powder*
*1¾ teaspoons garlic powder*
*1¾ teaspoons dried oregano*
  *leaves*
*1½ teaspoons white pepper*
*1¼ teaspoons dried thyme leaves*
*1¼ teaspoons dry mustard*
*1 teaspoon black pepper*

☆

*1 (12-ounce) bag medium egg*
  *noodles*
*2 tablespoons plus 1 teaspoon*
  *vegetable oil, in all*
*1½ pounds ground sirloin*

*4 ounces cream cheese*
*½ cup sour cream*
*1 tablespoon fresh lime juice*
*1 cup chopped green onions*
  *(tops and bottoms)*
*¼ cup chopped fresh parsley*
*1½ cups chopped onions*
*1 cup chopped celery*
*1 teaspoon minced fresh garlic*
*2½ cups beef stock (see*
  *page 11), in all*
*4 tablespoons unsalted butter*
*1 (8-ounce) can tomato sauce*
*1 cup grated Monterey Jack*
  *cheese*
*1 cup grated sharp Cheddar*
  *cheese*

Preheat the oven to 350°.

Combine the seasoning mix ingredients thoroughly in a small bowl.
Makes ¼ cup plus 1¼ teaspoons.

Cook the noodles *al dente* according to the package directions. Rinse
under hot water, then cold water, and drain. Pour *1 teaspoon* of the oil

into your hands and rub into the noodles. Sprinkle *2 teaspoons* of the seasoning mix over the noodles and blend well with your hands.

Place the ground sirloin in a bowl, add *1 tablespoon plus 1 teaspoon* of the seasoning mix, and blend it in well with your hands.

Combine the cream cheese, sour cream, lime juice, green onions, and parsley in a bowl and mix thoroughly with a spoon until completely blended.

Heat the *remaining 2 tablespoons* oil in a 10-inch skillet over high heat until very hot, about 4 minutes. Add the onions, celery, garlic, and the *remaining* seasoning mix and cook, stirring occasionally, until the vegetables are golden brown and sticking to the bottom of the skillet, about 7 to 8 minutes. Add *½ cup* of the beef stock, scrape the crust from the bottom of the skillet, and cook until another crust forms on the skillet bottom, about 3 minutes. Add another *½ cup* stock, scrape up the crust on the skillet bottom, and cook 2 minutes. Add the seasoned meat, breaking it up with a spoon, and cook, scraping occasionally, until most of the liquid has evaporated, about 7 to 9 minutes. (Be careful not to let the meat get too dry.) Add the butter and cook 3 to 5 minutes, without stirring, to allow another crust to form. Stir in the tomato sauce, scrape the bottom of the skillet, and cook 3 to 4 minutes. Add the *remaining 1½ cups* stock and bring to a boil. Remove from the heat and stir in the sour cream mixture until thoroughly blended.

Spread half the seasoned noodles in the bottom of a deep 10-inch square casserole. Pour about 3 cups of the meat mixture over the noodles and sprinkle with the Monterey Jack cheese. Add the remaining noodles, cover with the remaining meat mixture, and sprinkle the Cheddar cheese evenly over the top. Bake, uncovered, 25 to 30 minutes, or until brown and bubbly.

Spoon up and serve with a crisp salad.

# Polenta
# with Meat Sauce

MAKES 4 TO 6 SERVINGS

*Color photograph 39*

★

Italian-Americans have their own version of the cornmeal mush first cooked here by the Plains Indians. The Indians fried or baked a ground maize mush, and later the pioneers ate their cornmeal fried, as well. But the Italians serve theirs with a wonderful meat sauce. This particular recipe comes from Kansas.

**SEASONING MIX**

2 tablespoons light brown sugar

1 tablespoon salt

2¹⁄₂ teaspoons dried sweet basil leaves

2 teaspoons dry mustard

2 teaspoons white pepper

1¹⁄₂ teaspoons dried thyme leaves

1¹⁄₂ teaspoons garlic powder

1 teaspoon onion powder

1 teaspoon black pepper

1 teaspoon dried marjoram leaves

1 teaspoon dried oregano leaves

☆

**POLENTA**

1 cup yellow cornmeal

1 tablespoon plus 1¹⁄₂ teaspoons Seasoning Mix (see above)

3 tablespoons unsalted butter

1 cup grated onions

1 teaspoon salt

¹⁄₂ teaspoon ground cinnamon

¹⁄₂ teaspoon ground allspice

4 cups chicken stock (see page 11)

Vegetable oil cooking spray

**MEAT SAUCE**

3 tablespoons olive oil

1¹⁄₂ cups chopped onions, in all

¹⁄₂ cup chopped green bell peppers

1 cup chopped celery, in all

6 tablespoons Seasoning Mix (see above), in all

1 pound lean ground beef

2 teaspoons minced fresh garlic

¹⁄₂ cup diced carrots

¹⁄₂ cup chopped fresh parsley

1 (16-ounce) can whole tomatoes, with their liquid

1 cup heavy cream

Preheat the oven to 350°.

Combine the seasoning mix ingredients thoroughly in a small bowl. Makes 7 tablespoons plus 1½ teaspoons.

**FOR THE POLENTA,** combine the cornmeal with *1½ teaspoons* of the seasoning mix in a small bowl and set aside.

Melt the butter in a heavy 3-quart pot over high heat. When the butter sizzles, add the onions and cook, stirring once or twice, until browned, about 6 minutes. Add the salt, cinnamon, and allspice, stir, and cook 3 minutes. Stir in the remaining *1 tablespoon* seasoning mix, scrape the pot, and cook 2 minutes. Add the chicken stock, scrape the bottom of the pot, and bring to a rolling boil. Slowly add the seasoned cornmeal, whipping constantly with a wire whisk. Reduce the heat to low and simmer, scraping from time to time to prevent burning, about 10 minutes. Remove from the heat.

Coat a 12-cup muffin tin with cooking spray and fill each cup about half full with the polenta mixture. Bake until golden brown, about 30 to 40 minutes. Remove from the oven and let cool at least 10 minutes.

**FOR THE SAUCE,** heat the oil in a 12-inch skillet over high heat. When the oil is hot, add *1 cup* of the onions, the bell peppers, *½ cup* of the celery, and *1 tablespoon* of the seasoning mix. Stir well and cook until the onions are browned and sticking a bit, about 8 minutes. Move the vegetables to one side of the skillet. Place the meat in the cleared space and sprinkle with the *remaining 5 tablespoons* seasoning mix. Cook, breaking up any lumps of meat with a spoon as it browns, about 3 minutes. Add the garlic, carrots, the *remaining ½ cup* each onions and celery, and the parsley, to the meat, stir, and cook 3 minutes. Stir the meat into the vegetable mixture and cook 3 minutes. Stir in the tomatoes, breaking them up with the spoon, and cook 5 minutes. Add the cream and bring just to the boiling point, then reduce the heat to low and simmer 10 minutes. Remove from the heat.

Remove the polenta rounds from the muffin tin. Place 2 or 3 polenta rounds on each plate and cover with sauce. Serve with a cool green salad.

# Texas Chili (Texas Red)

MAKES 12 GENEROUS SERVINGS

*Color photograph 40*

★

As everyone knows, chili is about as American as apple pie and is eaten almost everywhere in the United States. In fact, many states claim to have invented the dish and promote a wide range of unusual variations on the theme. But chili was actually created in San Antonio, Texas, around the middle of the nineteenth century. Our version is based on a true Texas-style chili, which in San Antonio would be called a "bowl of red." When he tasted it, Dudley Passman, our director of sales, told us it was his best bowl of red—ever.

SEASONING MIX
*1 tablespoon salt*
*1 tablespoon ground guajillo chile pepper (see Note)*
*1 tablespoon ground arbol chile pepper (see Note)*
*2 teaspoons dried sweet basil leaves*
*1½ teaspoons garlic powder*
*1 teaspoon onion powder*
*1 teaspoon paprika*
*1 teaspoon black pepper*
*1 teaspoon cayenne pepper*
*1 teaspoon ground cumin*
*1 teaspoon dry mustard*
*1 teaspoon dried thyme leaves*
*½ teaspoon ground nutmeg*
*½ teaspoon ground cinnamon*

☆

*5 pounds beef top round, cut into ½-inch dice*
*3 dried ancho or poblano peppers (see Note)*
*3 dried arbol peppers or any small, thin hot red chile peppers (see Note)*
*6 dried serrano or guajillo peppers (see Note)*
*½ cup yellow cornmeal*
*1¼ pounds salt pork, Boston pork butt, or bacon, cut into ¼-inch dice (if you use salt pork, rinse some of the salt from the rind and pat dry)*
*6 cups chopped onions,* in all
*6 cups chopped green bell peppers,* in all
*3 cups chopped celery,* in all
*2 tablespoons minced fresh garlic*
*4 bay leaves*
*6 cups beef (preferred), pork, or chicken stock (see page 11),* in all
*8 medium fresh tomatoes, peeled and smashed, with their juices*
*1 tablespoon ground cumin*

Preheat the oven to 350°.

Combine the seasoning mix ingredients thoroughly in a small bowl. Makes 6 tablespoons plus 2½ teaspoons.

Sprinkle ¼ *cup* of the seasoning mix all over the meat and work it in well with your hands.

Place the dried anchos, arbols, and serranos—or whatever chile peppers you were able to find—on a baking pan and dry them in the oven until brittle, about 10 to 13 minutes. Let cool. When the peppers are cool enough to handle, crush them with your hands into the bowl of a food processor and blend into a fine powder. There should be about 7 tablespoons in all.

Place the cornmeal in a small skillet over medium-high heat and toast, flipping the cornmeal and shaking the skillet constantly, until the cornmeal is light brown, about 4 minutes. Remove from the heat and set aside.

Place the salt pork, pork butt, or bacon in a large heavy pot over medium heat. Cover and cook, uncovering the pot occasionally to scrape the bottom, until the salt pork is a deep brown color, about 30 minutes. There should be a film on the bottom of the pot that looks like ground red pepper. Remove the salt pork from the pot with a slotted spoon and set aside.

Turn the heat up to high, and when the fat remaining in the pot is hot, add half the beef to the pot. Cook, turning once or twice, until browned, about 5 minutes. Remove with a slotted spoon to a bowl. Then brown the remaining beef and remove to the bowl.

Add *4 cups* each of the onions and bell peppers, *2 cups* of the celery, the garlic, and the *remaining* seasoning mix to the pot. Stir well, cover, and cook 8 to 10 minutes. Add the bay leaves, cover, and cook, uncovering occasionally to stir, about 15 minutes. Remove the lid and cook until the vegetables are sticking to the bottom of the pot, about 6 minutes. Stir in the ground peppers and the browned beef. Cook until the meat sticks hard and forms a hard crust on the bottom of the pot, about 20 to 25 minutes.

Meanwhile, place the browned salt pork and *1 cup* of the stock in the container of a blender and process until thoroughly blended.

When the meat has formed a crust on the bottom of the pot, stir in the salt pork/stock mixture and scrape the bottom of the pot. Add the tomatoes, the *remaining* 2 cups onions, *2 cups* bell peppers, *1 cup* celery, and *1 cup* of the stock. Scrape the bottom of the pot well and cook, uncovered, 12 minutes. Cover the pot and cook over high heat 8 minutes. Add the toasted cornmeal and *1 cup* more stock to the pot and scrape the bottom. Stir in the *remaining 3 cups* stock and the cumin. Bring to a boil, cover, lower the heat, and simmer, scraping occasionally if the mixture starts to stick, about 1 hour and 10 minutes. Remove from the heat. Makes about 18 cups.

Serve immediately or refrigerate overnight and reheat before serving. Fantastic with toasted corn tortillas!

NOTE: These are the chile peppers we used. You can use whatever is available in your area, whole dried or ground, but be sure to buy pure ground chile peppers, not commericial chili powder.

# Midtown Meat Loaf

MAKES 6 TO 8 SERVINGS

★

Meat loaf is the younger cousin of the European pâté, although one would hardly be mistaken for the other. Since the recipe first appeared in print in this country in 1900, meat loaf hasn't been the most popular dish. You rarely hear "Oh, boy, we're having meat loaf for dinner!" or "Let's send out for some meat loaf!" But that's probably because many people, when cooking it, don't give meat loaf the attention it deserves. In order to make it a treat, instead of a treatment, meat loaf must be juicy and tasty. Seems basic, but somehow there exists a legacy of dry, tasteless slabs of cooked ground meat. We think this recipe will make you a meat loaf lover. If you like your meat loaf crusty, try brushing some ketchup on the top of the loaf before baking.

SEASONING MIX

2 teaspoons dry mustard

2 teaspoons paprika

1½ teaspoons salt

1½ teaspoons dried thyme leaves

1½ teaspoons dried sweet basil
   leaves

1 teaspoon black pepper

1 teaspoon garlic powder

1 teaspoon onion powder

½ teaspoon white pepper

☆

8 slices bacon, diced

1½ cups chopped onions

1 cup chopped green bell peppers

1 cup chopped celery

4 bay leaves

1 cup tomato juice

½ cup evaporated milk

1½ pounds ground beef

½ pound ground veal

2 eggs, lightly beaten

½ cup unsalted saltine cracker
   crumbs (about 12 crackers)

Vegetable oil cooking spray

Preheat the oven to 350°.

Combine the seasoning mix ingredients thoroughly in a small bowl. Makes ¼ cup.

Cook the bacon in a 10-inch skillet over high heat until brown and crispy, about 7 to 9 minutes. If the fat starts to smoke before the bacon is brown, lower the heat to medium. Remove the bacon with a slotted spoon and set aside.

Add the onions to the skillet and cook until the onions are golden brown, about 5 to 6 minutes. Add the green peppers, celery, bay leaves, and *2 tablespoons* of the seasoning mix and cook, stirring and scraping occasionally, about 4 minutes. Add the *remaining* seasoning mix and cook, stirring often, about 5 to 6 minutes. Remove from the heat and remove and discard the bay leaves.

Combine the tomato juice, evaporated milk, and the cooked bacon in a large bowl. Add the cooked vegetable mixture and blend well.

Gently combine the meat, eggs, and cracker crumbs in another large bowl. Add the vegetable mixture and, being careful not to pack too tightly, incorporate everything thoroughly.

Spray a 13- by 9-inch loaf pan or rectangular casserole dish with cooking spray. Turn the meat mixture into the pan and mold it into a thick loaf. Bake 30 minutes, turn the pan around, and bake another 15 minutes.

Cut into slices about ¾ inch thick and serve.

# German-Style Meatballs

MAKES 6 TO 8 SERVINGS

★

The German immigrants who brought this recipe with them to the New World were definitely fond of the tangy flavors prevalent in their cooking. This dish is a great example of flavorful German food and a surprise for those of us who have never expected much from a meatball.

SEASONING MIX
1 tablespoon salt
2½ teaspoons dry mustard
2½ teaspoons paprika
2 teaspoons onion powder
2 teaspoons garlic powder
1½ teaspoons white pepper
1 teaspoon black pepper
1 teaspoon ground savory
½ teaspoon ground cloves

☆

1 (2-ounce) can anchovy fillets
8 tablespoons (1 stick) unsalted butter, in all
3 cups chopped onions
2 cups chopped celery
1¼ cups sauterne wine, in all

1 tablespoon juice from the jar of capers (see below)
3 eggs
3 tablespoons drained capers, in all
1 teaspoon minced fresh garlic
¼ cup chopped fresh parsley
2 tablespoons sugar
¾ cup evaporated milk
1 pound ground beef
½ pound ground veal
½ pound ground pork
1 cup bread crumbs
3 tablespoons all-purpose flour
3 cups beef stock (see page 11), in all
3 thin lemon slices
1 (12-ounce) package broad egg noodles

Combine the seasoning mix ingredients thoroughly in a small bowl. Makes 5 tablespoons plus 1 teaspoon.

Drain the anchovy fillets and soak them in water to cover for 20 minutes.

Preheat the oven to 450°.

Melt *4 tablespoons* of the butter in a 10-inch skillet over high heat. When the butter sizzles, add the onions and celery and cook until the vegetables are lightly browned, about 6 to 8 minutes. Add *1 tablespoon* of the seasoning mix and cook, stirring occasionally, until a dark crust forms on the bottom of the *skillet*, about 2 to 3 minutes. Add ¼ *cup* of the sauterne and the caper juice and scrape the skillet clean. Remove from the heat.

Put the eggs, *2 tablespoons* of the capers, the anchovy fillets, garlic, parsley, sugar, evaporated milk, ¼ *cup* of the sauterne, and *1 tablespoon* of the seasoning mix into the container of a blender and process 20 seconds. Add 1 packed cup of the cooked onions and celery and process 25 seconds. Set aside 1 cup of this mixture.

Combine all the ground meat in a mixing bowl, add the bread crumbs and *2 tablespoons plus 2 teaspoons* of the seasoning mix, and blend well with your hands. Gently fold in the remaining mixture from the blender, taking care not to overmix. Using your hands, gently form the mixture into 1½-inch meatballs (we got 24) and put them in a large baking pan with an ovenproof handle. Bake, uncovered, 20 minutes.

Meanwhile, set the skillet of onions and celery over high heat and add the *remaining 4 tablespoons* butter. When the butter has melted, add the flour and cook, stirring constantly, 2 minutes. Stir in ¼ *cup* of the sauterne and cook until a film forms on the bottom of the skillet, about 1 minute. Add the *remaining 1 tablespoon* capers and cook, scraping the skillet bottom, until the mixture starts to brown, about 1 minute. Add *1 cup* of the stock and cook, scraping the skillet bottom, about 1 minute. Add ¼ *cup* more sauterne, thoroughly scrape the bottom of the skillet, and cook, stirring occasionally, about 4 minutes. Add the *remaining 2 cups* stock and bring to a rolling boil, stirring occasionally. Add the lemon slices, the reserved caper/anchovy mixture, and the *remaining ¼ cup* sauterne. Bring to a boil and cook over high heat until the sauce is slightly thickened, about 6 minutes. Remove from the heat.

With a metal spatula, loosen the baked meatballs from the baking pan. Pour the sauce over the meatballs, return the pan to the oven, and bake, basting once, about 17 minutes.

Meanwhile, cook the noodles according to the package directions. Sprinkle the *remaining* seasoning mix over the hot noodles and mix well with your hands. Keep warm.

Spread the noodles on a large serving platter, arrange the meatballs over the noodles, and pour the sauce over the top. Serve immediately.

# Michigan Miner's Pasties

MAKES 5 SERVINGS

*Color photograph 41*

★

There have been attempts to have the Cornish or miner's pasty (pronounced with a soft "a") declared the state food of Michigan. The pasty
was brought to Michigan's upper peninsula by Cornish miners who settled
there in the middle of the nineteenth century. Today, these meat and
vegetable turnovers are so popular in Michigan that the pasty shops do
better business than the local hamburger joints.

**SEASONING MIX**

1 tablespoon salt

1½ teaspoons onion powder

1½ teaspoons dried thyme leaves

1 teaspoon black pepper

1 teaspoon garlic powder

1 teaspoon dried sweet basil
leaves

¾ teaspoon white pepper

¾ teaspoon ground savory

☆

**DOUGH**

2 cups all-purpose flour

1 teaspoon Seasoning Mix (see
above)

6 tablespoons unsalted butter

7 to 8 tablespoons cold water

**FILLING**

10 ounces lean pork, very finely
chopped

¾ pound lean beef, very finely
chopped

2 tablespoons plus 2½ teaspoons
Seasoning Mix (see above)

4 tablespoons unsalted butter

2 cups chopped onions

1 cup chopped celery

1½ cups finely diced turnips

1 teaspoon minced fresh garlic

**FINISH**

1 egg

2 tablespoons water

2 large potatoes, approximately

1 teaspoon Seasoning Mix
(see above)

All-purpose flour

Vegetable oil cooking spray

Combine the seasoning mix ingredients thoroughly in a small bowl. Makes
3 tablespoons plus 1½ teaspoons.

**FOR THE DOUGH,** combine the flour, the *1 teaspoon* seasoning mix, and the butter in a bowl and blend with a fork until the texture is mealy. Gradually add the water and work the dough lightly with your hands until all the ingredients are thoroughly incorporated. Form the dough into a ball. Refrigerate, covered, 1 hour.

**FOR THE FILLING,** combine the pork and beef in a bowl. Sprinkle *2 tablespoons* seasoning mix over the meat and work in well with your hands.

Melt the butter in a 12-inch skillet over high heat. When the butter begins to sizzle, add the onions and celery and cook, stirring occasionally, until the onions begin to brown, about 4 to 6 minutes. Stir in *2½ teaspoons* of the seasoning mix and cook 4 minutes. Push the vegetables to one side of the skillet, place the seasoned meat in the cleared space, and cook, stirring occasionally, just until brown, about 3 minutes. Mix the meat into the vegetables, add the turnips and garlic, and cook until the vegetables are tender, about 3 minutes. Pour the filling mixture into a shallow pan and refrigerate until cool. (The potatoes should be sliced just before filling the pasties so they don't discolor.)

Preheat the oven to 350°.

**TO FINISH,** make an egg wash by beating the egg and water together.

Remove the dough from the refrigerator and divide into 5 equal portions. Sprinkle a clean surface with flour and roll out each portion of dough to a thickness of about ⅟₁₆ inch. Using a plate or a pan as a guide, cut a 9-inch round from each portion.

Peel the potatoes and cut them into 30 thin slices. Sprinkle the *1 teaspoon* seasoning mix over both sides of the potato slices.

Remove the filling from the refrigerator. Place 3 potato slices on half of each dough round, cover the potatoes with 1 cup of the filling, and arrange 3 more potato slices over the filling. Bring the other half of each round of dough over the filling to make a half-moon shape. Brush the edges with the egg wash, fold them over to seal, and crimp with the tines of a fork. Brush egg wash over the top of each pasty.

Spray a large baking sheet with cooking spray and place the pasties on the sheet. (If you have trouble picking up the pasties, use a spatula.) Bake until golden brown, about 1 hour and 10 minutes.

Serve warm.

# Iowa Stuffed Pork Chops

MAKES 4 SERVINGS

*Color photograph 42*

★

The state of Iowa is known for its quality pork, particularly its outstanding pork chops. This recipe for corn-stuffed pork chops is a favorite Iowa dish.

SEASONING MIX
2 teaspoons paprika
1½ teaspoons salt
1 teaspoon garlic powder
1 teaspoon onion powder
1 teaspoon dried sweet basil
   leaves
1 teaspoon dried thyme leaves
¾ teaspoon black pepper
½ teaspoon dry mustard
½ teaspoon white pepper
½ teaspoon ground sage

☆

4 lean rib pork chops, each
   about 1½ inches thick

4 tablespoons unsalted butter
1 cup chopped onions
½ cup chopped green bell
   peppers
½ cup chopped celery
½ cup fresh corn kernels (about
   1 ear)
½ cup chopped fresh mushrooms
2 bay leaves
2 cups chicken stock
   (see page 11), in all
2 cups plain dry bread cubes or
   plain croutons
½ cup chopped green onions
1 egg, lightly beaten

Preheat the oven to 300°.

Combine the seasoning mix ingredients thoroughly in a small bowl. Makes 3 tablespoons plus ¾ teaspoon.

Using a small, sharp knife, cut a 1-inch slit in the top edge of each chop. Stick the tip of the knife into the slit and cut a large pocket inside each chop, being careful not to enlarge the slit. Put ¼ *teaspoon* of the seasoning mix into the opening of each chop and rub into the pocket with your finger. Then sprinkle ¼ *teaspoon* of the seasoning mix on each side of each chop (½ teaspoon total per chop) and rub it in with your hands.

Melt the butter in an 8-inch skillet over high heat. When the butter is sizzling, add the onions and cook 3 minutes. Stir in the bell peppers, celery, and *2 tablespoons* of the seasoning mix and cook until the mixture is sticking to the bottom of the skillet, about 3 minutes. Scrape up the crust on the bottom of the skillet, stir in the corn and mushrooms, and cook 2 minutes. Add the bay leaves and scrape the skillet bottom clean. Cook until the mixture starts to stick hard to the bottom of the skillet, about 4 minutes. Stir in *1 cup* of the stock, scrape up the crust on the bottom of the skillet, and cook 1 minute. Remove from the heat and add the bread cubes. Mix the bread thoroughly into the vegetable mixture. Remove the bay leaves. Sprinkle the green onions over the stuffing mixture, add the beaten egg, and blend thoroughly.

Using a teaspoon, stuff each chop with about one quarter of the stuffing mixture.

Pour the *remaining 1 cup* stock into a baking pan and place the chops in the pan, standing them up on the bone edge if possible. Place the remaining stuffing in a small casserole. Bake the chops until light brown but tender, about 25 to 30 minutes; bake the casserole of stuffing along with the chops.

Remove the baking pan and the casserole from the oven and turn the broiler on. Lay the chops flat, baste with the pan juices, and broil until golden brown and juicy, about 2 to 3 minutes on each side.

To serve, place each chop on a small bed of the baked stuffing.

# Ohio Ham Loaf

MAKES 6 TO 8 SERVINGS

★

Americans surely do love ground meat, and not only beef. In the 1930s, a lot of experimenting was done with dishes using ground pork, lamb, and even ham. Homemakers across the country relied on a good meat loaf as a dinner staple. This ham loaf is from a recipe found in Ohio, but we've given it a more intricate seasoning blend to complement the flavor of the meat. We've also combined cooked ham with fresh pork for a "round" flavor. It's equally delicious served hot or cold, with your favorite mustard sauce, gravy, or just as is. Or use it for scrumptious sandwiches.

SEASONING MIX

1½ teaspoons paprika
1¼ teaspoons garlic powder
1 teaspoon onion powder
1 teaspoon salt
1 teaspoon white pepper
1 teaspoon dry mustard
¾ teaspoon black pepper
¾ teaspoon dried dill weed
¾ teaspoon ground cloves
¾ teaspoon ground allspice
½ teaspoon ground ginger

2 tablespoons unsalted butter
1 cup chopped onions
½ cup chopped celery
½ teaspoon minced fresh garlic
¼ cup packed light brown sugar
¾ cup evaporated milk
1 pound ground (cooked) ham
1 pound ground pork
1 cup unsalted saltine cracker
    crumbs (about 24 crackers)
4 eggs
Vegetable oil cooking spray

☆

Preheat the oven to 325°.

Combine the seasoning mix ingredients thoroughly in a small bowl. Makes 3 tablespoons plus 1¼ teaspoons.

Melt the butter in a 10-inch skillet over high heat. When the butter sizzles, add the onions and celery and cook, stirring occasionally, 3 minutes. Stir in *1 tablespoon* of the seasoning mix and cook, occasionally scraping the bottom of the skillet, until the vegetables are lightly browned, about 2 minutes. Stir in the *remaining* seasoning mix and cook 1 minute. Add the garlic, brown sugar, and evaporated milk, and cook, stirring, until the sugar is dissolved. Remove from the heat and let cool a few minutes.

Meanwhile, in a large bowl, combine the ground ham and pork, cracker crumbs, and eggs.

Add the contents of the skillet to the meat mixture and mix well with a large spoon. Try not to overmix or the texture of the loaf will be too dense.

Spray a rectangular baking pan with vegetable-oil spray. Turn the meat mixture into the pan and form it into a loaf. Bake until browned and juicy, about 50 minutes.

Cut into 6 or 8 slices and serve.

# Pontchartrain Smoked Pork Chops Maque Choux

MAKES 6 SERVINGS

★

*Maque choux*, pronounced "mock-shoe," is a well-seasoned dish of corn. When I was a boy my mother made chicken or crawfish *maque choux*. I thought pork would work well, too, and so it does—in this case the deep, smoky flavor of the chops blends wonderfully with the seasoned corn.

SEASONING MIX

*1 tablespoon paprika*
*1 tablespoon dried chopped chives*
*1 tablespoon dried parsley flakes*
*2 teaspoons salt*
*2 teaspoons garlic powder*
*2 teaspoons onion powder*
*2 teaspoons dry mustard*
*1½ teaspoons black pepper*
*1 teaspoon white pepper*
*1 teaspoon dried thyme leaves*
*1 teaspoon dried sweet basil leaves*
*1 teaspoon ground nutmeg*

*6 smoked pork chops, each about*
   *1 inch thick*
*5 tablespoons unsalted butter*
*4 cups chopped onions, in all*
*3 cups chopped celery, in all*
*1 cup chopped green bell peppers*
*½ cup chopped fresh parsley*
*8 cups fresh corn kernels (about*
   *10 to 12 large ears), in all*
*4 cups chopped peeled fresh*
   *tomatoes*

☆

Combine the seasoning mix ingredients thoroughly in a small bowl. Makes 7 tablespoons plus 1½ teaspoons.

Trim the fat from the pork chops, and cut the fat into small dice.

Using a small, sharp knife, cut a 1-inch slit in the top edge of each chop. Stick the tip of the knife into the slit and cut a large pocket inside each chop, without enlarging the slit; the slit should be just large enough to get the stuffing in using a teaspoon.

Place the diced pork fat in a large heavy pot over high heat. Cook until the fat renders to a liquid with some crispy pieces, about 6 minutes. Add the butter, and when it has melted, add *2 cups* of the onions, *2 cups* of the celery, the bell peppers, parsley, *1 cup* of the corn, and *3 tablespoons* of the seasoning mix. Stir well, cover, and cook, uncovering the pot occasionally to scrape the bottom, about 16 to 18 minutes. Remove 1½ cups of the mixture from the pot and set aside.

Add the *remaining 2 cups* onions and *1 cup* celery and the *remaining* seasoning mix to the pot. Stir well, cover, and cook, occasionally uncovering to stir, about 7 minutes. Add the tomatoes and scrape the bottom of the pot. Stir in the *remaining 7 cups* corn, cover, and cook 5 minutes. Remove from the heat. Makes about 9 cups.

Preheat the oven to 250°.

Use a teaspoon to stuff the pork chops with the reserved cooked vegetable mixture, allowing ¼ cup per chop. Place the chops, standing on the bone end if possible, in a baking pan approximately 15 by 10 inches. Carefully spoon the corn mixture around and between the pork chops. Cover loosely with a tent of aluminum foil and bake until the chops are cooked through, tender, and juicy, about 2 hours.

Allow 1 pork chop served over 1½ cups of the *maque choux* per person.

# Chicago Pork Roast
# with Dill Sauce

MAKES 6 SERVINGS

Pork has been a popular meat in the American diet since the first European settlers arrived in the New World. In the late nineteenth century, Chicago became the center of the pork-processing industry, and pork consumption began to rise in the Midwest. Today, as at the turn of the century, no one would be surprised to see a succulent pork roast on a Midwesterner's Sunday dinner table. Or on mine!

*1 tablespoon salt*

*2 teaspoons ground Anaheim
   chile pepper (see Note)*

*2 teaspoons ground Corona
   chile pepper (see Note)*

*1 teaspoon white pepper*

*1 teaspoon black pepper*

*1 teaspoon dry mustard*

*1 teaspoon dried thyme leaves*

*¾ teaspoon onion powder*

*½ teaspoon garlic powder*

*½ teaspoon ground cumin*

*½ teaspoon dried dill weed*

☆

*4 tablespoons unsalted butter,
   in all*

*1 cup chopped onions*

*1 cup chopped celery*

*1 tablespoon plus 1 teaspoon
   grated fresh ginger, in all*

*1 (5½-pound) boneless pork
   loin, from the sirloin end*

*3 branches fresh dill plus ¼ cup
   minced fresh dill, in all*

*¼ cup all-purpose flour*

*½ teaspoon minced fresh garlic*

*3 cups beef stock (see page 11),
   in all*

*1½ cups heavy cream, in all*

Preheat the oven to 350°.

Combine the seasoning mix ingredients thoroughly in a small bowl. Makes ¼ cup plus 1¼ teaspoons.

Melt *2 tablespoons* of the butter in an 8-inch skillet over high heat. When the butter sizzles, add the onions and celery, *2 teaspoons* of the seasoning mix, and *1 teaspoon* of the ginger. Cook, stirring once or twice, until the vegetables are browned, about 6 to 7 minutes. Remove from the heat and let cool.

Using a small, sharp knife, make small slits about 1 inch apart in the top of the meat, taking care not to cut all the way through. Using your fingers, stuff the holes with sprigs of dill pulled from the 3 branches (reserve 1 large sprig for garnish). Sprinkle *1 tablespoon plus 1 teaspoon* of the seasoning mix all over the meat and work it in well with your hands. Spread the vegetable mixture over the top and sides of the roast. Place the meat in a roasting pan and roast until the pork is fork tender and juicy, about 2¼ hours.

Pour off the drippings from the pan, and cover the pork to keep warm. Skim *⅓ cup* of fat from the drippings. Combine this fat with the *remaining 2 tablespoons* butter in a 10-inch skillet over high heat. When the butter has melted, whisk in the flour. Add the garlic and *2 teaspoons* of the fresh ginger and cook, whisking constantly, 2 minutes. Add the minced dill and

*1½ cups* of the stock and cook, whisking, 2 minutes. Add *1 tablespoon plus 1 teaspoon* of the seasoning mix and cook 1 minute, whisking. Add *1 cup* of the cream and cook, whisking, 5 minutes. Add the *remaining ½ cup* cream, *1 teaspoon* ginger, and *1½ cups* stock and cook, whisking, 4 minutes. Add *2 teaspoons* of the seasoning mix, cook 2 minutes, and remove from the heat. Makes about 4½ cups sauce.

To serve, slice the pork, drizzle the sauce over, and garnish with a sprig of dill.

NOTE: These are the chile peppers we used. You can use whatever is available in your area, but be sure to buy pure ground chile peppers, not commercial chili powder.

# Chinatown Chop Suey and Twice-Fried Rice

### MAKES 4 TO 6 SERVINGS

★

*Tsap sui* is a Cantonese term meaning "miscellaneous fragments" or "chopped-up odds and ends"—and that about approximates the essence of chop suey. It was probably created by a Chinese cook who was feeding indentured Chinese laborers on the Central Pacific Railroad in the middle of the last century. We put our chop suey together with a double-fried rice that complements it beautifully and elevates it almost to elegance. Almost. But the real point is, it tastes incredibly good. Because of the way the rice is cooked, it comes out both juicy and crunchy all at once. The crispness of the vegetables and the blend of flavors combine to make this dish irresistible. Have all the ingredients ready before you begin, because it cooks very quickly.

SEASONING MIX

2 teaspoons salt
2 teaspoons dried cilantro leaves
1½ teaspoons dry mustard
1½ teaspoons onion powder
1½ teaspoons ground ginger
1 teaspoon white pepper
1 teaspoon garlic powder
1 teaspoon dried thyme leaves
1 teaspoon black pepper
½ teaspoon sugar

☆

1 pound pork tenderloin
  (chilled, for easy slicing)
1 tablespoon soy sauce
2 tablespoons dry sherry
2 tablespoons unsalted butter
3 tablespoons chopped onions
2 tablespoons chopped green bell
  peppers
1 cup uncooked converted rice
3½ cups chicken stock
  (see page 11), in all

½ cup plus 1 tablespoon peanut
  oil, in all
1½ cups julienned onions
1 tablespoon plus 2 teaspoons
  cornstarch, in all
1 tablespoon finely minced fresh
  ginger
1 large garlic clove, finely minced
⅓ cup sliced canned water
  chestnuts
⅓ cup sliced canned bamboo
  shoots
¼ cup julienned red bell pepper
¼ cup julienned yellow bell
  pepper
1 celery stalk, thinly sliced on the
  bias
1¾ cups small fresh mushrooms,
  thinly sliced
1 cup fresh bean sprouts or
  sunflower sprouts
3 eggs
½ cup chopped green onion tops

Preheat the oven to 350°.

Combine the seasoning mix ingredients thoroughly in a small bowl. Makes ¼ cup plus 1 teaspoon.

Cut the pork into paper-thin slices and place in a bowl. Sprinkle *1 tablespoon* of the seasoning mix, the soy sauce, and sherry over the pork and work in well with your hands. Set aside.

Melt the butter in a 12-inch skillet over high heat. When the butter is sizzling, add the chopped onions and peppers, stir, and cook 1 minute. Stir in the rice and cook until it begins to brown, about 2 minutes. Stir in *2 cups* of the chicken stock and bring to a simmer. Cover the skillet tightly and bake until all the liquid is absorbed by the rice, about 17 minutes. Remove from the oven and set aside.

Meanwhile, heat *2 tablespoons* of the peanut oil in an 8-inch skillet over high heat. When the oil is very hot, add the shredded onions and *1 teaspoon* of the seasoning mix. Cook, stirring and shaking the pan occasionally, until the onions are browned and caramelized, about 4 to 6 minutes. Remove from the heat and set aside.

Heat ¼ *cup* of the peanut oil in a 12-inch skillet over high heat. While the oil is heating, sprinkle *1 tablespoon* of the cornstarch over the meat and rub it in with your hands. When the oil is very hot, add the pork to the skillet. Cook, turning once or twice, until the meat is browned, about 2 to 3 minutes. Stir in the fresh ginger and garlic and cook, stirring occasionally, about 2½ minutes. Add the water chestnuts, bamboo shoots, shredded bell peppers, celery, and mushrooms and cook, stirring occasionally, 1 minute. Stir in *2 teaspoons* of the seasoning mix and cook 30 seconds. Sprinkle over the *remaining 2 teaspoons* cornstarch and cook 1 minute, stirring, then add *1 cup* of the chicken stock, scrape the bottom of the skillet, and cook 1 minute. Add the *remaining* ½ *cup* stock, bring to a simmer, and remove from the heat. Stir in the caramelized onions and the sprouts. Makes 5 cups.

Heat the *remaining 3 tablespoons* peanut oil in a 10-inch skillet over high heat. Whip the eggs in a small bowl, and, when the oil is very hot, pour the eggs into the skillet. Immediately stir in the cooked rice, the green onions, and the *remaining* seasoning mix. Cook, stirring continuously and shaking the pan often, until the eggs are set, about 5 minutes. Remove from the heat and serve immediately.

To serve 6 portions, allow each person ⅓ cup of the fried rice with a generous ¾ cup of the chop suey on top; for 4 servings, give each person about ½ cup rice and 1¼ cups chop suey.

**44.**

# Three-Bean Salad with Hot Bacon Dressing

*page 226*

45.

# San Diego Shrimp Salad

*page 233*

46.

# Connecticut Corn Pudding

*page 238*

**47.**

Baked Onions Stuffed with Pork and Mushrooms

*page 242*

**48.**

# Hoppin' John

*page 248*

49.

# Maids of Honor

*page 269*

50.

# Down-Home Coconut-Pecan Candy Bar Cake

*page 272*

*Clockwise from top:*

51. Shaker Apple Dumplings *page 281*

52. Berry Cobbler (with blueberries) *page 287*

53. Strawberry Shortcake *page 288*

# Chuck Wagon Beans

MAKES 6 SERVINGS

★

Many wonderful recipes for bean dishes were handed down from one generation of chuck wagon cooks to another, some cooked with beef, others with pork. The most important thing to remember is that a pot of beans must be watched closely so the beans won't burn. Our thanks to Paula LaCour, who is our chief accountant and our very best eater, for retesting these at home.

*1 pound dried pinto beans*

SEASONING MIX
*1 tablespoon salt*
*2 teaspoons paprika*
*1½ teaspoons onion powder*
*1 teaspoon garlic powder*
*1 teaspoon black pepper*
*1 teaspoon white pepper*
*1 teaspoon ground cumin*
*1 teaspoon dried thyme leaves*
*½ teaspoon ground coriander*
*½ teaspoon ground savory*

☆

*1 pound pork spareribs,*
*    separated and cut into 2-inch*
*    lengths*
*2 cups chopped onions*
*1 cup chopped green bell peppers*
*1 cup chopped celery*
*¼ cup chopped fresh jalapeño*
*    peppers (see Note)*
*1½ cups chopped fresh Anaheim*
*    peppers (see Note), in all*
*11 cups pork or chicken stock*
*    (see page 11), in all*
*1 (6-ounce) can tomato paste*

**DAY 1:** Put the beans in a large bowl, add hot water to cover, and let soak overnight.

**DAY 2:** Combine the seasoning mix ingredients thoroughly in a small bowl. Makes ¼ cup plus ½ teaspoon. Sprinkle *2 teaspoons* of the seasoning mix all over the ribs and pat in well with your hands.

Drain the beans.

Heat a large heavy pot or kettle (preferably cast iron) over high heat until smoking hot, about 4 to 5 minutes. Place the ribs in the pot and cook until browned, about 3 minutes. Turn the ribs over and cook until browned on the second side, about 3 minutes. Stir in the onions, bell peppers, celery, jalapeño peppers, *½ cup* of the Anaheim peppers, and *1 tablespoon* of the seasoning mix. Cover and cook, uncovering occasionally to stir, until a crust begins to form on the bottom of the pot, about 3 to 4 minutes. Stir in *1 cup* of the stock, scrape up the crust on the pot bottom, and cook 3 minutes. Stir in the drained beans, cover, and cook, uncovering occasionally to scrape the pot bottom, about 4 to 5 minutes. Stir in *1 tablespoon* of the seasoning mix, cover, and cook, uncovering occasionally to scrape, until the mixture is sticking hard (but not burning), 8 to 10 minutes. Add *5 cups* more stock, the tomato paste, the *remaining 1 cup* Anaheim peppers, and the *remaining* seasoning mix. Stir, cover, and bring to a boil. Reduce the heat to low and simmer, uncovering often to scrape the pot, about 35 minutes. Stir in *2 cups* more stock, scrape the pot bottom, cover, and bring back to a boil. Lower the heat and simmer, covered, 30 minutes. Stir in the *remaining 3 cups* stock, scrape, and bring back to a boil. Reduce the heat to low, cover, and simmer 15 minutes. Uncover and cook, scraping often, 30 minutes. Serve with warm corn bread and a hearty salad.

NOTE: These are the peppers we used. If you can't find them, substitute peppers of similar heat intensities.

# Navajo Tacos

MAKES 10 SERVINGS

*Color photograph 43*

★

Many native Americans living in the Southwest make a kind of fry-bread, which tastes good with just about anything—especially a spicy chili or stew. But even more fun is topping a crisp fry-bread with seasoned meat and salsa for a meal-in-one Navajo treat. Make the salsa and the filling first. Then fry the bread right before you plan to eat it, because the texture changes as it cools. And be prepared for the most delicious tacos you've ever eaten!

### SALSA

2 fresh serrano chile peppers,
   chopped (see Note)
3 large fresh Anaheim peppers,
   chopped (see Note)
2 fresh cayenne peppers,
   chopped (see Note)
3 fresh jalapeño peppers,
   chopped (see Note)
¾ cup chopped green bell
   peppers
1½ cups chopped onions
1 cup packed chopped fresh
   cilantro
4 large fresh tomatoes,
   coarsely chopped
2 tablespoons distilled white
   vinegar
Juice of 1 lemon
2 tablespoons dark brown
   sugar

### SEASONING MIX

2 teaspoons salt
2 teaspoons ground guajillo
   chile pepper (see Note)
1¾ teaspoons ground arbol chile
   pepper (see Note)
1½ teaspoons ground cumin
1½ teaspoons dried oregano
   leaves
1 teaspoon garlic powder
1 teaspoon onion powder
1 teaspoon black pepper
1 teaspoon white pepper

☆

### FILLING

1 small lamb roast,
   approximately 1½ pounds
   if boneless, 2 pounds
   if bone-in, or 1½ pounds
   lamb stew meat
2 cups chopped onions
4 tablespoons unsalted butter
1 (4-ounce) can chopped green
   chiles
2 large garlic cloves, sliced
1 cup chopped green bell
   peppers
½ cup chopped fresh Anaheim
   peppers or any fresh mild
   chile peppers
¼ cup all-purpose flour
2¾ cups chicken stock
   (see page 11), in all

### INDIAN FRY-BREAD

5 cups all-purpose flour,
   in all
½ cup powdered nondairy
   creamer
1 tablespoon plus 1 teaspoon
   baking powder
½ cup powdered milk
1 teaspoon salt
2 cups water
3 to 4 cups vegetable oil

**FOR THE SALSA,** combine the peppers, onions, and cilantro in a large bowl. Stir in the tomatoes, vinegar, lemon juice, and sugar. Blend thoroughly with a spoon and set aside.

Combine the seasoning mix ingredients thoroughly in a small bowl. Makes ¼ cup plus ¾ teaspoon.

**FOR THE FILLING,** cut all the visible fat from the lamb, chop the fat into small pieces, and set aside.

Cut the lamb into 1-inch cubes and place in a small bowl. Sprinkle *1 tablespoon plus 1 teaspoon* of the seasoning mix over the lamb cubes and work it in well with your hands.

Render the reserved lamb fat in a 10-inch skillet over high heat until fairly dark and smoky, about 4 to 6 minutes. Add the onions and *1 tablespoon* of the seasoning mix. Stir once and cook until the onions start sticking to the bottom of the pan, about 4 minutes. Stir in the butter. As soon as the butter has melted, add the lamb. Scrape up the crust on the bottom of the skillet and cook, scraping the pan bottom occasionally, about 10 minutes. Stir in the chilies and garlic and cook 2 minutes. Stir in the bell peppers, Anaheim peppers, and *2 teaspoons* of the seasoning mix and cook 2 minutes. Stir in the flour and cook, scraping the bottom of the pan occasionally, 3 minutes. Stir in *2 cups* of the chicken stock, scrape up the crust on the bottom of the skillet, and bring the stock to a bubbling boil. Reduce the heat to medium and simmer, uncovered, 5 minutes. The mixture should be thick and dark. Stir in the *remaining ¾ cup* stock and cook until the mixture reduces slightly, about 11 minutes. Remove from the heat and keep warm. Makes about 5 cups.

**FOR THE FRY-BREAD,** sift *4 cups* of the flour, the nondairy creamer, baking powder, powdered milk, and salt together into a mixing bowl. Add the water and mix well until a soft dough forms. Sift the *remaining 1 cup* flour over the board or counter on which you'll be working the dough, and flour your hands thoroughly. Pull off a large handful of dough and pat it out with floured hands into a thin, flat, round cake. Keep flouring the work area and your hands as you form cakes from the remaining dough; you should get 10 cakes.

Heat *2 cups* of the oil in an 8-inch skillet over high heat until very hot (about 350°). Fry the cakes one at a time, turning two or three times, until golden brown, about 30 to 45 seconds. Drain thoroughly on paper towels. Add oil as necessary, and allow it to get hot before adding additional cakes.

Cover each fry-bread with ½ cup of the lamb mixture. Top with salsa and serve immediately.

NOTE: If you can't find the fresh peppers we used, substitute peppers of similar heat intensities. The cayennes are the hottest of those we used, the serranos almost as hot, the jalapeños a bit milder, and the Anaheims very mild.

We used ground guajillo and arbol chile peppers. You can use whatever is available in your area, but be sure to buy pure ground chile peppers, not commercial chili powder.

# Empanadas

MAKES ABOUT 14 EMPANADAS

Empanadas and other little turnovers or pies were brought to this country by Hispanic immigrants from Mexico, Cuba, and Puerto Rico. Sometimes they're filled with sweets and served for dessert, sometimes they're filled with leftovers the day after a big dinner. Ours are sweet-spicy meat pies filled with pork, raisins, and almonds and laced with enough chile peppers to make anyone sit up and pay attention. Once you get the knack of making these, you're sure to start coming up with your own ideas for fillings.

SEASONING MIX

2¾ teaspoons salt

2½ teaspoons ground ancho
   chile pepper (see Note)

2 teaspoons ground guajillo
   chile pepper (see Note)

¾ teaspoon ground pasilla chile
   pepper (see Note)

½ teaspoon ground New Mexico
   chile pepper (see Note)

1½ teaspoons dried oregano
   leaves

¾ teaspoon dried sweet basil
   leaves

¾ teaspoon ground cumin

¾ teaspoon onion powder

¾ teaspoon garlic powder

½ teaspoon white pepper

½ teaspoon ground cinnamon

¼ teaspoon ground allspice

☆

FILLING

½ cup slivered almonds

3 tablespoons peanut oil

2 cups chopped onions

1 cup chopped green bell peppers

1½ pounds lean pork, cut into
   small cubes

1¼ cups grated potatoes (about
   1 medium potato)

2 cups beef stock (see page 11),
   in all

1 teaspoon minced fresh garlic

½ cup raisins

4 cups finely diced peeled apples


DOUGH

1 cup raisins

3¼ cups all-purpose flour

3 tablespoons sugar

1 teaspoon salt

8 ounces cream cheese, cut in
   cubes

14 tablespoons (1¾ sticks)
   unsalted butter, cut into about
   14 pats

2 to 2½ tablespoons cold water


FINISH

1 egg

2 tablespoons water

Vegetable oil cooking spray

All-purpose flour


Combine the seasoning mix ingredients thoroughly in a small bowl. Makes ¼ cup plus 2¼ teaspoons.

**FOR THE FILLING,** toast the almonds in a dry 8-inch skillet over medium-low heat, shaking the pan and stirring frequently, until the almonds are a light golden brown, about 4 to 5 minutes. Set aside.

Heat the oil in a 12-inch skillet over high heat. When the oil is very hot, add the onions and bell peppers and cook, stirring occasionally, until the onions start to brown, about 4 to 5 minutes. Stir in *1 tablespoon* of the seasoning mix and cook 2 minutes. Move the vegetables to one side of the skillet and add the pork to the cleared space. Sprinkle *2 tablespoons* of the seasoning mix over the meat and cook 2 minutes without stirring. Stir the meat and cook, stirring occasionally, until the pork is sticking to the bottom of the skillet, about 4 to 5 minutes. Stir the vegetables into the pork and scrape up any brown crust on the bottom of the skillet. Stir in the potatoes and cook until a hard crust forms on the bottom of the skillet, about 2 to 3 minutes. Add *1 cup* of the beef stock and scrape up the crust on the skillet bottom. Stir in the garlic and *1 tablespoon* of the seasoning mix and bring to a boil. Cook 4 minutes, scraping the bottom of the skillet to prevent sticking. Add the *remaining 1 cup* stock, scrape the skillet bottom, and cook 1 minute. Add the raisins, scrape the bottom of the skillet, and cook 3 minutes. Add the apples and *1 teaspoon* of the seasoning mix. Cook, scraping the skillet bottom occasionally, about 2 minutes. Remove from the heat and stir in the toasted almonds. Let cool. Makes 7 cups.

Preheat the oven to 400°.

**FOR THE DOUGH,** place the raisins in the bowl of a food processor and whirl them until finely ground, about 1 to 2 minutes. Add the flour, sugar, and salt, and then distribute the cream cheese and butter pats evenly over the dry ingredients. Process until well blended, about 45 to 55 seconds. With the food processor running, add *2 tablespoons* of the water in a thin stream and process until the mixture becomes a cohesive dough; add some or all of the *remaining* water if necessary.

**TO FINISH,** lightly beat together the egg and water to make an egg wash.

Coat 2 baking sheets with cooking spray.

Sprinkle a light coating of flour over a clean countertop. Pull off a fistful of dough and roll out to a thickness of about ¼ inch. Using a 7-inch plate as a guide, cut out a round. Save the scraps to reroll, and repeat with the remaining dough. You should get 14 circles. If the scraps won't cooperate, moisten your hands with water before kneading them back into a ball of dough.

Brush each round of dough with egg wash. Heap 4 to 5 tablespoons filling on one half of each round and fold over into a half-moon shape. Fold over the edges and press with the tines of a fork to seal. Place the empanadas about 1 inch apart on the baking sheets and brush the tops with egg wash.

Bake until golden brown, about 25 to 30 minutes.

Serve warm.

NOTE: These are the ground chile peppers we used. You can use whatever is available in your area, but be sure to buy pure ground chile peppers, not commercial chili powder.

# SALADS
## *and*
# DRESSINGS

The salad offers a great opportunity to create truly different combinations of taste, and it can be a very important part of the meal or a wonderful meal in itself. For me, the fun is in being able to get spectacular taste and texture using a variety of greens and other vegetables. And the possibilities are almost endless; they run the gamut from greens that are peppery tasting and heavy textured or even spiny and sharp tasting to vegetables that seem buttery and even sweet, like Vidalia or Walla Walla onions.

For a long time, salads took a back seat to heavier foods, but in the nineteenth century, Delmonico's restaurant in New York City helped make the salad a fashionable food item. In the twentieth century, California became the state most identified with salads, and it is the birthplace of a number of famous ones, including Cobb and Green Goddess.

When a salad is to be part of a larger meal, it should complement the other dishes. If the main course is heavy, rich, or saucy, the salad should be a simple one of crisp greens with a light vinaigrette. But if the main course is lighter and unsauced, do get more creative with your salad: Try greens and vegetables with lots of texture and a creamy dressing with some sweetness and some wonderful acids from citrus or fruit vinegars.

# Connecticut Coleslaw

MAKES 16 TO 20 SIDE-DISH SERVINGS

★

Coleslaw has become a familiar accompaniment everywhere in the United States, although the Germans who settled in Pennsylvania probably made it first. Sometimes it's just a limp mass of oversweetened, overmayo-ed cabbage, a garnish to be nudged to the side as one eats the "real" food on the plate. But a good coleslaw can be a wonderful catalyst, enhancing the flavors of fried chicken or any other food it happens to escort to the table. This coleslaw recipe comes from the Northeast, and we think it's dynamite!

| | |
|---|---|
| 1 egg | 2 tablespoons apple cider |
| 2 egg yolks | vinegar |
| 2 teaspoons dry mustard | 1 tablespoon fresh lemon juice |
| 1½ teaspoons salt | 3 tablespoons sugar |
| 1¼ teaspoons white pepper | 10 cups coarsely chopped green |
| ½ teaspoon minced fresh | cabbage |
| garlic | 2 cups coarsely chopped purple |
| 1 cup vegetable oil, in all | cabbage |
| ¾ cup chopped onions | 2 cups coarsely grated carrots |

Place the egg, egg yolks, mustard, salt, white pepper, and garlic in the container of a blender and process 5 seconds. Add ½ cup of the oil in a steady stream. Add the onions, vinegar, and lemon juice and process. Add the sugar and the *remaining ½ cup* oil and process about 20 seconds or until thoroughly combined and creamy.

Toss the cabbage and carrots together in a bowl; pour the dressing over and toss again. Serve immediately.

# Iowa Dutch Lettuce

MAKES 10 LUNCH SERVINGS

A hot salad popular in the small towns of Iowa, Dutch Lettuce can be made with numerous variations. The one we've created is so satisfying, it could even be the main course.

SEASONING MIX
1 tablespoon salt
1 teaspoon white pepper
1 teaspoon dry mustard
1 teaspoon paprika
½ teaspoon garlic powder
½ teaspoon onion powder
½ teaspoon celery seed

☆

¾ pound bacon, diced
14 tablespoons (1¾ sticks)
    unsalted butter, or more, as
    necessary, in all
1 egg

2 egg yolks
1½ cups plus 2 tablespoons
    white wine vinegar, in all
6 peeled hard-boiled eggs, in all
5 tablespoons sugar, in all
2 cups chopped onions
5¼ cups mashed potatoes (from
    about 6 to 8 large potatoes),
    in all
2 cups chicken stock (see page 11)
1 head iceberg lettuce, in all
½ cup chopped green onion tops
Paprika

Combine the seasoning mix ingredients thoroughly in a small bowl. Makes 2 tablespoons plus 1½ teaspoons.

Cook the bacon in a 10-inch skillet over high heat until light brown, about 8 to 9 minutes. Add *8 tablespoons (1 stick)* of the butter and heat just until the butter melts. Leaving the bacon in the pan, strain off the butter/bacon fat into a measuring cup. Add enough melted butter to make 1 cup if necessary. Set the skillet aside.

Place the raw egg and yolks in a food processor or blender. Add *2 tablespoons* of the vinegar and the *1 cup* butter/bacon fat, and process to blend well. Add *2* of the hard-boiled eggs, one at a time, then add *1 tablespoon* of the sugar and *1½ teaspoons* of the seasoning mix. Blend thoroughly and set this mayonaisse dressing aside.

Return the skillet with the bacon to high heat. Add the *remaining 6 tablespoons* butter and the onions and cook 5 minutes. Stir in the *remaining* seasoning mix and cook 3 minutes. Add *1 cup* of the mashed potatoes and cook 4 minutes or until the potatoes are sticking hard to the bottom of the pan. Stir in the chicken stock, *2 tablespoons* of the sugar, and the *remaining 1½ cups* vinegar. Bring to a boil and cook 10 minutes. Add ¼ *cup* more of the mashed potatoes and the *remaining 2 tablespoons* sugar and cook 17 to 20 minutes, or until most of the liquid has evaporated. Remove from the heat.

Meanwhile, cut out the core from the lettuce and cut the head of lettuce in half. Coarsely chop half the lettuce, finely shred the other half, and keep separate.

Combine the *remaining 4 cups* mashed potatoes with the coarsely chopped lettuce. Stir in the mixture from the skillet and turn it into a large casserole. Scatter the finely shredded lettuce over the top, and pour the mayonnaise dressing over all. Slice the *remaining 4* hard-boiled eggs and arrange on top. Sprinkle with the green onions and paprika and serve.

# Three-Bean Salad
# with Hot Bacon
# Dressing

MAKES APPROXIMATELY 6 CUPS; 4 LUNCH SERVINGS
OR 6 SIDE-DISH SERVINGS
*Color photograph 44*

This salad's probably an offshoot of the bean salads the Amish people brought with them to the New World. The seasoning mix we've created for it really pushes the sweet and sour flavors, and with its crunchy freshness this makes a terrific lunch.

1 cup dried red beans
1 cup dried chick peas
1 cup plus 6 tablespoons distilled
  white vinegar, in all
6 tablespoons sugar, in all


SEASONING MIX
2 teaspoons paprika
1 teaspoon dry mustard
1 teaspoon garlic powder
1 teaspoon onion powder
1 teaspoon salt
1 teaspoon white pepper
½ teaspoon black pepper
☆

1 tablespoon cornstarch
2 tablespoons water
8 slices bacon, diced
2½ cups chopped red onions,
  in all
1 cup chopped celery
4 small bay leaves
2 teaspoons minced fresh garlic,
  in all
4 cups chicken stock (see page
  11), in all
1 pound fresh green beans,
  trimmed and cut into 2-inch
  pieces
1 cup chopped green onion tops

**DAY 1:** Soak the red beans overnight in hot water to cover and *3 tablespoons* of the vinegar in a covered bowl. Soak the chick peas overnight in hot water to cover, *3 tablespoons* of the vinegar, and *2 tablespoons* of the sugar in another covered bowl.

**DAY 2:** Drain and rinse the red beans and chick peas.

Combine the seasoning mix ingredients thoroughly in a small bowl. Makes 2 tablespoons plus 1½ teaspoons.

Combine the cornstarch and water well and set aside.

Cook the bacon in an 8-inch skillet over high heat until soft and lightly browned, about 6 minutes. Stir in *1½ cups* of the red onions and cook until golden, about 4 minutes. Add the celery, red beans and chick peas, and *2 tablespoons* of the seasoning mix, and cook, occasionally scraping up the crust that forms on the bottom of the skillet, about 3 minutes. Stir in the bay leaves and the *remaining* seasoning mix, and cook, scraping the skillet occasionally, 3 minutes. Stir in the *remaining 1 cup* vinegar, *1 teaspoon* of the garlic, and *2 cups* of the stock. Bring to a boil, reduce the heat to medium, and cover the skillet. Cook, uncovering occasionally to stir, until the liquid is almost completely absorbed, about 30 to 40 minutes. Turn the heat up to high and add *1 cup* more stock. Bring to a boil, reduce the heat to medium, cover, and cook 15 minutes. Turn the heat up to high, stir in the green beans, and cook, uncovered, 1 minute. Stir the cornstarch/water mixture thoroughly, stir into the beans, and cook until the green beans turn a bright green color, about 2 minutes.

Turn the contents of the skillet into a large bowl. Add the green onion tops and the *remaining ¼ cup* sugar, *1 cup* red onion, *1 teaspoon* garlic, and *1 cup* stock. Toss well and serve hot or allow to cool to room temperature.

# Hot German Potato Salad

## MAKES 8 SIDE-DISH SERVINGS

★

The German immigrants brought a load of hearty fare to this country, and this dish is no exception. In German communities all over America, hot potato salad is a familiar side dish. It's particularly popular at large parties and events because it keeps well without refrigeration, since there's no mayonnaise in it.

**SEASONING MIX**
*1 teaspoon dry mustard*
*1 teaspoon onion powder*
*1 teaspoon garlic powder*
*1 teaspoon white pepper*
*½ teaspoon black pepper*
*½ teaspoon salt*

*20 unpeeled small red new*
  *potatoes*
*4 hard-boiled eggs, peeled and*
  *chopped*
*8 slices bacon, diced*
*1 cup chopped onions*
*¼ cup all-purpose flour*
*1 cup chicken stock (see page 11)*
*¾ cup distilled white vinegar*
*½ cup sugar*
*½ cup chopped green onion tops*
  *or chives*

Combine the seasoning mix ingredients thoroughly in a small bowl. Makes 1 tablespoon plus 2 teaspoons.

Cook the potatoes in a large pot of water until just tender (about 5 minutes from when the water starts to boil). Drain and cool under cold running water. Slice the potatoes ¼ inch thick and place in a large bowl. Add the eggs and mix well. Set aside.

Sauté the bacon in a 10-inch skillet over high heat until browned, about 7 minutes. Remove the bacon from the skillet with a slotted spoon and set aside.

Pour off all but 2 tablespoons bacon fat from the skillet and set the skillet over high heat. Add the onions and cook, scraping the bottom of the skillet occasionally, until the onions are golden, about 3 to 5 minutes. Add all of the seasoning mix, and then whisk in the flour. Slowly add the chicken stock, vinegar, and sugar, whisking constantly. Cook, whisking frequently, until the mixture is thick, about 5 to 6 minutes. Remove from the heat. Makes about 2¾ cups.

Fold the sauce into the potato and egg mixture, add the green onions and the cooked bacon, and combine thoroughly. Makes about 8 cups.

This is best served warm, but it's also good at room temperature.

# Crab Louis

MAKES 4 LUNCH SERVINGS

★

Most reports agree that this dish was first created in San Francisco around the turn of the century, although there is some dispute as to whether it originated at the St. Francis Hotel or Solari's restaurant. We don't care, we just love it, especially when it's seasoned properly to get the best taste from the fresh ingredients. You might want to prepare and garnish this salad in the morning and pull it out of the refrigerator just in time for a special lunch.

SEASONING MIX
*1½ teaspoons salt*
*1½ teaspoons white pepper*
*1 teaspoon dried sweet basil
 leaves*
*1 teaspoon garlic powder*
*1 teaspoon onion powder*
*1 teaspoon dry mustard*
*¾ teaspoon dried thyme leaves*
*½ teaspoon black pepper*
*½ teaspoon ground cinnamon*

☆

*2 tablespoons olive oil*
*1 cup chopped onions*
*1 cup chopped green bell peppers*
*½ cup chopped celery*
*2 eggs*

*1 egg yolk*
*¼ cup tarragon vinegar*
*1 cup vegetable oil, in all*
*1 tablespoon prepared Dijon
 mustard*
*1 fresh tomato, cut into 8 wedges*
*1 pound lump crabmeat, picked
 over for shells and cartilage*
*½ cup diced tomatoes*
*½ cup chopped green onion
 tops, plus extra for garnish*
*3 hard-boiled eggs, peeled and
 chopped*
*2 cups shredded lettuce*
*Tomato wedges*
*Sliced black olives*

Combine the seasoning mix ingredients thoroughly in a small bowl. Makes 2 tablespoons plus 2¾ teaspoons.

Heat the olive oil in an 8-inch skillet over high heat. When the oil is hot, add the onions, bell peppers, and celery and *1 tablespoon plus 2 teaspoons* of the seasoning mix. Cook, stirring and shaking the pan occasionally, until the onions are golden brown, about 5 to 6 minutes. Remove from the heat and set aside to cool.

Process the raw eggs, egg yolk, and vinegar in a food processor or blender, until blended, about 10 to 15 seconds. With the machine running, slowly drizzle in *½ cup* of the vegetable oil in a thin stream. Add the mustard, tomato wedges, *1 teaspoon* of the seasoning mix, and the cooled cooked vegetables, scraping all the seasoning from the skillet. Process until thoroughly blended, about 1 minute. Drizzle in the *remaining ½ cup* vegetable oil and process until the dressing is creamy and smooth, about 1 minute.

Combine the crabmeat, diced tomatoes, green onions, hard-boiled eggs, and the *remaining* seasoning mix in a large bowl. Toss well. Gently fold in 1½ cups of the dressing.

For each serving, place ½ *cup* of the shredded lettuce on a plate and sprinkle 2 tablespoons of the dressing over the lettuce. Cover with about 1 cup of the crab mixture and top with 2 tablespoons more dressing. Garnish with tomato wedges, sliced olives, and green onions.

# New Jersey Dilled Steak Salad

## MAKES 6 LUNCH SERVINGS

Although it took a long time for salads to catch on in this country, once they did they became very popular, and they continue to become even more so in the ongoing quest for lighter, healthier meals. Main-course salads with meats seem to have originated in the eastern part of the United States, and this one has its roots in New Jersey.

SEASONING MIX
1 tablespoon salt
2 teaspoons dried sweet basil
  leaves
1¾ teaspoons dried thyme leaves
1½ teaspoons paprika
1½ teaspoons dry mustard
1½ teaspoons black pepper
1½ teaspoons onion powder
1 teaspoon white pepper
1 teaspoon ground savory
1 teaspoon dried dill weed
½ teaspoon garlic powder
½ teaspoon dried marjoram
  leaves
½ teaspoon ground nutmeg

2 pounds boneless sirloin tip
  roast, sliced into ½-inch slivers
3 tablespoons olive oil, in all
6 tablespoons white wine vinegar
½ cup snipped fresh dill
1¾ cups chopped celery, in all
1½ cups chopped onions, in all
2 cups sliced fresh mushrooms
12 cherry tomatoes, halved
½ cup finely chopped chives or
  green onions
1 small jar marinated artichoke
  hearts, drained

Combine the seasoning mix ingredients thoroughly in a small bowl. Makes 5 tablespoons plus 2¼ teaspoons.

Sprinkle *3 tablespoons* of the seasoning mix and *2 tablespoons* of the olive oil over the meat and work it in well with your hands.

Combine the vinegar, fresh dill, and *1 tablespoon* of the seasoning mix in a small bowl. Add the *remaining 1 tablespoon* oil, and mix well with a fork. Set aside.

Heat a large heavy skillet over high heat. When the skillet is very hot, add the meat and brown it quickly on both sides until just medium-rare, about 2 to 3 minutes. Remove the meat with a slotted spoon and set aside. Add *1¼ cups* of the celery, *1 cup* of the onions, and *1 tablespoon* of the seasoning mix to the skillet, stir, cover, and cook over high heat, uncovering once or twice to stir, until the onions are browned, about 7 minutes. Stir in the *remaining* seasoning mix, cover, and cook, scraping the bottom of the skillet once or twice when the mixture sticks, about 8 minutes. Return the meat to the skillet, stir well, and transfer the mixture to a large bowl.

Add the mushrooms, cherry tomatoes, chives or green onions, artichoke hearts, and the *remaining ½ cup* each celery and onions to the beef mixture. Add the dill dressing, toss well, cover, and marinate at least 8 hours in the refrigerator.

Serve cold or at room temperature.

# San Diego Shrimp Salad

MAKES 6 LUNCH SERVINGS

*Color photograph 45*

★

When I think of a great salad, I automatically think of California, since that state is where some of our most memorable salads, like Cobb and Green Goddess, were created. The dressing for this salad combines some of the flavors associated with the West Coast, and the blend of sweet and tangy, cool and hot pleases the tongue and complements the ingredients in the salad itself.

*1 cup (4 ounces) sliced almonds, in all*

*1 pound cooked peeled shrimp*

*1 pound plus 1 cup seedless white grapes*

*6 celery stalks, thinly sliced on the diagonal*

*1 (8-ounce) can sliced water chestnuts, drained*

*1 small pineapple, peeled, cored, and cut into bite-size pieces*

*1½ cups mayonnaise*

*2 tablespoons plus 1½ teaspoons curry powder*

*2 tablespoons orange marmalade*

*2 tablespoons honey*

*2 teaspoons Worcestershire sauce*

*2 tablespoons apple cider vinegar*

*½ teaspoon ground cardamom*

*¾ teaspoon dry mustard*

*¾ teaspoon Creole (preferred) or other prepared brown mustard*

*1 teaspoon dried dill weed*

*1 teaspoon dried sweet basil leaves*

*½ teaspoon finely minced fresh garlic*

*Juice of ½ lime*

*½ cup olive oil*

*2 teaspoons salt*

*Belgian endive leaves*

*Boston or limestone lettuce leaves*

Toast the almonds in a small skillet over medium heat, shaking the pan constantly until the almonds are light brown, about 4 to 6 minutes. Remove from the heat and set aside.

Combine the shrimp, *1 pound* of the grapes, the celery, *¾ cup* of the toasted almonds, the water chestnuts, and pineapple in a large bowl.

Combine the mayonnaise, curry powder, marmalade, honey, Worcestershire sauce, vinegar, cardamom, dry and prepared mustards, dill weed, basil, garlic, and lime juice in the container of a blender. Process at high speed about 30 seconds. Add the *remaining 1 cup* grapes and ¼ *cup* almonds and process about 20 seconds. Add the oil and salt and process until completely smooth and creamy, about 30 to 40 seconds. Makes about 3 cups.

Arrange a bed of lettuce and endive leaves on each serving dish. Scoop about 1½ cups salad onto the lettuce and cover with ½ cup dressing.

# SIDE DISHES
## *and*
# NOSHES

In the American quest to eat nourishing, well-rounded meals, side dishes became essential. If the main dish was meat or fowl, the cook was likely to serve a starch and a vegetable as well. The starch might be in the form of a potato or rice dish; the vegetable would be whatever was grown fresh and in season at the time.

Unfortunately, side dishes were misunderstood for a long time and were simply "go-alongs"—overcooked, underseasoned necessities. Now we take side dishes far more seriously, knowing they can make a meal more memorable with their own exciting flavors and eye appeal.

Side dishes can also be functional. For instance, starches such as rice, pasta, or potatoes in dishes like Idaho Potato Cake or Savannah Red Rice can be a counterpoint to harsher, hotter, or spicier flavors in the main dish, or they can add a different texture to the meal. Vegetables such as Connecticut Corn Pudding and Kansas Stuffed Squash can add art to the table because they're colorful and thoughtfully prepared and arranged.

# Connecticut Corn Pudding

MAKES 6 TO 8 SERVINGS

*Color photograph 46*

★

Corn—the oldest staple of the American diet—lends itself deliciously to hundreds of recipes. This one is a favorite all over the country, although the ingredients vary slightly from region to region. We chose a recipe from the Northeast and added a simple seasoning mix that brings out the individual flavors of the corn, bell peppers, and ham while blending them together in the happiest way.

SEASONING MIX
*1½ teaspoons salt*
*1 teaspoon white pepper*
*1 teaspoon garlic powder*
*1 teaspoon dried sweet basil
   leaves*
*½ teaspoon black pepper*
*½ teaspoon onion powder*

☆

*5 tablespoons unsalted butter*
*1½ cups diced lean ham (about
   6 ounces)*
*1½ cups chopped onions*
*1 cup chopped green bell peppers*
*3 cups fresh corn kernels (about
   6 ears)*
*½ cup yellow cornmeal*
*1 cup canned evaporated milk*
*1½ cups whole milk,* in all
*4 eggs*
*Vegetable oil cooking spray*

Preheat the oven to 350°.

Combine the seasoning mix ingredients thoroughly in a small bowl. Makes 1 tablespoon plus 2½ teaspoons.

Melt the butter in a 10-inch skillet over high heat. When the butter is sizzling, add the ham, onions, and bell peppers. Cook, stirring, until the vegetables are soft, about 4 minutes. Stir in the seasoning mix and cook, stirring once, until a light crust forms on the bottom of the skillet, about 4 minutes. Add the corn, scrape the bottom of the skillet, and cook 4 minutes. Stir in the cornmeal and cook, scraping the bottom of the skillet to keep the cornmeal from burning, about 1 to 2 minutes. Add the evaporated milk and scrape the bottom of the skillet well. Add $\frac{1}{2}$ *cup* of the whole milk, scrape the bottom of the skillet again, and remove from the heat. Let cool a few minutes.

Whip the eggs with a wire whisk in a medium-size mixing bowl until frothy, about 45 seconds. Add the *remaining 1 cup* whole milk and whip until thoroughly blended. Fold the cooled corn mixture into the egg mixture.

Coat a 9- by 9- by 2-inches deep casserole with cooking spray, pour in the corn mixture, and bake until the pudding is set, about 35 to 45 minutes.

Cut into wedges or spoon the pudding onto plates, and serve warm.

# Upstate New York Mushroom Turnovers

MAKES 12 TURNOVERS

★

Both wild and cultivated mushrooms are abundant in the United States, especially throughout New York, Connecticut, Delaware, and Pennsylvania. Americans eat their mushrooms raw in salads, sautéed, sauced, steamed, stewed, souffléed, deep-fried, deviled, dilled, boiled, broiled, buttered, and creamed. One of our favorite mushroom dishes is this one for turnovers, which came to us from New York State farm country. The filling is a medley of two kinds of mushrooms, chopped pork, onions, and cream—and an exciting blend of seasonings—all wrapped in a crisp and tasty pastry casing. If you have some filling left over after you've made the turnovers, you can have a dynamite mushroom omelet the next day!

SEASONING MIX

2 teaspoons dry mustard

2 teaspoons dried sweet basil
   leaves

2 teaspoons dried thyme leaves

1½ teaspoons salt

1½ teaspoons dried marjoram
   leaves

1¼ teaspoons white pepper

1 teaspoon onion powder

1 teaspoon garlic powder

¾ teaspoon black pepper

☆

FILLING

3 cups small fresh mushrooms
   (about ½ pound)

6 tablespoons unsalted butter,
   in all

2 cups chopped onions

½ pound ground pork

1 cup beef stock (see page 11),
   in all

3 tablespoons all-purpose flour

1¼ cups heavy cream

¼ pound fresh shiitake or oyster
   mushrooms, sliced

¼ pound large fresh mushrooms,
   sliced

TURNOVER DOUGH

3¼ cups all-purpose flour, in all

¼ cup sugar

8 ounces cream cheese, cut into
   cubes

14 tablespoons (1¾ sticks) butter,
   cut into about 14 pats

¼ cup cold water

FINISH

Vegetable oil cooking spray

1 egg

2 tablespoons water

All-purpose flour

Combine the seasoning mix ingredients thoroughly in a small bowl. Makes
¼ cup plus 1 teaspoon.

**FOR THE FILLING,** place the small mushrooms in a food processor and pulse
about 15 seconds or until finely chopped. Set aside.

Melt *2 tablespoons* of the butter in a 10-inch skillet over high heat.
When the butter sizzles, add the onions and cook, stirring and flipping them,
until the onions begin to brown, about 5 to 6 minutes. Move the onions
to one side of the skillet and add the pork to the cleared space. Sprinkle
*2 teaspoons* of the seasoning mix over the pork and break up the meat
with a large spoon. Then stir the onions into the pork and cook 3 minutes,
breaking up any lumps of meat and stirring occasionally. Add the reserved
chopped mushrooms and cook 2 minutes, stirring and scraping the bottom

of the skillet well. Add the *remaining 4 tablespoons* butter and the *remaining* seasoning mix and cook, stirring occasionally, until a crust forms on the bottom of the skillet, about 8 minutes. Add $\frac{1}{2}$ *cup* of the beef stock, scrape up the crust, and cook about 5 minutes, allowing a new crust to form the same way. Stir in the *remaining $\frac{1}{2}$ cup* stock and the flour and scrape the bottom of the skillet thoroughly. Cook 1 minute, stirring and scraping to prevent the flour from getting too brown. Add the cream and all the sliced mushrooms and cook, scraping the bottom of the skillet from time to time, about 2 minutes. Remove from the heat and set aside.

Preheat the oven to 325°.

**FOR THE DOUGH,** place the flour and sugar in the bowl of a food processor. Distribute the cubes of cream cheese and the butter pats evenly on top. Process about 25 to 30 seconds. With the processor running, add the water in a steady stream and process until well blended and the mixture forms a dough.

Spray 2 baking sheets with cooking spray.

Beat the egg lightly with the water to make an egg wash. Sprinkle a light coating of flour over a clean countertop and turn the dough out of the food processor. Pull off a fistful of dough at a time and roll out to a thickness of about ⅛ inch. Using a 7-inch plate as a guide, cut out a pastry round. Repeat with the remainder of the dough, reflouring the counter often, until you have 12 rounds. To reuse the scraps, wet your hands with water and smooth the scraps together into a ball. Roll out as above.

**TO FINISH,** brush a round of dough with egg wash and place about ¼ cup of the mushroom mixture on one half of the pastry. Fold over the pastry to form a half-moon shape, and press the seams together with a fork. Place on a baking sheet and brush the top with egg wash. Form the remaining turnovers the same way and place on the baking sheet 1 inch apart.

Bake until golden brown, about 50 minutes.

Serve warm.

# Baked Onions
# Stuffed with Pork
# and Mushrooms

MAKES 6 SERVINGS

*Color photograph 47*

★

Onions were one of the earliest cultivated crops in this country, and it wasn't long before our ancestors were growing variations as well, including scallions and shallots. While we all know the benefits of adding chopped or grated onions in some form as a seasoning to many other dishes, the onion makes a pretty satisfying—and pretty—side dish all by itself, especially when stuffed with all sorts of good things.

SEASONING MIX

2 teaspoons salt

2 teaspoons dry mustard

1½ teaspoons dried sweet basil
  leaves

1½ teaspoons dried thyme leaves

1 teaspoon black pepper

1 teaspoon white pepper

1 teaspoon garlic powder

1 teaspoon paprika

☆

6 large or 8 medium onions

½ cup coarsely chopped pecans
  (preferred) or Brazil nuts,
  filberts, or peanuts

4 tablespoons unsalted butter

1¼ cups chopped onions, in all

½ cup chopped green bell
  peppers

¼ cup chopped celery

½ pound lean ground pork

½ teaspoon minced fresh garlic

¾ cup uncooked converted rice

2 cups sliced or chopped fresh
  mushrooms (depending on
  their size—they have to fit in
  the onion cups)

2 cups pork or chicken stock (see
  page 11), in all

1 (12-ounce) can evaporated
  milk

2 cups shredded Monterey Jack
  cheese

Combine the seasoning mix ingredients thoroughly in a small bowl. Makes 3 tablespoons plus 2 teaspoons.

Reserve 2 tablespoons seasoning mix if you're using 6 onions, or 2 tablespoons plus 2 teaspoons for 8 onions.

Peel the onions and cut a thin slice off the top of each so it will stand without tipping. Turn each onion over and scoop out the insides with a melon baller, leaving a shell about ½ inch thick. Cut a very thin slice off each of the 4 sides of each onion to keep the onions from rolling in the skillet, so they'll brown evenly.

Toast the nuts in a dry 10-inch skillet over medium heat, flipping and shaking them, until they're light brown, about 3 minutes. Remove from the skillet and set aside.

Wipe the skillet clean, return it to high heat, and add the butter. When the butter is sizzling, add the onion cups, laying them on their sides, and cook, turning them occasionally, until they're browned on all sides, about 2 minutes. Remove the onion cups and set aside.

Add *¾ cup* of the chopped onions, the bell peppers, and celery to the skillet and cook until browned, about 6 minutes. Add the pork and garlic, and cook until browned, breaking up the meat with a spoon, about 3 minutes. Stir in *1 tablespoon* of the seasoning mix and the *remaining ½ cup* chopped onions and cook 1 minute. Stir in the rice and the *remaining* seasoning mix and cook 3 minutes. Add the mushrooms and cook 1 minute, scraping as the mixture begins to stick to the bottom of the skillet. Stir in *1¼ cups* of the stock and cook until the stock is reduced and the mixture forms another crust on the bottom of the skillet, about 8 minutes. Add the evaporated milk and the toasted nuts and scrape the skillet bottom. Bring to a rolling boil, cover, and remove from the heat. Allow to sit, covered, 20 minutes.

Preheat the oven to 375°.

Sprinkle each onion cup all over with *1 teaspoon* of the reserved seasoning mix, rubbing the mixture inside and out.

Place the onions, open ends up, in a 9½-inch by 2-inch-deep cake pan or a springform pan or other pan just large enough to hold them. Stuff them with the pork/rice mixture, heaping it up as much as possible, and sprinkle the shredded cheese on top. Pour the *remaining ¾ cup* stock into the bottom of the pan. Bake 20 minutes, then turn the oven heat up to 550° and bake another 10 minutes or until brown and bubbly on top.

Serve with a little stock from the pan spooned over each onion.

# Succotash

MAKES 6 SERVINGS

★

Now a familiar side dish, succotash was originally a creation of Native American Indians, whose staples included corn and beans. Although it has become a requisite of cafeteria offerings, especially in the South, succotash can be wonderful if made with loving care. You must always use corn, but you can get creative with the beans and use any variety you prefer. If you live where it's impossible to get fresh produce, you may substitute frozen—but the result will never be as delicious as that made with fresh vegetables.

SEASONING MIX
1 teaspoon salt
1 teaspoon paprika
¾ teaspoon dried thyme leaves
½ teaspoon garlic powder
½ teaspoon onion powder
½ teaspoon ground cumin
½ teaspoon dried dill weed
¼ teaspoon black pepper
¼ teaspoon white pepper

☆

4 tablespoons unsalted butter,
  in all
1½ cups chopped onions
4½ cups fresh corn kernels
  (about 8 or 9 ears), in all
2½ cups chicken stock (see page
  11), in all
3 cups shelled fresh or frozen
  lima beans
2 cups fresh or frozen green
  beans, cut into 1-inch pieces
1 cup beef stock (see page 11)

Combine the seasoning mix ingredients thoroughly in a small bowl. Makes 1 tablespoon plus 2¼ teaspoons.

Melt *2 tablespoons* of the butter in a 12-inch skillet over high heat. When the butter sizzles, add the onions, shake the pan, stir once, and cook until the onions start to brown, about 4 minutes. Stir in *2 cups* of the corn and *2 teaspoons* of the seasoning mix and cook until a light crust forms on the bottom of the skillet, about 1 minute. Add ½ *cup* of the chicken stock and scrape well to remove all of the crust from the skillet bottom. Cook without stirring until another hard crust forms on the bottom of the skillet, about 6 to 8 minutes. Add the *remaining 2½ cups* corn, the lima beans, the *remaining* seasoning mix, and *1 cup* more chicken stock. Scrape the pan bottom well, stir, and cook 2 minutes. Add the green beans, stir, and bring to a simmer. Add the *remaining 2 tablespoons* butter, stir, and cook, shaking the pan and flipping its contents from time to time, 6 minutes. Stir in the *remaining 1 cup* chicken stock and cook, stirring occasionally, 7 minutes. Add the beef stock, stir, and cook 10 minutes, or until the lima beans are tender.

Serve with meat, poultry, or fish.

# Kansas Stuffed Squash

## MAKES 6 SERVINGS

Acorn squash was enjoyed by the early settlers in the colonies, and it moved west with the pioneers, becoming a colorful fall favorite throughout the young country. Squashes of varying types were consumed by the Indians who lived in Kansas, and they taught the settlers how to cook them. This recipe, of course, is a bit tangier than the one the Indians made, and it creates a very pretty dish that would look especially nice on your Thanksgiving table.

SEASONING MIX
*2 teaspoons salt*
*1 teaspoon white pepper*
*1 teaspoon onion powder*
*1 teaspoon garlic powder*
*1 teaspoon dried sweet basil leaves*
*1 teaspoon dried dill weed*
*1 teaspoon black pepper*
*1 teaspoon dark brown sugar*
*1 teaspoon ground nutmeg*
*½ teaspoon turmeric*
*Large pinch of saffron*

☆

*3 medium acorn squash*
*2 cups chicken stock (see page 11)*
*4 tablespoons unsalted butter*
*1 cup chopped onions*
*5 cups chopped yellow summer squash*
*1 cup grated Monterey Jack cheese*
*1 cup grated mozzarella cheese*
*¼ cup grated Parmesan cheese*

Preheat the oven to 350°.

Combine the seasoning mix ingredients thoroughly in a small bowl. Makes about 3 tablespoons plus 2 teaspoons.

Cut each acorn squash in half crosswise, remove the seeds and membranes, and slice a thin piece off the bottom of each to make it sit without falling over. Pour the chicken stock into a baking pan. Place the acorn squash cups upside down in the stock and bake until just tender, about 20 to 25 minutes.

Meanwhile, melt the butter in a 12-inch skillet over high heat. When the butter sizzles, add the onions and cook until the onions are lightly browned, about 6 minutes. Stir in *1 tablespoon plus 2 teaspoons* of the seasoning mix and cook 2 minutes. Add the yellow squash and cook, stirring occasionally, about 8 to 10 minutes. Remove from the heat and stir in the Monterey Jack and mozzarella.

Remove the squash from the oven, turn the cups right side up in the pan, and rub the inside of each with *½ teaspoon* of the seasoning mix. Baste the squash cups with a little of the chicken stock. Fill each cup with approximately ½ cup of the cooked yellow squash mixture, and top each with *2 teaspoons* of the Parmesan. Bake until the acorn squash is very tender and brown and bubbly on top, about 25 minutes.

Allow 1 stuffed squash cup per serving, as an accompaniment to a roast beef, chicken, or turkey.

# Turnips in Cream

MAKES 4 TO 6 SERVINGS

★

The turnip wasn't cultivated in this country until the early part of the eighteenth century. Turnip greens are often cooked with bacon as a vegetable and the turnip itself is usually thought of as common and homely. But prepared properly in a savory cheese/cream sauce, turnips can steal the show at a company dinner. Our CEO, Shawn McBride, who tested this at home, said even a turnip-hater would love this dish.

*1½ teaspoons salt*

*½ teaspoon white pepper*

*½ teaspoon garlic powder*

*½ teaspoon onion powder*

*½ teaspoon ground nutmeg*

*½ teaspoon dried cilantro leaves*

*½ teaspoon dried sweet basil
  leaves*

*½ teaspoon dried thyme leaves*

*¼ teaspoon dried oregano leaves*

*¼ teaspoon dried marjoram
  leaves*

*3½ tablespoons sugar,* in all

*½ teaspoon salt*

*1¾ pounds white turnips, peeled
  and cut into ⅛-inch slices*

*2 tablespoons unsalted butter*

*1 cup sliced onions*

*1 cup heavy cream*

*Vegetable oil cooking spray*

*1 cup lightly packed shredded
  Swiss cheese,* in all

*¼ cup grated Parmesan cheese*

☆

Preheat the oven to 400°.

Combine the seasoning mix ingredients thoroughly in a small bowl. Makes 1 tablespoon plus 2½ teaspoons.

Bring a large pot of water to a boil over high heat. Add *2 tablespoons* of the sugar, the salt, and turnips and cook until the turnips are just tender, about 9 to 11 minutes. Drain and set aside.

Melt the butter in a 10-inch skillet over high heat. Add the onions, tossing them to coat evenly with the butter, and cook 4 minutes. Add *1 tablespoon plus 1 teaspoon* of the seasoning mix and the *remaining 1½ teaspoons* sugar and cook, stirring occasionally, until the onions are golden brown, about 3 minutes. Stir in the cream, simmer 2 minutes, and remove from the heat.

Coat a small baking pan or casserole with cooking spray. Cover the bottom with a generous layer of turnips. Sprinkle the *remaining* seasoning mix evenly over the turnips, *½ cup* of the Swiss cheese over that, and the Parmesan over the Swiss cheese. Distribute the remaining turnips over the cheese. Spoon the creamed onions evenly over the turnips and sprinkle with the *remaining ½ cup* Swiss cheese. Bake until brown and bubbly, about 30 minutes.

Serve as a delicious side dish with roasts or broiled meat, poultry, or fish.

# Hoppin' John

Here's one of those wonderful Southern dishes with a quaint name and fuzzy origins. Most likely, it was a staple dish of the African slaves on the plantations and before that, it was found throughout the Caribbean. The name has its roots in American folklore, and one theory is that hospitable hosts would invite their guests to stay for supper by saying, "Hop in, John." But who knows. Today, Hoppin' John is a traditional dish served on New Year's Day to bring luck in the coming year. It's usually accompanied by a dish of cabbage or greens, meant to ensure a wealthy year. We don't soak our black-eyed peas because we feel that proper cooking is all that's needed to ensure a perfect texture. The mixture of seasonings and herbs saves the dish from its traditional blandness. We think if you eat it often you'll have luck any time of the year or at least your taste buds will!

SEASONING MIX
*1 tablespoon salt*
*1 tablespoon paprika*
*2½ teaspoons black pepper*
*1½ teaspoons garlic powder*
*1 teaspoon onion powder*
*1 teaspoon white pepper*
*1 teaspoon dried sweet basil leaves*
*1 teaspoon dried thyme leaves*

☆

*5 slices bacon, cut into small dice*
*3 cups chopped onions,* in all

*2 cups chopped green bell peppers,* in all
*1½ cups chopped celery,* in all
*3 bay leaves*
*1 pound dried black-eyed peas, rinsed and picked over*
*11 cups chicken stock (see page 11),* in all
*1 teaspoon minced fresh garlic*
*1 pound smoked sausage (the best you can find), cut into ½-inch-thick slices*
*2 cups uncooked converted rice*

Combine the seasoning mix ingredients thoroughly in a small bowl. Makes ¼ cup plus 2 teaspoons.

Place the bacon in a heavy ovenproof 5-quart pot over high heat and cook until the bacon starts to brown, about 6 minutes. Stir in *2 cups* of the onions, *1 cup* of the bell peppers, *1 cup* of the celery *2 tablespoons plus 1 teaspoon* of the seasoning mix, the bay leaves, and *half* the black-eyed peas. Cover and cook, uncovering the pot once or twice to stir, about 10 minutes. Stir in *2 cups* of the chicken stock and the garlic and scrape up any crust that's formed on the bottom of the pot. Bring to a boil and cook, stirring occasionally, about 20 minutes. Add *1 cup* more stock and scrape the bottom of the pot clean. Add the sausage, *6 cups* more stock, the *remaining 1 cup* onions, *1 cup* bell peppers, and ½ *cup* celery, the *remaining* black-eyed peas, and the *remaining* seasoning mix. Cover and bring to a boil over high heat. Reduce the heat to low and simmer, covered, until the peas are tender and creamy, about 1¼ hours.

Preheat the oven to 350°.

Stir the rice and the *remaining 2 cups* stock into the black-eyed peas, turn up the heat to high, and bring to a boil. Cover the pot and bake 15 minutes.

Serve alongside roast chicken and greens.

# Southern Smothered Potatoes

MAKES 6 SERVINGS

★

Almost any type of food—meat, poultry, fish, vegetables—can be "smothered," or cooked in gravy and vegetables in a covered pot, for a nostalgic "down-home" American flavor. The important thing to remember when cooking this dish is that to get the most flavor from the potatoes, they should be allowed to stick to the bottom of the pot and then scraped up. So don't be afraid to let them stick, but be careful not to let them stick too hard or get too brown, or you'll wind up with a burnt taste. Always use our times as guides, but use your common sense and watch the pot.

SEASONING MIX

1 tablespoon paprika
2 teaspoons salt
1 teaspoon black pepper
1 teaspoon dry mustard
1 teaspoon dried cilantro leaves
1 teaspoon dried sweet basil
  leaves
1 teaspoon onion powder
¾ teaspoon garlic powder
½ teaspoon white pepper
¼ teaspoon ground allspice

4 tablespoons unsalted butter
3 medium potatoes, peeled and
  cut into ⅛-inch-thick slices
3 cups sliced onions
1 cup chicken stock (see
  page 11)

☆

Combine the seasoning mix ingredients thoroughly in a small bowl. Makes 3 tablespoons plus 2½ teaspoons.

Melt the butter in a large heavy pot over high heat. When the butter starts to sizzle, add the potatoes and *2 tablespoons* of the seasoning mix. Cover the pot and cook over high heat until the potatoes start turning golden and sticking hard to the pot bottom, about 4 to 6 minutes; uncover the pot occasionally to scrape up the crust as it forms on the bottom of the pot. Add the onions and the *remaining* seasoning mix. Cover and cook, scraping the pot bottom occasionally, until the potatoes are sticking hard to the bottom of the pot and a golden brown crust has formed, about 6 to 8 minutes. Add the chicken stock and scrape the bottom of the pot clean. Cook, uncovered, until the stock is completely absorbed by the potatoes, about 3 to 4 minutes. Remove from the heat, cover, and let sit 5 minutes before serving.

# Potatoes au Gratin

## MAKES 8 TO 10 SERVINGS

★

Although this dish has its origins in France, it has become truly an all-American masterpiece—a wonderful blend of cheese and cream and potatoes with a brown, bubbly crust. It is to this crisp golden crust that the term *au gratin* refers.

SEASONING MIX
1 tablespoon salt
2½ teaspoons paprika
2 teaspoons dry mustard
1½ teaspoons garlic powder
1½ teaspoons onion powder
1½ teaspoons dried thyme leaves
1 teaspoon white pepper
½ teaspoon ground nutmeg
¼ teaspoon black pepper

☆

10 cups sliced peeled potatoes
(about 7 medium-large
potatoes, sliced ¼ inch thick)

8 tablespoons (1 stick) unsalted
butter, in all
¾ cups grated onions
2½ cups grated peeled potatoes
2 cups chicken stock (see page
11), in all
½ cup finely diced red bell peppers
¼ cup finely chopped fresh parsley
2 cups milk
1 cup heavy cream
3 cups grated sharp Cheddar
cheese, in all
1 cup grated Monterey Jack
cheese

Preheat the oven to 375°.

Combine the seasoning mix ingredients thoroughly in a small bowl. Makes ¼ cup plus 1¾ teaspoons.

Bring a large pot of water to a boil over high heat. Add the sliced potatoes, return to a boil, and cook until just firm-tender, about 2 to 3 minutes. Drain and rinse under cold running water.

Melt *4 tablespoons* of the butter in a 12-inch skillet over high heat. When the butter begins to sizzle, add the onions and cook, stirring occasionally, until the onions are golden, about 4 to 5 minutes. Stir in *1 tablespoon* of the seasoning mix, the grated potatoes, and the *remaining 4 tablespoons* butter. Cook, scraping often with a metal spatula to keep a crust from forming on the bottom of the skillet, about 5 minutes. Add *1 tablespoon* of the seasoning mix and *1 cup* of the chicken stock and cook, scraping the bottom of the pan occasionally, until the mixture is thick, light brown in color, and sticking hard to the bottom of the skillet, about 5 to 6 minutes. Add the red bell peppers, parsley, *remaining 1 cup* chicken stock, and the *remaining* seasoning mix and cook, stirring occasionally, 3 minutes. Using a wire whisk, whip in the milk, breaking up the grated potatoes (they will act as a thickening starch). Bring to a rolling boil and cook, whisking occasionally, until the sauce is light brown, about 4 minutes. Add the cream and return to a boil, whisking occasionally. Reduce the heat to low and simmer, whisking occasionally, until very thick, about 4 to 5 minutes. Add *1 cup* of the Cheddar and the Monterey Jack cheese and cook, whisking, until the sauce returns to a boil. Remove from the heat.

Pour a thin layer of sauce over the bottom of a large, deep casserole dish, about 10 by 10 by 4 inches. Add the boiled sliced potatoes and pour the *remaining* sauce over the potatoes. Sprinkle the top with the *remaining 2 cups* grated Cheddar. Bake, uncovered, until brown and bubbly on top, about 25 minutes.

Serve immediately.

# Lower East Side Latkes

MAKES 15 TO 20 POTATO PANCAKES, OR
5 TO 7 SIDE-DISH SERVINGS
OR 10 PARTY APPETIZER SERVINGS

★

Latkes are potato pancakes traditionally served during the celebration of Chanukah, but many smart people, especially those who live in New York City, eat these crispy pancakes all year round. Jessie Tirsch, who is the project manager of this book, remembers that her mother, Bea Badash, made the best latkes. But even though these are a bit different because of the seasoning mixture we added to the traditional recipe, Jessie says she loves the tangy new flavor. You can serve them as either a side dish or party food. You can accompany them with applesauce or sour cream, but they're so delicious we found ourselves gobbling them up without any accompaniment at all. We tested this recipe twice, once using a food processor, once grating the potatoes by hand. The difference was amazing—the hand-grated potatoes tasted so much sweeter.

SEASONING MIX
*2 teaspoons salt*
*1 teaspoon sugar*
*³⁄₄ teaspoon white pepper*
*¹⁄₂ teaspoon garlic powder*
*¹⁄₂ teaspoon onion powder*
*¹⁄₂ teaspoon dry mustard*
*¹⁄₂ teaspoon ground ginger*
*¹⁄₄ teaspoon ground allspice*
*¹⁄₈ teaspoon ground nutmeg*

*2 large potatoes, peeled*
*1 large onion, peeled*
*1 egg*
*1 tablespoon plus 2 teaspoons*
   *matzo meal*
*1 cup vegetable oil*

☆

Combine the seasoning mix ingredients thoroughly in a small bowl. Makes 2 tablespoons plus ⅛ teaspoon.

Place a colander over a mixing bowl and using a hand grater, grate the potatoes into the colander. Grate the onion directly into the potatoes and blend together with a spoon. Let drain about 3 minutes.

When the mixture has drained thoroughly, transfer it to a large bowl. Add the egg, matzo meal, and *2 tablespoons* of the seasoning mix, and whip with a wire whisk or a large wooden spoon.

Heat the oil in a 10-inch skillet over high heat. When the oil is very hot, carefully drop in large spoonfuls of the latke mixture, being careful not to crowd the pan. Fry about 3 minutes, turning once or twice, until browned on both sides. Watch the frying closely: If the oil is too hot the latkes will brown too quickly, or even burn. If yours start getting brown too fast, lower the heat to medium.

These are best eaten immediately. If they have to wait, put them on a baking sheet in a 200° oven until you're ready for them—but for no longer than a few minutes.

Serve with applesauce, sour cream, or nothing at all.

# Idaho Potato Cake

MAKES 6 SERVINGS

★

Many nineteenth-century cowboys on the plains of Idaho and Oregon were of Basque origins and they cooked the foods that reminded them of their ancestral homes. This potato cake is an excellent example. Serve it alongside a roast, or for lunch with just a green salad.

SEASONING MIX
*2½ teaspoons garlic powder*
*2 teaspoons onion powder*
*2 teaspoons white pepper*
*2 teaspoons dry mustard*
*1½ teaspoons salt*
*1 teaspoon dried thyme leaves*

☆

*4 large potatoes, peeled and cut*
*   in half crosswise*
*8 slices bacon, diced*
*4 tablespoons unsalted butter*

*2 medium onions, thinly sliced*
*3 eggs*
*½ cup heavy cream*
*1 cup grated Monterey Jack*
*   cheese*
*1 cup grated mozzarella cheese*

*Two heavy ovenproof skillets that*
*   can nest one inside the other,*
*   one about 10 inches in*
*   diameter and the other 8 or 9*
*   inches*

Combine the seasoning mix ingredients thoroughly in a small bowl. Makes 3 tablespoons plus 2 teaspoons.

Cook the potatoes in a large pot of boiling water until tender, about 15 to 20 minutes. Drain, pat dry, and slice very thin. Set aside.

Place the bacon in the larger skillet over high heat, and cook 6 minutes. Reduce the heat to medium and cook until the bacon is browned and crisp, about 2 minutes. Using a slotted spoon, remove the bacon and set aside. Pour the bacon drippings into a cup, add the butter, and stir until the butter melts.

Preheat the oven to 400°.

Layer the sliced potatoes and onions in the large skillet, starting with the potatoes and alternating the layers. Sprinkle each layer of onions evenly with *1½ teaspoons* of the seasoning mix; you should have 6 layers in all.

Pour the bacon drippings/butter mixture over the potatoes and onions.

Place the skillet over high heat and cook 5 minutes. Then place the smaller skillet on top of the potatoes and onions to weight them down. Cook 7 minutes. Remove the top skillet and cook until the bottom of the cake is crisp and brown (check by lifting some of the potatoes from the edge to check doneness), about 3 to 5 minutes. Transfer the skillet to the oven and bake 15 minutes.

Meanwhile, beat the eggs, cream, and the *remaining* seasoning mix in a small bowl with a wire whisk until frothy.

Remove the potato cake from the oven and reduce the oven heat to 325°. Pour the egg/cream mixture over the cake and sprinkle with the cooked bacon and the cheeses. Bake until the cheese is melted, bubbly, and brown, about 20 to 25 minutes.

Cut into wedges or remove from the skillet with a large flat spoon and serve warm with meat, poultry, or fish.

# Big Hole Valley Cowpoke Beans

MAKES 8 TO 10 SERVINGS

★

Many ranch hands and wranglers worked the livestock in Montana's range cattle industry in the early 1800s, long before Montana achieved statehood. Snowy winters and long hours put in at places like Big Hole Valley in southwestern Montana made for some pretty mean appetites, which were often appeased with a big black kettle of beans. In our version of the cowpoke's traditional beanpot, we combined the heat of ground chile peppers with the sweetness of brown sugar and a special mix of herbs and spices. This would be a wonderful treat after spending a chilly day out on the ski slopes.

1 pound dried red, pink, or
   pinto beans

SEASONING MIX
1 tablespoon paprika
2 teaspoons black pepper
2 teaspoons dry mustard
1½ teaspoons dried sweet basil
   leaves
1 teaspoon dried oregano leaves
1 teaspoon garlic powder
1 teaspoon onion powder
1 teaspoon ground New Mexico
   chile pepper (see Note)
1 teaspoon ground pasilla chile
   pepper (see Note)

½ pound salt pork, finely diced
2 cups chopped onions
2 cups chopped green bell
   peppers
1 cup chopped celery
3 bay leaves
2 cups chopped peeled, fresh
   tomatoes
2 cloves garlic, sliced
3 tablespoons dark brown sugar
5 cups chicken stock (see page
   11), in all

☆

**DAY 1:** Put the beans in a large pot, add hot water to cover, and let soak overnight.

**DAY 2:** Combine the seasoning mix ingredients thoroughly in a small bowl. Makes ¼ cup plus 1½ teaspoons.

Drain the beans.

If the salt pork has a heavy coating of salt, rinse it off and pat dry.

Place the salt pork in a 5-quart pot over high heat. Cover and cook, uncovering to stir once or twice, until golden brown, about 7 to 8 minutes. Add the onions, bell peppers, celery, and bay leaves. Scrape the bottom of the pot, cover, and cook until the onions are lightly browned, about 3 to 4 minutes. Add *2 tablespoons* of the seasoning mix and the drained beans, and scrape the pot bottom. Cover the pot and cook, occasionally scraping the bottom of the pot, about 7 minutes. Add the tomatoes and scrape the pot bottom well. Cover and cook, stirring from time to time, about 8 minutes. Stir in the garlic, cover, and cook 4 to 5 minutes. Stir in the brown sugar, *2 cups* of the chicken stock, and *2 tablespoons* of the seasoning mix. Bring to a boil, cover, reduce the heat to low, and simmer, stirring occasionally, 20 minutes. Add *2 cups* more stock, cover, and cook, stirring occasionally, about 50 minutes. Stir in the *remaining* seasoning mix, if you like your beans highly seasoned, and the *remaining 1 cup* stock. Cover and cook until the beans are tender, about 20 minutes.

Serve in bowls with warm thick slices of bread, alongside a dinner of ribs or pork roast.

NOTE: These are the chile peppers we used. You can use whatever is available in your area, but be sure you buy pure ground chile peppers, not commercial chili powder.

# San Francisco Rice

MAKES 4 TO 6 SERVINGS

★

Although this old favorite is a familiar side dish in San Francisco, many people have tasted only the commercially packaged version. We've rescued it from the ordinary by using a rich, thick stock, adding herbs and spices, and browning the rice and pasta well to give it a rich, nutty flavor and interesting texture.

**SEASONING MIX**
*2 teaspoons salt*
*2 teaspoons dry mustard*
*1½ teaspoons dried cilantro leaves*
*1 teaspoon white pepper*
*1 teaspoon dried sweet basil leaves*
*¾ teaspoon ground ginger*
*½ teaspoon black pepper*
*½ teaspoon onion powder*
*½ teaspoon garlic powder*

*¼ cup peanut oil*
*1 cup uncooked converted long-grain rice*
*1 cup 2-inch pieces uncooked #4 spaghetti*
*2 cups chopped onions*
*1 cup chopped celery*
*2 tablespoons unsalted butter*
*¼ cup sesame seeds*
*2 teaspoons minced fresh garlic*
*½ cup chopped fresh parsley*
*3 cups chicken stock (see page 11)*

Combine the seasoning mix ingredients thoroughly in a small bowl. Makes 3 tablespoons plus ¾ teaspoon.

Heat the oil in a 12-inch skillet over high heat until very hot, about 4 minutes. Add the rice, spaghetti, onions, celery, butter, and *2 tablespoons* of the seasoning mix. Stir well and cook, shaking the pan and stirring occasionally, until the rice and spaghetti are golden brown, about 6 minutes. Add the sesame seeds and the *remaining* seasoning mix. Stir well and cook 2 minutes. Add the garlic and cook, stirring occasionally, until the rice and spaghetti are brown, about 3 to 5 minutes. Stir in the parsley and chicken stock, cover the skillet, and bring to a boil over high heat. Reduce the heat to low and simmer 12 minutes. Remove from the heat and let the skillet sit, covered, 8 minutes.

This is a great dinner side dish to accompany almost any kind of meat, poultry, or fish. Or serve for lunch with a salad.

# Savannah Red Rice

MAKES 10 TO 12 SERVINGS

★

Despite the fact that this is a traditional dish from Savannah, Georgia, for some reason it's known elsewhere in America as "Spanish rice"—but no one seems to know why. Anyway, it'll certainly add color to your meal in a delicious way. Serve with foods that are more subtle in flavor—such as simple roasts—rather than those likely to fight the rice for your palate.

**SEASONING MIX**
2 tablespoons dark brown sugar
2 teaspoons salt
2 teaspoons paprika
1½ teaspoons white pepper
1¼ teaspoons dry mustard
1 teaspoon black pepper
1 teaspoon onion powder
1 teaspoon garlic powder
½ teaspoon dried thyme leaves
½ teaspoon ground cumin

☆

10 slices bacon, diced
2 bay leaves
2 cups chopped onions
1½ cups chopped green bell peppers
1 cup chopped celery
2½ cups uncooked converted rice
1 (16-ounce) can whole or chopped tomatoes
1 teaspoon minced fresh garlic
5 cups chicken stock (see page 11)
¼ cup finely minced fresh parsley

Combine the seasoning mix ingredients thoroughly in a small bowl. Makes 5 tablespoons plus 1¾ teaspoons.

Place the bacon in a heavy 5-quart pot, cover, and cook over high heat until the bacon starts to brown, about 5 to 6 minutes. Add the bay leaves, onions, bell peppers, and celery, cover, and cook, stirring occasionally, until the onions and bacon are golden brown, about 14 to 15 minutes. Stir in the rice and *5 tablespoons* of the seasoning mix. Cover and cook, occasionally scraping up the crust that forms on the bottom of the pot, until the rice is golden, about 5 minutes. Stir in the tomatoes, mashing them with the spoon, then add the garlic and the *remaining* seasoning mix, cover, and cook 2 minutes. Add the stock and scrape the bottom of the pot. Cover, bring to a boil, reduce the heat to low, and simmer, uncovering the pot to scrape the bottom as the mixture sticks, about 25 minutes. Stir in the parsley, remove from the heat, and let sit, covered, 10 minutes before serving.

This is just great with roast beef or chicken and a light salad.

# SWEETS
## *and*
# MORE SWEETS

There's no doubt about it—Americans have a collective sweet tooth. From soft drinks and ice cream to candy bars and chewing gum, there are few other places in the world where sweets are in such demand.

I myself am a big fan of all things sweet because they bring a high level of emotional satisfaction. As a child I ate caramel popcorn balls and pralines. But as I grew up I realized there are many basic similarities between Cajun sweets and desserts and those throughout the rest of America. The main differences are usually in the kinds of fruits or nuts used.

I've also developed a great appreciation for the artistic possibilities sugar has. Sugar is a rewarding and pleasurable medium for a professional chef to work with. Although this is not an extensive section of this cookbook, you may find that the recipes for desserts here transport you in delight back to your childhood.

# Black Bottom Pie

## MAKES 8 SERVINGS

★

Take a perfectly made graham cracker crust, line the bottom with rich, dark chocolate, and top it with a light, rummy cream, and you've got black bottom pie, one of the most sinfully sensational desserts you'll ever taste. If you care to be even more sinful, add whipped cream—you may never recover.

**CRUST**

2¼ cups graham cracker crumbs

½ cup firmly packed dark brown sugar

½ pound (2 sticks) unsalted butter, melted

**CHOCOLATE FILLING**

3 cups semisweet chocolate pieces

6 tablespoons unsalted butter

¾ cup evaporated milk

**RUM CREAM**

8 egg yolks

3 tablespoons cornstarch

3 tablespoons water

1 quart heavy cream

8 tablespoons (1 stick) unsalted butter, cut into pats

1 cup plus 2 tablespoons white sugar, in all

1 teaspoon vanilla extract

3 tablespoons dark or light rum, in all

**FOR THE CRUST,** combine the graham cracker crumbs and brown sugar in a medium mixing bowl and mix thoroughly with a spoon. Add the butter and mix until thoroughly blended. Press the mixture into the bottom and halfway up the sides of a 10-inch springform cake pan and refrigerate at least 30 minutes.

**FOR THE FILLING,** put the chocolate pieces, butter, and evaporated milk in the top of a 1½-quart double boiler set over boiling water. Cook, stirring, until the butter and chocolate are melted and thoroughly blended with the milk, about 6 minutes. Remove from the heat and stir 1 minute. Pour the chocolate mixture into the chilled crust, spreading it evenly over the bottom. Refrigerate 30 minutes.

**FOR THE RUM CREAM,** place the egg yolks in a medium mixing bowl and whip until frothy, about 10 seconds. Set aside.

Combine the cornstarch and water, mix well, and set aside.

Put the cream and butter in the top of the (cleaned) double boiler set over gently boiling water. As soon as the butter has melted, start whipping with a wire whisk. Cook, whisking occasionally, about 3 minutes. Whisk in the sugar and cook, whisking constantly, until the sugar has dissolved, about 1 minute. Whisk in the cornstarch/water mixture. Cook, whisking occasionally as the mixture thickens, about 18 minutes. Remove 1 cup of the cream mixture from the pot and whisk it into the egg yolks; then whisk in another cup of the cream mixture. Return the egg yolk/cream mixture to the double boiler and cook, whisking constantly, until the mixture is the consistency of a thin custard and thick enough to coat the back of a spoon, about 15 minutes.

Stir in the vanilla and rum and cook, whisking constantly, until the mixture becomes the consistency of pudding, about 25 minutes. Remove from the heat and whisk constantly for 4 minutes, then whisk once every minute or so until the mixture has cooled down to 120° on a thermometer, about 15 to 18 minutes.

Remove the crust from the refrigerator. Pour the rum cream over the chocolate filling and refrigerate overnight, or until set.

Cut the pie into wedges with a warm knife and serve topped with whipped cream, if desired.

# St. Louis Peanut Butter Banana Cream Pie

MAKES 8 SERVINGS

★

Peanuts have been an important staple crop in the South since the last part of the nineteenth century, when George Washington Carver promoted their versatility in cooking. Around the end of the century, peanut butter was developed by a St. Louis doctor who recognized the healthful aspect of the peanut and sought to make it more palatable to children. A far better place for peanut butter than between two pieces of bread, swamped with a layer of jelly is, in our opinion, this incredibly delicious pie. We've taken peanut butter pie to new heights with the addition of fresh bananas and—well, you decide for yourself.

| | |
|---|---|
| *5 eggs* | *3 very ripe medium bananas, cut* |
| *3 egg yolks* | *into large pieces* |
| *8 tablespoons (1 stick) unsalted* | *3 tablespoons cornstarch* |
| *butter, cut into pats* | *3 tablespoons water* |
| *½ cup packed light brown sugar* | *1 quart heavy cream* |
| *1 cup crunchy peanut butter* | *1 (12-ounce) can evaporated* |
| *½ cup honey* | *milk* |
| *1 tablespoon vanilla extract* | *1 baked 10-inch pie shell* |

Combine the eggs, egg yolks, butter, brown sugar, peanut butter, honey, vanilla, and bananas in the bowl of a food processor and process until completely blended, about 1½ minutes. Leave the mixture in the food processor.

Combine the cornstarch and water in a small bowl and stir until well blended. Set aside.

Place the cream and evaporated milk in the top pot of a double boiler set over boiling water and heat, stirring occasionally, until light bubbles start forming around the edges and the mixture is hot, about 6 to 7 minutes.

Stir the cornstarch mixture and whisk it into the cream/milk. Then, with the food processor running, add the cream mixture to the banana mixture in a steady stream and process 45 to 60 seconds. Pour the mixture back into the top of the double boiler and cook over high heat, whisking constantly, until the temperature reaches 165°, about 10 minutes. Remove from the heat and allow the filling to cool to about 120°, whisking frequently, about 15 minutes.

Pour the filling into the prepared pie shell and refrigerate 6 to 8 hours, until set.

Serve as is or with whipped cream.

# St. Landry Parish Sweet Potato Pecan Praline Pie

MAKES 10 TO 12 SERVINGS

★

It would be difficult to find a combination as delicious as sweet potatoes and pecan pralines. Bake them together in a pie crust, top with whipped cream, and you're almost in heaven. This is an impressive dessert that makes a beautiful appearance. Serve only to those who deserve it!

**DOUGH**

1 cup all-purpose flour

2 tablespoons sugar

1/4 teaspoon salt

3 tablespoons unsalted butter, softened, cut into 6 pats

1/2 egg (see Note)

2 tablespoons cold milk

**PRALINE SAUCE**

1 1/2 cups pecan pieces, in all

5 tablespoons unsalted butter

1/2 cup packed light brown sugar

1/2 cup white sugar

1/4 cup heavy cream

1/2 cup milk

1 tablespoon vanilla extract

**SWEET POTATO FILLING**

2 1/2 cups baked peeled, sweet potatoes (about 4 1/2 potatoes), cut up

3 eggs

3 tablespoons plus 1 teaspoon heavy cream

4 tablespoons unsalted butter, cut into 8 pats

2 tablespoons vanilla extract

3/4 teaspoon salt

1/2 teaspoon ground cinnamon

1/4 teaspoon ground allspice

1/4 teaspoon ground nutmeg

**WHIPPED CREAM**

2 cups heavy cream

1 teaspoon vanilla extract

2 tablespoons white sugar

**FOR THE DOUGH,** combine the flour, sugar, and salt in the bowl of a food processor, and process until blended, about 20 to 30 seconds. With the machine running, add the butter pats one at a time, then the egg, and then the milk, a tablespoon at a time. Process until thoroughly blended, about 2 minutes. Turn the dough into a bowl, cover, and refrigerate 1 hour.

Remove the dough from the refrigerator and turn out onto a lightly floured surface. Roll out into a large circle about ¼ inch thick and press into a 10-inch cake pan. Refrigerate 1 hour.

**FOR THE SAUCE,** toast *1 cup* of the pecan pieces in a small skillet over medium heat, shaking the skillet, and flipping the pecans, until the pecans are golden brown, about 4 minutes. Remove from the heat and set aside.

Melt the butter in an 8-inch skillet over high heat. When the butter starts to sizzle, add the brown and white sugars, cream, milk, and the *remaining ½ cup* pecan pieces. Bring to a rolling boil, whipping the mixture constantly with a wire whisk until thickened, about 3 minutes. Then cook, whisking frequently, about 5 minutes. Whisk in the vanilla and the toasted pecan pieces and cook, whisking, 1 minute. Remove from the heat.

Pour the praline sauce into the chilled pie shell and spread it evenly over the bottom.

Preheat the oven to 250°.

**FOR THE FILLING,** combine all the ingredients in the bowl of a food processor and process until thoroughly blended, about 3 to 4 minutes.

Pour the filling over the praline sauce in the pie shell and bake 1 hour and 45 minutes. Let cool to room temperature and refrigerate overnight, or until set.

**FOR THE WHIPPED CREAM,** combine the cream, vanilla, and sugar in the container of a blender or food processor (or use a hand or electric mixer) and whip until thick.

Invert the pie onto a serving platter, leaving it upside down, and cut into wedges. Serve in a cloud of whipped cream.

NOTE: Beat an egg in a small cup or ramekin, then measure out half.

# Maids of Honor

MAKES 24 TARTS

*Color photograph 49*

★

This charming and delicious dessert came to the New World with the first settlers from England. Individual tarts of raspberry or plum jam and almonds, they were named for the maids of honor at the court of Elizabeth I. These are best eaten warm, when every mouthful carries a burst of warm jam. These incredible tarts come with a challenge: Try eating just one.

**DOUGH**

*1½ cups plus a little extra all-purpose flour*

*3 tablespoons light brown sugar*

*½ teaspoon salt*

*1 teaspoon strawberry extract*

*½ teaspoon almond extract*

*12 tablespoons (1½ sticks) unsalted butter, cut into 12 pats*

*½ cup heavy cream or milk*

**FILLING**

*1 cup sliced or slivered almonds*

*3 eggs*

*1 cup packed dark brown sugar*

*4 tablespoons unsalted butter, cut into 4 pats*

*2 tablespoons all-purpose flour*

*½ teaspoon ground nutmeg*

*½ teaspoon ground cinnamon*

*5 tablespoons Grand Marnier or other orange-flavored liqueur*

*Vegetable oil cooking spray*

*All-purpose flour*

*¼ cup raspberry or damson plum jam (or your favorite fruit jam)*

**FOR THE DOUGH,** place the flour, brown sugar, salt, and strawberry and almond extracts in the bowl of a food processor and process until blended, about 30 to 45 seconds. With the food processor running, add the butter pats one at a time and process until thoroughly blended, about 45 to 60 seconds.

Turn the dough into a medium-size mixing bowl and break up any lumps with your hands. Add the cream or milk and mix thoroughly with a fork. Form the dough into a ball, flour it lightly, place it in a plastic bag, close the bag tightly, and refrigerate for 30 minutes to 1 hour. (If you don't flour the ball of dough, it will stick to the plastic bag.)

**FOR THE FILLING,** toast the almonds in an 8-inch skillet over medium heat until just golden, about 4 minutes. Remove from the heat and set aside.

Place the eggs, brown sugar, and butter in the bowl of the food processor and process until well blended, about 30 to 45 seconds. Add the almonds and process about 20 seconds. With the processor running, add the flour, nutmeg, cinnamon, and liqueur and process until thoroughly blended, about 45 seconds. Makes about 2¼ cups.

Preheat the oven to 350°. Coat 2 muffin tins with cooking spray.

Remove the dough from the refrigerator. Sprinkle a clean surface with flour, sprinkle more flour on the dough, and roll out about one quarter of the dough at a time to a thickness of ⅛ inch. Keep reflouring dough as needed. Use a glass or cup to cut out twenty-four 3-inch circles. Press the dough circles into the muffin cups. (If you find the dough too sticky to roll out, divide the dough into 24 small pieces and press 1 piece into the bottom and up the sides of each cup. Be sure to keep your hands floured.)

Place ½ teaspoon of the jam in each dough cup and top the jam with about 1 tablespoon of filling. Bake the tarts until the tops are golden brown and cracking open, about 20 to 25 minutes.

Serve warm.

# Joe Froggers

MAKES ABOUT 4 DOZEN COOKIES

★

Joe Froggers are big molasses cookies from Marblehead, Massachusetts. As the story goes, the best molasses cookies in town were baked by an old man called Uncle Joe, who lived on the edge of a frog pond. These cookies keep so well that fishermen going on long sea voyages would trade rum for Uncle Joe's Joe Froggers. There's no molasses in our cookies, but the brown sugar more than does the job.

*1¾ cups yellow cornmeal*
*1¼ cups all-purpose flour, plus*
  *extra for rolling out dough*
*1 cup packed dark brown sugar*
*1 tablespoon baking powder*
*1 teaspoon ground ginger*
*¾ teaspoon ground cloves*
*1 teaspoon ground cinnamon*

*¾ teaspoon ground nutmeg*
*¾ teaspoon ground allspice*
*1 teaspoon salt*
*½ cup heavy cream*
*3 eggs*
*12 tablespoons (1½ sticks)*
  *unsalted butter, cut into*
  *20 pats*

**DAY 1:** Combine the cornmeal and flour in a large mixing bowl.

Place the brown sugar, baking powder, ginger, cloves, cinnamon, nutmeg, allspice, salt, cream, and eggs in the bowl of a food processor. Process until thoroughly blended, about 1 minute. With the food processor running, add the butter one pat at a time, then process another 30 seconds.

Turn out the contents of the food processor into the dry ingredients and blend well with a wooden spoon. Refrigerate overnight.

**DAY 2:** Preheat the oven to 350°.

Sprinkle a clean surface with flour and roll out the dough to a thickness of ¼ inch. Cut out 2 ½-inch rounds with a glass; if the dough sticks to the glass, dip the rim in flour. Place the rounds on ungreased cookie sheets and bake until brown, about 20 to 23 minutes. Transfer the cookies to a plate to cool.

# Down-Home Coconut-Pecan Candy Bar Cake

MAKES 10 TO 12 SERVINGS

*Color photograph 50*

★

There's nothing quite as special as the taste of fresh coconut, and I strongly urge you not to make this cake with the packaged kind. This is a very pretty cake, and its texture makes us think of wonderful, chewy candy.

*3 large fresh coconuts*

**COCONUT MILK GLAZE**
*3 cups reserved coconut milk
  (see above)*
*1 cup white sugar*

**FILLING**
*4½ cups pecan pieces, in all*
*½ pound (2 sticks) unsalted
  butter*
*¾ cup white sugar*
*1½ cups firmly packed dark
  brown sugar*
*3¼ cups heavy cream, in all*
*3 cups shredded coconut (see
  above)*
*1 tablespoon vanilla extract*

**FROSTING**
*16 ounces cream cheese, cut into
  pieces*
*1½ cups confectioner's sugar*
*1 teaspoon ground cinnamon*
*½ teaspoon ground allspice*
*2 cups shredded coconut (see
  above)*
*2 teaspoons vanilla extract*

**CAKE**
*1 cup all-purpose flour*
*2 cups cake flour*
*1 tablespoon baking powder*
*½ teaspoon salt*
*1½ cups white sugar*
*7 eggs*
*1½ cups evaporated milk*
*½ pound plus 4 tablespoons (2½
  sticks) unsalted butter, melted*
*1 tablespoon vanilla extract*
*1¾ cups toasted coconut (see
  above)*
*Vegetable oil cooking spray*

Punch holes through the eyes of the coconuts with a screwdriver or other sturdy sharp pointed tool or instrument, and pour off the milk. Set aside.

Crack open the coconuts with a hammer and remove the meat. Remove the thin brown layer from the meat and discard; rinse the meat. Place the coconut meat in the bowl of a food processor and process until finely shredded. Measure out 3 cups and reserve the rest.

Toast the 3 cups of coconut in a 10-inch nonstick skillet over high heat, flipping the coconut and shaking the skillet frequently, until the coconut is a deep brown (don't burn it!), about 14 to 15 minutes. The coconut will reduce to about 1¾ cups. Remove from the heat and set aside.

**FOR THE GLAZE,** combine the coconut milk and sugar in a 10-inch skillet over high heat. Bring to a boil, stirring frequently. Reduce the heat to low and simmer, stirring occasionally, until the liquid has reduced to 1½ cups, about 25 to 30 minutes. Remove the skillet from the heat and set aside.

**FOR THE FILLING,** toast the pecan pieces in a medium skillet over medium heat until golden brown, about 4 minutes. Remove from the heat. Measure out 2 cups of the toasted pecans, place in the bowl of a food processor, and process until finely chopped. Set aside. Set aside the remaining 2½ cups toasted pecans.

Melt the butter in a 12-inch skillet over high heat. When the butter starts to sizzle, add the white sugar and whisk just until it begins to brown, about 2 minutes. Whisk in the brown sugar and then *2¾ cups* of the cream and cook, whisking occasionally, 2 minutes. Add the reserved 2½ cups toasted pecan pieces and the coconut and cook, stirring often with a wooden spoon, about 17 minutes. (Watch carefully, because the mixture burns easily around the edges.) Stir in the 2 cups chopped pecans and cook 3 minutes. Remove from the heat and whisk in the vanilla and the *remaining ½ cup* cream. Pour the mixture into a mixing bowl and whip vigorously with a wire whisk as it cools slightly. Then spread in a large, shallow pan to cool to room temperature. Makes about 8 cups.

**FOR THE FROSTING,** combine all of the ingredients in the bowl of a food processor and process until thoroughly blended, about 1 to 2 minutes. Pour into a bowl and refrigerate until ready to use.

Preheat the oven to 350°.

**FOR THE CAKE,** combine both flours, the baking powder, salt, and sugar in the bowl of a food processor and process until well blended, about 25 seconds. Add the eggs and process to blend. With the processor running, drizzle in the evaporated milk, butter, and vanilla. Add the coconut and process 10 to 15 seconds.

Coat four 9-inch cake pans with cooking spray and divide the batter evenly among the pans. Bake until a toothpick inserted in the middle of each comes out dry, about 30 minutes. About 3 minutes before the cakes are finished baking, set the coconut milk glaze over high heat and bring it back to a boil. Remove the cake pans from the oven and turn the cake layers out onto wire racks. Immediately spread the hot glaze over the layers with a pastry brush. Then turn the layers over and brush the other sides. Repeat the process to brush each side of each layer 6 times. Let the cake layers cool completely.

Choose the best layer for the top of the cake, and set it aside. Place a second layer top side down on a cake plate and spread 2 cups of the filling over the top. Place another layer on top and cover it with another 2 cups of filling. Repeat the process with the third layer. Then place the remaining layer on top, right side up, and spread the remaining filling in the middle of the top of the cake.

Remove the frosting from the refrigerator and frost the sides of the cake, then the top to meet the filling.

# Pat's Raisin Pralines

MAKES 15 TO 20 PRALINES

★

I had never eaten a praline with raisins, and since I've never met a praline I didn't like, I decided to try it. But the consistency wasn't coming out quite right in the test kitchen, so my assistant, Pat Scanlan, took the recipe home and mixed up a batch of incredibly wonderful raisin pralines. They're easy to make and truly unforgettable. Be sure to work quickly once the praline mixture is ready to be formed into cookies.

*Vegetable oil cooking spray*

*12 tablespoons (1½ sticks)*
  *unsalted butter*
*1 cup packed light brown sugar*
*1 cup white sugar*

*1 cup milk*
*½ cup heavy cream*
*1 cup raisins*
*2 teaspoons ground cinnamon*
*2 tablespoons vanilla extract*

Coat 2 baking sheets with cooking spray.

Melt the butter in a 10-inch skillet over high heat. As soon as the butter melts, add both sugars, the milk, cream, and raisins and cook, whisking constantly, 11 minutes. (The mixture should be at a rolling boil.) Add the cinnamon and cook, whisking constantly, 2 minutes. Add the vanilla and cook, whisking constantly, until the mixture forms strings when you pull the whisk through it from the sides of the skillet, about 3 to 4 minutes. Remove from the heat and immediately spoon out the praline batter onto the baking sheets with a large kitchen spoon. You should get 15 to 20 pralines depending on the size of your spoon.

Allow the pralines to cool at room temperature 15 to 20 minutes. Wrap each praline individually in waxed paper or plastic wrap and store at room temperature. The pralines should keep 5 days to a week if properly wrapped.

# South Dakota Kuchen

MAKES 6 SERVINGS

★

German immigrants who settled in the Dakotas did a lot of baking, and they were especially known for their yeast dough coffee cakes, or *kuchen*. Sometimes the kuchen was simply a plain sweet dough, but more often it was topped with fresh fruit, cottage cheese, or custard. We used apples on ours, but feel free to get creative with this.

FILLING

4 tablespoons unsalted butter

4 medium apples, peeled, cored, quartered, and cut lengthwise into 1/4-inch slices (about 6 cups)

3/4 cup packed dark brown sugar

1 teaspoon ground nutmeg

1 teaspoon ground cinnamon

1/2 cup milk

2 eggs, lightly beaten

DOUGH

1 cup milk

2 cups all-purpose flour

4 ounces cream cheese, cut into small pats

4 tablespoons unsalted butter, cut into pats

1/4 teaspoon salt

1 (1/4-ounce) package active dry yeast

3 tablespoons white sugar

1/2 teaspoon ground nutmeg

1/2 teaspoon ground cinnamon

3 eggs

FINISH

Vegetable oil cooking spray

**FOR THE FILLING,** place the butter and apple slices in a heavy 3-quart pot over high heat. Add the brown sugar, nutmeg, and cinnamon and cook, stirring occasionally, until apples are soft and golden brown, about 5 to 6 minutes. Stir in the milk and cook 2 minutes. Remove from the heat and let cool a few minutes. Stir the beaten eggs into the apple mixture. Let the filling cool while you prepare the dough.

Preheat the oven to 400°.

**FOR THE DOUGH,** bring the milk to a boil in a small saucepan. Remove from the heat and set aside.

Place the flour in the bowl of a food processor and distribute the cream cheese and butter pats evenly over the flour. Add the salt, yeast, sugar, nutmeg, and cinnamon and process 15 to 20 seconds. With the machine running, add the eggs one at a time. With the machine running, add the hot milk in a steady stream. Process, stopping to scrape the sides of the bowl if necessary, until thoroughly blended, about 10 to 15 seconds. The dough will be very soft, almost like wet putty.

**TO FINISH,** coat a baking pan or casserole approximately 15 by 10½ by 2¼ inches deep with cooking spray. Turn the dough into the pan and spread as evenly as possible with a rubber spatula. Pour the apple mixture over the dough and place the pan in a warm spot to rise until doubled in size, about 35 minutes.

Bake until baked through, about 30 to 40 minutes. (Test with a toothpick; if the toothpick comes out dry, the kuchen is done.)

Serve warm, with heavy cream or vanilla ice cream if desired.

# Minnesota Cranberry Nut Pudding

MAKES 8 TO 10 SERVINGS

This would be a special side dish for any holiday, but Marti Dalton, our marketing assistant, said the first thing she tasted was "Christmas," and we agree. This is an extraordinary pudding, with a moist, rich texture and a festive air. Cranberry pudding is popular throughout New England, but we patterned ours after a recipe from Minnesota. When you cook down the berries, you'll find most of them will purée, but some of them will remain whole, adding to the interesting textures in each mouthful. Serve the pudding in a puddle of Chantilly cream or with hard sauce.

1 cup pecan pieces

2 cups hot water

2 (12-ounce) bags cranberries

8 tablespoons (1 stick) unsalted
   butter, in all

1¼ cups sugar

1 tablespoon grated orange zest

2 teaspoons grated lemon zest

2 teaspoons grated lime zest

2½ cups all-purpose flour

2 tablespoons baking powder

1 cup light molasses

1 cup light corn syrup

Vegetable oil cooking spray

Preheat the oven to 325°.

Toast the pecan pieces in a 10-inch skillet over low heat, flipping the nuts and shaking the pan, until the nuts are golden brown, about 8 to 10 minutes. Remove from the heat and set aside.

Bring the hot water to a simmer in another 10-inch skillet over high heat. Add the cranberries, *4 tablespoons* of the butter, the sugar, and orange, lemon, and lime zests and bring to a rolling boil. Cook, occasionally scraping the bottom of the skillet to prevent sticking, about 10 to 12 minutes. Remove from the heat. Cut the *remaining 4 tablespoons* butter into pats, add to the cranberries, and stir until melted.

Combine the flour and baking powder in a large bowl. Add the molasses and corn syrup and mix thoroughly. Add the cranberry mixture to the bowl and combine thoroughly. Stir in the toasted pecans.

Coat a 9-inch springform pan or other deep round cake pan with cooking spray. Pour in the cranberry mixture and place in a rectangular pan approximately 10 by 14 inches. Pour enough water into the larger pan to come halfway up the sides of the cake pan. Bake 2 hours.

Serve the pudding warm, in a puddle of heavy cream if desired.

# Indian Pudding

MAKES 6 TO 8 SERVINGS

★

The early settlers tagged almost anything made with corn or cornmeal as "Indian," since corn was always known as "Indian corn." This dessert pudding, called *sagamite* by Native Americans, is usually made with molasses. Our version omits the molasses, but adds toasted pine nuts for flavor and texture. Be sure to whip everything in the food processor until it's airy and then bake immediately for the lightest, most delicious results.

½ cup pine nuts
6 tablespoons unsalted butter
¾ teaspoon ground allspice
¾ teaspoon ground mace
½ cup plus 3 tablespoons dark
   brown sugar

2 (12-ounce) cans evaporated
   milk
½ teaspoon salt
2 eggs
1 teaspoon baking soda
1 teaspoon vanilla extract
1 cup yellow cornmeal

Preheat the oven to 350°.

Toast the pine nuts in a small skillet over medium heat until light brown, about 3 minutes.

Melt the butter in a small saucepan over high heat. When the butter begins to sizzle, stir in the allspice and mace and cook 2 minutes. Stir in the brown sugar and cook just until the sugar has dissolved, about 30 seconds. Add the evaporated milk and salt and cook, stirring occasionally, until the milk is just ready to boil. Remove from the heat.

Process the eggs in the bowl of a food processor until very frothy, about 20 to 30 seconds. Add the baking soda and vanilla and process 5 seconds. Add the cornmeal and process until thoroughly blended, about 35 to 40 seconds. With the processor running, add the milk mixture in a steady stream and process until thoroughly blended, about 1 minute.

Immediately pour the mixture into a casserole 10 by 10 by 4 inches deep. Sprinkle the toasted pine nuts evenly over the top and place the casserole in a large baking pan. Pour enough water into the pan to come about 1 inch up the sides of the casserole. Bake until it is the consistency of pudding on top, about 45 to 55 minutes.

Serve warm, with heavy cream if desired.

# New Mexico Apple Bread Pudding

MAKES 6 SERVINGS

This is our version of *capirotado*, a New Mexican bread pudding that is often made with wine, but without the usual eggs and milk. We made ours without wine and fell in love with it as it is.

*2 medium red baking or Granny Smith apples, peeled, cored, and sliced (reserve the peels and cores)*
*3 cups water*
*1¼ cups packed dark brown sugar*
*2 cloves*
*1 cinnamon stick*
*¾ cup blanched almonds*

*3 cups toasted unseasoned bread cubes (from good, dense white bread)*
*8 tablespoons (1 stick) unsalted butter, cut into 20 pats, in all*
*½ teaspoon ground cinnamon, in all*
*½ teaspoon ground nutmeg, in all*
*½ cup raisins*
*½ pound Monterey Jack cheese, thinly sliced*

Preheat the oven to 350°.

To make an apple stock, place the apple peels and cores and the water in a saucepan and bring to a boil over high heat. Add the brown sugar, cloves, and cinnamon stick and cook 20 minutes. Remove from the heat and set aside.

Toast the almonds in an 8-inch skillet over medium heat, shaking the pan and flipping the almonds almost constantly, until the nuts are light brown, about 4 minutes. Don't let them burn!

Spread *half* the bread cubes in the bottom of a small casserole. Distribute *10 pats* of the butter evenly over the bread. Add a layer of *half* the sliced apples and distribute *5 pats* of the butter over the apples. Sprinkle on ¼ *teaspoon* each of the ground cinnamon and nutmeg. Cover with about half the toasted almonds, spreading them as evenly as possible. Cover the almonds with a layer of *half* the raisins. Then add *half* the sliced cheese in an even layer. Spread the *remaining* bread cubes over the cheese, the *remaining* apple slices over that, and the *remaining 5 pats* of butter over the apples. Sprinkle with the *remaining* ¼ *teaspoon* cinnamon and nutmeg. Cover with the *remaining* almonds, raisins, and sliced cheese.

Strain the apple stock and measure out 1½ cups. (If necessary, add water to make 1½ cups.) Pour this over the contents of the casserole and bake, uncovered, until golden brown and bubbly, about 25 to 30 minutes.

Delicious by itself or served with whipped cream.

# Shaker
# Apple Dumplings

MAKES ABOUT 25 DUMPLINGS

*Color photograph 51*

This delicious dessert originated with the Shakers, who emigrated to America from England in the eighteenth century and established communities throughout the Northeast and Midwest. The ingenious Shakers devised wonderful recipes, many of them meatless. In the traditional version of this dish the apples are baked in pastry, but our translation is much more frivolous, as you will see.

½ cup pecan pieces

8 tablespoons (1 stick) unsalted
butter

½ cup packed light brown sugar

1½ teaspoons ground cinnamon

1½ teaspoons ground nutmeg

½ cup heavy cream

3 Granny Smith apples

1½ cups all-purpose flour

½ cup packed grated Cheddar
cheese

1 tablespoon baking powder

½ teaspoon salt

2 cups vegetable oil

Confectioner's sugar

Toast the pecans in a small skillet over medium-low heat, shaking the pan and flipping them constantly, until golden, about 3 to 4 minutes. Remove from the heat and set aside.

Heat the butter, brown sugar, cinnamon, and nutmeg in an 8-inch skillet over high heat, stirring once, until the butter has melted and the sugar has dissolved, about 4 minutes. Add the cream and cook, stirring constantly, until the mixture is dark brown. Remove from the heat.

Core the apples but do not peel. Grate them on the large holes of a hand grater into a medium-size mixing bowl. With a large spoon, stir in the flour, cheese, toasted pecans, baking powder, and salt until thoroughly blended. Add the butter/brown sugar mixture and stir well.

Heat the oil in a 10-inch skillet over high heat. When the oil is very hot, drop in 4 spoonfuls of the dumpling mixture. (Do not cook more than 4 dumplings at a time, or the oil will cool down. Try to keep the temperature of the oil above 340° at all times.) Fry until the dumplings are golden brown, about 30 to 45 seconds on each side. Remove with a slotted spoon and drain on paper towels. Repeat with the remaining dumpling mixture.

Allow the dumplings to sit several minutes, so they will be light and crunchy. Then sift confectioner's sugar over them and serve.

# Apple Pan Dowdy

## MAKES 6 TO 8 SERVINGS

★

"As American as apple pie" should really be "As American as Apple Pan Dowdy," since apple pie actually originated in England. A very old dessert from the early colonies, Apple Pan Dowdy, or Apple Jonathan as it is also known, is not too different from Apple Grunt or Apple Charlotte. Sometimes it's made with a pie crust and sometimes with a biscuit topping, as ours is.

**FILLING**

5 baking apples, such as Granny
    Smiths
2 cups water
1 cup packed light brown sugar,
    in all
1½ teaspoons ground
    cinnamon, in all
½ teaspoon ground nutmeg
½ teaspoon ground cloves
½ teaspoon ground mace
¾ teaspoon salt, in all
6 tablespoons unsalted butter,
    in all
½ teaspoon ground ginger

½ teaspoon ground allspice
¾ cup light molasses
2 tablespoons fresh lemon juice
2 eggs

**DOUGH**

1 cup yellow cornmeal
¾ cup all-purpose flour
2 teaspoons baking powder
2 tablespoons unsalted butter,
    chilled, cut into 4 pats
1 egg
1 cup reserved apple cooking
    liquid (see above)

Peel and core the apples and place the peelings, cores, and the water in a 5-quart pot over high heat. Bring to a boil and add ½ *cup* of the brown sugar, *¾ teaspoon* of the cinnamon, the nutmeg, cloves, mace, and ½ *teaspoon* of the salt. Cook 5 minutes. Stir in *2 tablespoons* of the butter, reduce the heat, and simmer until the liquid has reduced to 1 cup, about 15 to 20 minutes. Remove from the heat, strain the liquid, and set aside.

    Meanwhile slice the apples and place the slices in a bowl. Set aside. Preheat the oven to 350°.

Melt the *remaining 4 tablespoons* butter in a 2-quart pot over high heat. When the butter sizzles, add the ginger, allspice, and the *remaining ¾ teaspoon* cinnamon, *¼ teaspoon salt*, and *½ cup* brown sugar. Cook this seasoning mixture, whipping with a wire whisk, until it becomes a dark paste, about 3 to 4 minutes. Remove from the heat and whisk in the molasses and lemon juice. Let cool, then whisk in the eggs. (If the mixture is still warm, the eggs will cook.)

Add the seasoning mixture to the sliced apples and toss well until the apples are thoroughly coated. Set aside.

**FOR THE DOUGH,** combine the cornmeal, flour, and baking powder in the bowl of a food processor and process until throughly blended, about 1 minute. Add the butter and egg and process about 15 seconds. With the machine running, slowly add the reserved cooking liquid in a thin stream and process until thoroughly blended, about 30 to 45 seconds. The dough should be the consistency of pancake batter.

Pour the apples into a casserole approximately 10 by 10 by 2 inches deep. Pour the dough evenly over the apples.

Bake 40 minutes. Then turn the oven heat up to 475° and bake until golden and crusty, about 8 to 10 minutes.

Serve warm, with cream, if desired.

# Blackberry Buckle

MAKES 8 SERVINGS

★

Here's a buckle, which resembles a grunt, which is like a slump, which is to say, another one of those great old New England berry desserts. It's easier than pie to make, and you don't always have to use blackberries— blueberries or raspberries would work wonderfully.

*2½ cups all-purpose flour, in all*
*1 tablespoon baking powder*
*1 tablespoon grated lemon zest, in all*
*½ teaspoon salt, in all*
*½ pound (2 sticks) unsalted butter, room temperature*
*1½ cups sugar, in all*
*2 eggs*
*3 egg yolks*
*1 tablespoon grated orange zest, in all*
*1 teaspoon vanilla extract*
*1½ pounds (24 ounces) unsweetened frozen blackberries, thawed and all liquid drained and reserved (unsweetened blueberries or raspberries may be substituted)*
*¾ teaspoon ground cinnamon*
*¼ teaspoon ground nutmeg*
*¼ teaspoon ground mace*
*Vegetable oil cooking spray*
*Heavy cream*

Preheat the oven to 375°.

Combine *2 cups* of the flour, the baking powder, *1 teaspoon* of the lemon zest, and *¼ teaspoon* of the salt in a small bowl and mix well.

Cream *10 tablespoons* (*1¼ sticks*) of the butter in a food processor. Add *1 cup* of the sugar, the eggs, and egg yolks and process until well blended. Add *2 teaspoons* of the orange zest, the vanilla, and *1 teaspoon* of the lemon zest, and blend thoroughly. Add half the flour mixture and process 10 seconds. Add the remaining flour mixture and process until thoroughly blended, scraping the sides of the food processor if necessary. Transfer the mixture to a large bowl. Add the drained blackberries and fold in with a rubber spatula. Fold in ½ cup of the reserved blackberry juice.

To make the topping, combine the *remaining ½ cup* flour, the *remaining ½ cup* sugar, the cinnamon, nutmeg, mace, the *remaining ¼ teaspoon* salt, and the *remaining 1 teaspoon* each orange zest and lemon zest. Mix thoroughly with your hands. Add the *remaining 6 tablespoons* butter and mix with your hands until thoroughly combined.

Coat a 9- by 11-inch baking pan with cooking spray. Pour the blackberry mixture into the pan, spreading it evenly with a spatula. Sprinkle the topping mixture evenly over the blackberries.

Bake until browned and set, about 1 hour and 15 minutes.

Serve warm in a cool pool of heavy cream.

# Blueberry Slump

MAKES 8 TO 10 SERVINGS

★

Not a grunt or a buckle, this is a slump—a tasty dessert of sweet dumplings dropped onto a boiling blueberry mixture that has its roots along the New England coast. Spoon the warm slump over a puddle of cream and go for it!

*36 ounces (about 1 quart) fresh blueberries or 3 (12-ounce) bags unsweetened frozen blueberries (see Note)*
*1¼ cups sugar, in all*
*1 tablespoon vanilla extract, in all*
*2 tablespoons fresh lime juice*
*2 tablespoons fresh lemon juice*
*1 tablespoon raspberry or other fruit vinegar*

*½ cup all-purpose flour*
*¾ cup yellow cornmeal*
*1 tablespoon baking powder*
*¾ teaspoon ground cinnamon*
*½ teaspoon ground allspice*
*¼ teaspoon salt*
*¼ teaspoon ground mace*
*1¼ cups milk*
*5 tablespoons unsalted butter*
*Heavy cream*

Combine the blueberries, *1 cup* of the sugar, *2 teaspoons* of the vanilla, the lime juice, lemon juice, and vinegar in a medium-size bowl. Set aside.

Combine the flour, cornmeal, baking powder, the *remaining ¼ cup* sugar, the cinnamon, allspice, salt, mace, and the *remaining 1 teaspoon* vanilla in a large bowl.

Bring the milk just to a boil in a small saucepan over high heat, stirring to keep it from sticking to the bottom of the pot. Add the butter and heat just until the butter melts. Remove from the heat and gradually whisk into the flour mixture until the texture is thick, like a biscuit dough. (You may have to switch from the whisk to a spoon.)

Bring the blueberry mixture to a boil in a 10-inch skillet over high heat. As soon as the blueberries start to boil, drop heaping spoonfuls of the dough on top of the blueberries, using a large soup spoon or tablespoon (you should get about 10 dumplings out of the dough). Cover, reduce the heat to low, and cook until the dumplings are set, about 13 minutes.

For each serving, place 1 dumpling on a pool of heavy cream in a dessert plate and top with some of the blueberry mixture.

NOTE: If the blueberries are frozen, thaw and drain them in a colander.

# Berry Cobbler

MAKES 10 SERVINGS

*Color photograph 52*

The settlers of New England loved the wild berries they found in their new land and they used them to create many wonderful desserts. Berry cobbler is a treat still much loved by New Englanders, and it is especially good when made with fresh berries. Serve it warm with heavy cream or ice cream.

**FILLING**

*2¼ quarts (72 ounces) fresh or unsweetened frozen blackberries or blueberries, (if frozen, drain thoroughly in a colander)*
*1 cup sugar (see Note)*
*¾ teaspoon ground cinnamon*
*¾ teaspoon ground allspice*
*¾ teaspoon ground mace*
*2 tablespoons vanilla extract*

**BISCUIT DOUGH**

*2 eggs*
*4 tablespoons unsalted butter, cut into pats*
*½ cup plus 2 tablespoons sugar*
*1½ teaspoons vanilla extract*
*1 cup all-purpose flour*
*1 tablespoon baking powder*
*¾ cup evaporated milk*

Preheat the oven to 350°.

**FOR THE FILLING,** put the berries in a large mixing bowl. Add the sugar, cinnamon, allspice, mace, and vanilla and mix thoroughly with a large spoon. Set aside.

**FOR THE DOUGH,** place the eggs, butter, sugar, and vanilla in the bowl of a food processor and process 1½ minutes. Add the flour and baking powder and process 2 minutes. With the machine running, add the evaporated milk in a thin stream and process 1 to 2 minutes—stop when you have a good sticky dough; don't overprocess.

Spread the dough evenly over the bottom of a baking pan or casserole that measures approximately 13 by 9 by 2 inches deep. Pour the berries over the dough. Bake until the berry mixture is set and the dough is cooked through (test with a knife), about 50 to 60 minutes.

Serve warm, with cream or ice cream if desired.

**NOTE:** You may need to adjust the sugar depending on the sweetness of your berries.

# Strawberry Shortcake

MAKES 12 SHORTCAKES

*Color photograph 53*

★

The truth about strawberry shortcake is that it's not cake at all, but a delicious biscuit topped with crushed berries and whipped cream. If your strawberries are sweet, the proportions here will probably be just right. But if the berries are tart, you may want to increase the white sugar in the strawberry sauce by a tablespoon or two.

SHORTCAKE
2½ cups all-purpose flour
¼ cup white sugar
1 tablespoon plus 2 teaspoons
    baking powder
¼ teaspoon salt
14 tablespoons (1¾ sticks)
    unsalted butter, cut into pats
1 cup cold milk
2 tablespoons strawberry extract,
    optional

STRAWBERRY SAUCE
2 teaspoons strawberry extract
    (see Note)
10 cups hulled strawberries, in all

½ cup white sugar
¼ cup packed dark brown sugar
1 tablespoon vanilla extract
½ cup heavy cream
½ teaspoon ground savory

TOPPING
2 cups heavy cream
½ cup sour cream
3 tablespoons white sugar
1 teaspoon vanilla extract

FINISH
All-purpose flour
Vegetable oil cooking spray

**FOR THE SHORTCAKE,** combine the flour, sugar, baking powder, and salt in the bowl of a food processor. Process until blended, about 10 to 15 seconds. With the processor running, add the butter one pat at a time and process until the mixture resembles coarse meal.

Turn the dough into a large mixing bowl. Stir in the milk and the strawberry extract, if desired. The dough will be sticky. Place the dough in a bowl; cover and refrigerate 30 minutes.

Preheat the oven to 350°.

**FOR THE SAUCE,** place the strawberry extract, *4 cups* of the strawberries, the white and brown sugars, vanilla, cream, and savory in the bowl of a food processor. Process until thoroughly blended, about 45 to 60 seconds.

Place the *remaining 6 cups* strawberries in a bowl (if the strawberries are very large, cut them in half). Pour the sauce from the food processor over them. Set aside at room temperature about 45 minutes, or refrigerate if you plan to assemble the shortcake much later. Bring the berries to room temperature before serving if refrigerated.

**FOR THE TOPPING,** place all the ingredients in the bowl of a food processor and process until the consistency of thick whipped cream, about 1 to 3 minutes (depending on the size of your processor). Transfer to a bowl and refrigerate.

**TO FINISH,** lightly flour a work surface and roll out the dough to a 12-inch round about ¼ inch thick. Be careful not to roll out the dough too thin, or the shortcakes will be too crispy. If the dough is at all difficult to work with, try rolling one half or one quarter of the dough at a time. Cut the dough into 3- to 3½-inch circles with a glass; you should have 12 circles.

Coat a large baking sheet with cooking spray, place the dough circles on the sheet, and bake until light brown and crispy, about 20 to 25 minutes.

Place a shortcake on each dessert plate, spoon about ½ cup strawberry sauce over it, and top with about ¼ cup whipped topping.

NOTE: If your strawberries are very sweet, you can omit the strawberry extract.

# *Index*

★

onion(s):
    baked, stuffed with pork and
        mushrooms, 242–243
    cake, Indiana Amish, 18–19
    caramelizing of, 10
Opelousas crawfish stew, 80–81
oyster(s):
    and beef jambalaya, Bogue falayal,
        188–189
    Hangtown fry, 29–30
    pan roast, New York, 44
    pie, Island Beach, 47–49
    scalloped, 45–46
    stew, West Coast, 81–82

P
_____

pancakes:
    Indian pumpkin griddle cakes,
        19–20
    Lower East Side latkes, 252–253
pan dowdy, apple, 283
pan gravy, frontier chicken-fried steak
    with, 177–179
paprika, chicken, 160–161
pasta:
    beef noodle casserole, 192–193
    German-style meatballs, 200–201
    primavera, 116
    West Coast chicken Tetrazzini, 168–
        170
pasties, Michigan miner's, 202–203
Pat's raisin pralines, 275
peanut butter banana cream pie, St.
    Louis, 265–266
pecan:
    coconut candy bar cake, down-
        home, 272–274
    cranberry pudding, Minnesota, 277–
        278
    praline sweet potato pie, St. Landry
        Parish, 267–268

Pennsylvania Dutch cheese pie, 42–43
Pennsylvania Dutch chicken dumpling
    soup, 94–95
peppers:
    caramelizing of, 10
    stuffed, 117–119
peppers, chile:
    grinding of, 10
    posole stew, 110–112
    Texas chili (Texas red), 196–198
Philadelphia scrapple, 36–37
Philadelphia tomato chicken, 163–165
pie, dessert:
    black bottom, 264–265
    St. Landry Parish sweet potato pecan
        praline, 267–268
    St. Louis peanut butter banana
        cream, 265–266
pie, savory:
    Iowa chicken and corn pot, 170–
        172
    Island Beach oyster, 47–49
    jalapeño, 25–27
    La Jolla tamale, 63–64
    Pennsylvania Dutch, 42–43
pilau, Carolina chicken, 152–153
pinto beans:
    Big Hole Valley cowpoke, 255–257
    chuck wagon, 213–214
polenta with meat sauce, 194–195
Pontchartrain smoked pork chops
    maque choux, 207–208
pork:
    baked onions stuffed with
        mushrooms and, 242–243
    baked stuffed tomatoes, 119–120
    Chinatown chop suey and twice-
        fried rice, 210–212
    chops, Iowa stuffed, 204–205
    chops maque choux, Pontchartrain
        smoked, 207–208
    chuck wagon beans, 213–214

pork (*cont.*)
country ham with red-eye gravy,
33–34
empanadas, 217–220
German-style meatballs, 200–201
Indiana Dutch cabbage rolls, 123–
125
La Jolla tamale pie, 63–64
Michigan miner's pasties, 202–203
Ohio ham loaf, 205–206
Philadelphia scrapple, 36–37
posole stew, 110–112
roast with dill sauce, Chicago, 208–
210
sopa de albóndigas (Mexican
meatball soup), 99–101
South Miami Cuban stew, 104–105
stuffed peppers, 117–119
posole stew, 110–112
potato(es):
au gratin, 251–252
cake, Idaho, 254–255
Iowa Dutch lettuce, 225–226
Lower East Side latkes, 252–253
red flannel hash, 35
salad, hot German, 228–229
soup, Milwaukee, 72–73
southern smothered, 249–250
pot pie, Iowa chicken and corn, 170–
172
poultry:
arroz con pollo, 154–155
Atchafalaya roast boneless chicken,
144–145
Basque chicken and shrimp in wine,
155–157
Brunswick stew, 92–93
Buffalo chicken wings, 57–58
Carolina chicken pilau, 152–153
Chicago chicken à la king, 142–143
chicken, shrimp, and sausage
gumbo Hazel, 96–97

poultry (*cont.*)
chicken cacciatore, 157–158
chicken florentine, 146–147
chicken paprika, 160–161
chicken Stoltzfus, 166–168
country captain, 159–160
Iowa chicken and corn pot pie,
170–172
Kentucky burgoo, 105–107
Mulacalong chicken, 150–152
New World chicken fricassee, 147–
148
Oklahoma fried chicken and
biscuits, 162–163
Oklahoma honey chicken, 56–57
Pennsylvania Dutch chicken
dumpling soup, 94–95
Philadelphia tomato chicken, 163–
165
Tampa Bay chicken Marengo, 165–
166
Tex-Mex chicken mole tostadas,
173–175
turkey hash, 176–177
Vermont common cracker chicken
with cracker custard sauce,
149–150
Waikiki chicken, 59–61
West Coast chicken Tetrazzini, 168–
170
praline(s):
Pat's raisin, 275
pecan, sweet potato pie, St. Landry
Parish, 267–268
preparation of recipes, 9
pudding:
apple bread, New Mexico, 280–281
Connecticut corn, 238–239
cranberry nut, Minnesota, 277–278
Indian, 279–280
pumpkin griddle cakes, Indian, 19–
20